BLASTING THE FUTURE!

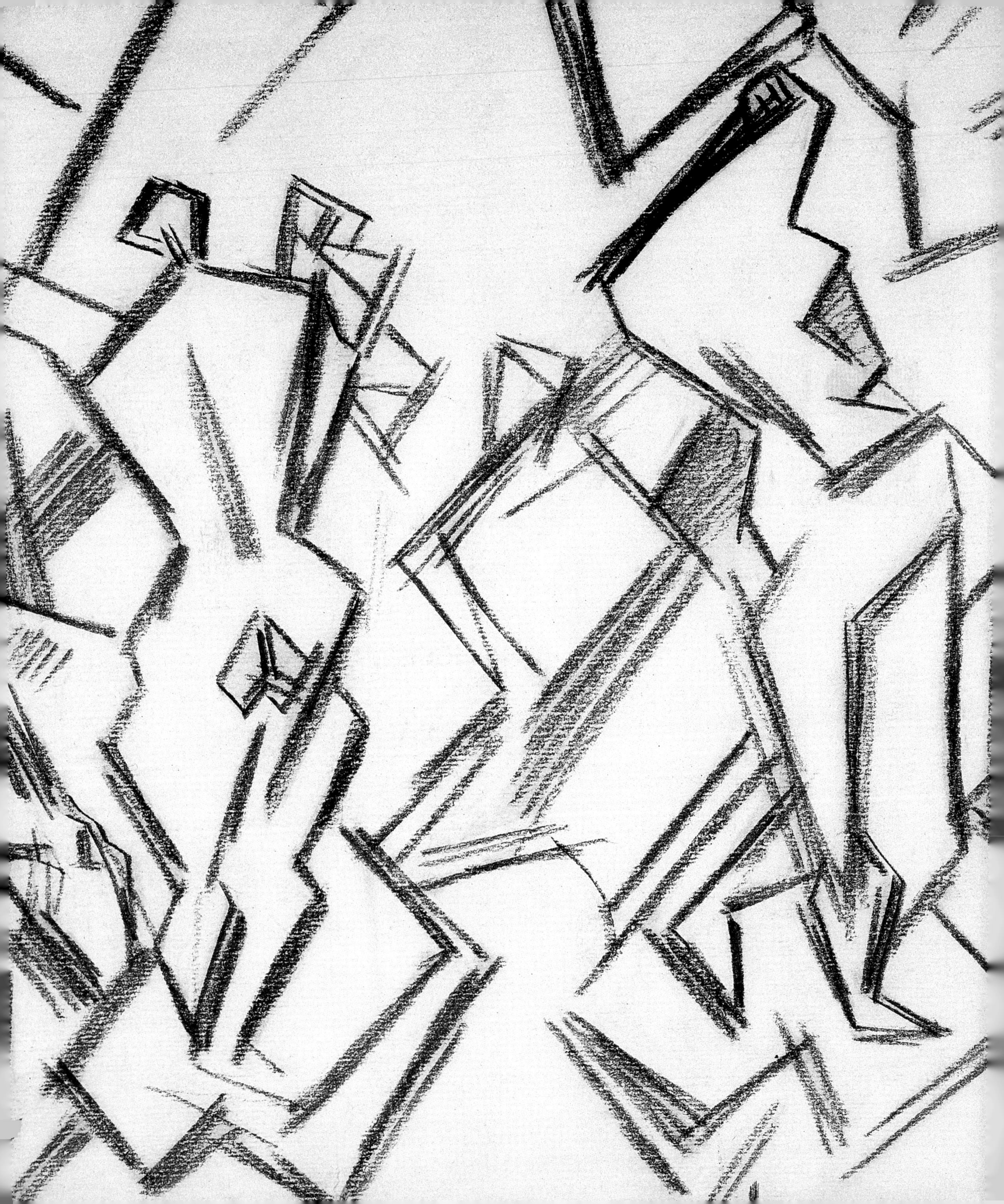

BLASTING THE FUTURE!

Vorticism in Britain 1910–1920

Jonathan Black
Christopher Adams
Michael J. K. Walsh
Jonathan Wood

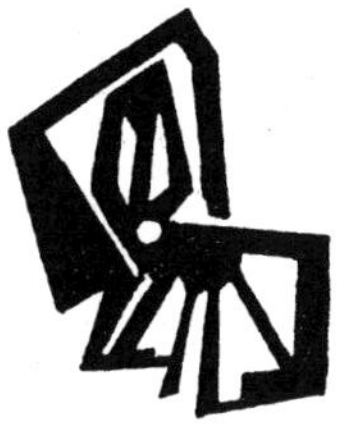

ESTORICK COLLECTION OF MODERN ITALIAN ART
PHILIP WILSON PUBLISHERS

Published on the occasion of the exhibition:
Blasting the Future! Vorticism in Britain 1910–1920

4 February–18 April 2004

Estorick Collection of Modern Italian Art
39a Canonbury Square
London N1 2AN

7 May–25 July 2004

The Whitworth Art Gallery
The University of Manchester
Oxford Road
Manchester M15 6ER

Exhibition curated by Jonathan Black

Exhibition organised by the Estorick Collection
Roberta Cremoncini
Christopher Adams
Lucy Bestwick
Leonie Taylor

First published in 2004 by
Philip Wilson Publishers
7 Deane House, 27 Greenwood Place
London NW5 1LB

Distributed throughout the world
(excluding North America) by
I. B. Tauris & Co. Ltd
6 Salem Road, London W2 4BU

Distributed in North America by
Palgrave Macmillan, a division of
St Martin's Press
175 Fifth Avenue
New York NY 10010

ISBN 0 85667 572 5 (hardback)
ISBN 0 85667 585 7 (paperback)

Designed by James Campus

Printed and bound in Italy by Editoriale Lloyd Srl

ACKNOWLEDGEMENTS

Our thanks are owed to the following individuals and institutions for their much-appreciated help in the realisation of this exhibition:

Sebastiano Barassi (Kettle's Yard, University of Cambridge); Janet Boston (Manchester City Galleries); Gordon Cooke (Fine Art Society plc, London); Stephen Coppel (Department of Prints and Drawings, British Museum, London); Andrew Cormack (Royal Air Force Museum, Hendon); Tim Craven (Southampton City Art Gallery); Jo Digger (New Art Gallery, Walsall); Tim Egan (National Museums & Galleries of Wales); Oliver Fairclough (National Museums & Galleries of Wales); Antony Griffiths (Department of Prints and Drawings, British Museum, London); Mary Griffiths (Whitworth Art Gallery, University of Manchester); Michael Harrison (Kettle's Yard, University of Cambridge); Alex Hollweg; Michael Houlihan (National Museums & Galleries of Wales, Cardiff); Neil Jennings; Mike Moody (Imperial War Museum, London); Charles Oldham; Brigid Peppin; Omar Pound; Russell Roberts (National Museum of Photography, Film and Television); Gordon Samuel (Scolar Fine Art); Sir Nicolas Serota (Tate, London); Jeffrey Sherwin; Peyton Skipwith (Fine Art Society plc, London); Alistair Smith (Whitworth Art Gallery, University of Manchester); Chris Stephens (Tate London); Virginia Tandy (Manchester City Galleries); David Thomson; Roger Tolson (Imperial War Museum); Michael Walsh (Department of Archaeology and Art History, Eastern Mediterranean University, Cyprus); Angela Weight (Imperial War Museum, London); Jonathan Wood (Henry Moore Institute, Leeds); Clara Young (McManus Galleries, Dundee Arts and Heritage Museum)

Supported by the Michael Marks Charitable Trust

With the support of The Paul Mellon Centre for Studies in British Art

Frontispiece: Wyndham Lewis: *Vorticist Figure Composition*, *c.*1914 (detail)
Private collection
Front cover: Cuthbert Hamilton: *Reconstruction*, 1919–20 (detail)
Tate, London
Back cover: Wyndham Lewis: *The Vorticist*, 1912 (detail)
Southampton City Art Gallery

CONTENTS

FOREWORDS

As a London based gallery devoted to Italian art, the Estorick Collection is naturally always keen to explore links between British and Italian culture. This exhibition represents perhaps the fullest expression of that desire to date, for the British Vorticist school very much defined itself through its relationship with Marinetti's Futurist movement.

Lewis and his colleagues were already alert to the implications of Post-Impressionism and Cubism, but it was Futurism's impact that proved to be decisive in energising the British art scene and inspiring the formation of the United Kingdom's first true avant-garde movement. Despite their often stormy and troubled relationship, both Futurism and Vorticism were essentially fighting for the same cause: the liberation of artistic expression from trite conventions and traditions. In Britain, this resulted in exciting experiments with abstraction that were only halted by the outbreak of World War I.

It is especially gratifying for us to host the first exhibition for several years to examine this important movement, as a number of major works from the 1912 Sackville Gallery show – which was so influential for young British artists of the day – belong to the Estorick Collection. As a consequence, the visitor will gain a unique insight into the relationship between the two movements.

This exhibition would not have been possible without the contribution of many people, and I would firstly like to thank Jonathan Black, the Curator of the show, who has been closely involved at every stage. My gratitude also goes to Jonathan Wood, Michael Walsh and Christopher Adams for their contributions to the catalogue, and I am naturally indebted to all the lenders, both public and private, who have so generously agreed to loan their works. I would also like to thank Alistair Smith, Director of The Whitworth Art Gallery, for sharing my enthusiasm for the project and for hosting the exhibition in Manchester. Finally, my thanks go to the Michael Marks Charitable Trust, for its contribution to the publication of this catalogue, and to The Paul Mellon Centre for Studies in British Art for its support. As always, I am indebted to my staff, Christopher Adams, Lucy Bestwick and Leonie Taylor for their consistent commitment to the project.

Roberta Cremoncini
Director
Estorick Collection

Since the Estorick Collection opened its doors in Canonbury Square in 1998 I have been a frequent visitor and an enthusiast for what has been achieved there. It has brought to Central London Italian art and design of the period after 1900, a subject all too often under emphasised through the pre-eminence of the Italian culture of earlier centuries. Thankfully, it has also provided exhibition rooms of domestic proportion for its permanent collection which is wholly appropriate to that setting, and for carefully tailored temporary exhibitions which encapsulate everything which blockbusters do not. Most memorable, perhaps, was the sensitive installation of Morandi's work in 2001; it synchronised tellingly with Tate Modern's Morandi exhibition, where the paintings and drawings, as intimate as they are small, died their death in the overpopulated vastness. To be with Morandi's works in the Estorick rooms, with committed visitors for company, was a privilege too rarely available in today's museums.

It was through admiration for these achievements that I approached Roberta Cremoncini, Director of the Estorick Collection, to propose a collaboration which has found its form in the exhibition *Blasting the Future!*, shown both in Canonbury Square, and, in amplified form, at The Whitworth Art Gallery on Oxford Road. The selection of works for the Manchester showing was researched by Dr Jonathan Black, aided by Mary Griffiths who carried out the organisation of the exhibition and its installation. To both, I am extremely grateful, as I am to all lenders. For making all possible through the most amicable of collaborations, we record the debt of The Whitworth Art Gallery and its viewing public to the Estorick Collection, in the persons of its staff and its Director, Roberta Cremoncini.

Alistair Smith
Director
The Whitworth Art Gallery,
The University of Manchester

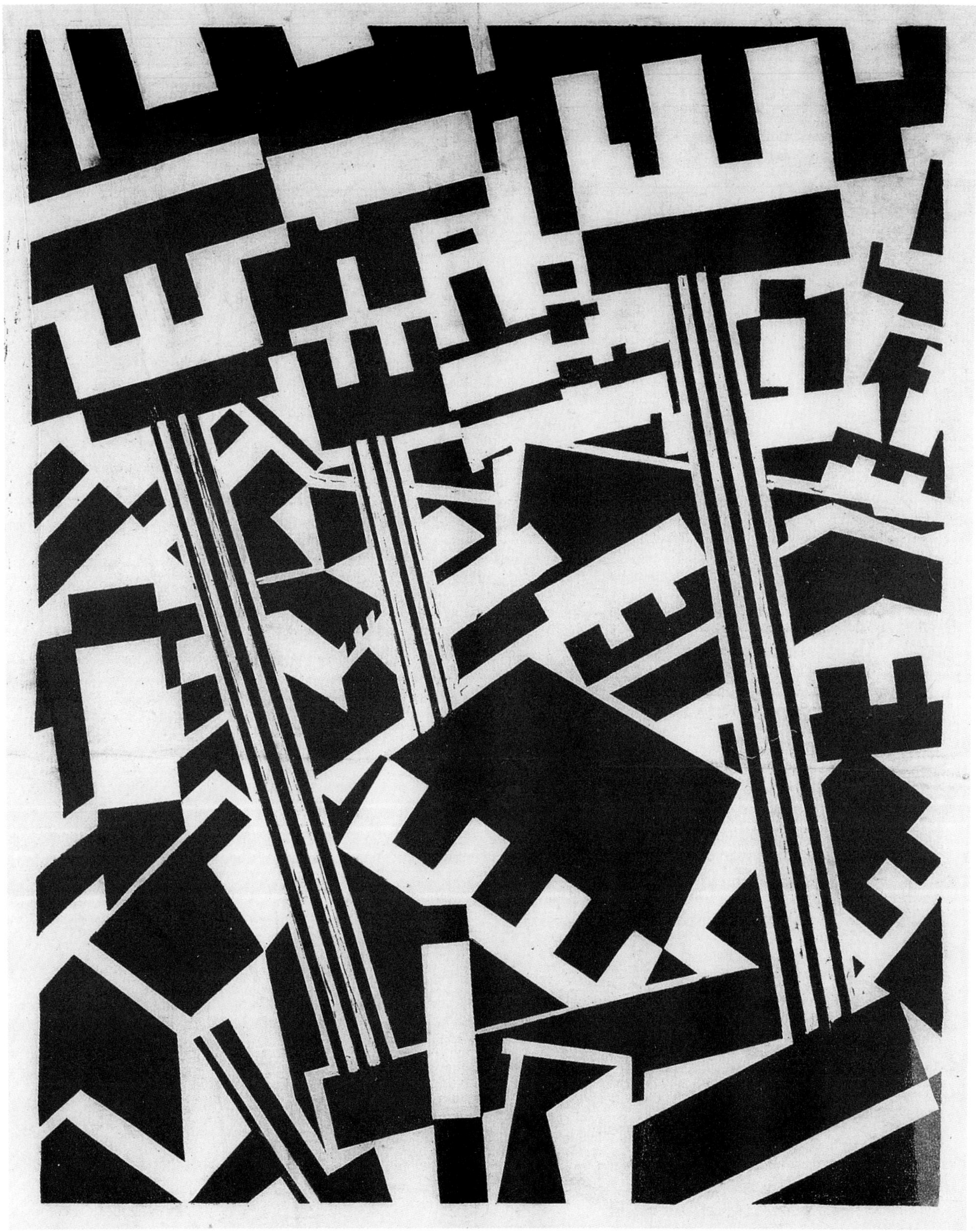

FUTURISM AND THE BRITISH AVANT-GARDE

Christopher Adams

Vorticism was – and remains – something of an oddity in Britain's artistic culture. Its programmatic and consciously 'modern' character goes against the grain of much twentieth-century and contemporary British painting where, as has been observed, progress has typically been achieved through 'a return to personal convictions or native traditions'.[1] Moreover, despite the fact that in Britain a much-cherished individualism has tended to free artists from an 'unthinking adoption of fashionable styles',[2] Vorticism owed much to the most sensationalist and high-profile avant-garde movement of the day – Italian Futurism.

Established in 1914, Vorticism was certainly a product of its time, reflecting early modernism's obsession with categorising its products in a desire to give the British avant-garde a sense of direction and identity. In its violent opposition to all retrogressive tendencies and concern with the machine and the urban world, Vorticism undoubtedly charted a course that was heavily influenced by Futurist ideology and aesthetics. However, those figures associated with the movement – dominated by that formidable polymath Wyndham Lewis – fiercely resisted lazy comparisons of their work with that of their Italian colleagues and stubbornly asserted their independence and autonomy. By way of an introduction to the current exhibition, this essay aims to briefly characterise the turbulent and complex relationship – both historical and aesthetic – between the two movements.

The Futurist movement burst onto an astonished world on 20 February 1909, with the publication of the Italian poet Filippo Tommaso Marinetti's 'Founding and Manifesto of Futurism' on the front page of the respectable French newspaper *Le Figaro*. The following year, the scope of the movement was expanded from literature to the visual arts through the allegiance of five painters – Umberto Boccioni, Carlo Carrà, Luigi Russolo, Gino Severini and Giacomo Balla. The Futurists considered the omnipresent, towering achievements of Italy's artistic heritage to be intimidating to young creative minds and, consequently, detrimental to the development of a vibrant and innovative modern Italian culture. They exhorted Italian youth to shake off this burden through metaphorical acts of destruction and desecration ('set fire to the library shelves! Turn aside the canals to flood the museums!')[3] and insisted that their own achievements should likewise be discarded by subsequent generations in order to

FIG. 1
EDWARD WADSWORTH
Rotterdam
1914
woodcut
26.7 × 19.7 cm
David Thomson

FIG. 2
CARLO CARRÀ
Leaving the Theatre
1909
oil on canvas
69 × 91 cm
Estorick Collection, London

ensure that Italian culture would remain in a perpetually healthy state of artistic revolution.

The basis of, and inspiration for, Futurist art and literature had of necessity to be modern life, they insisted, for by offering entirely novel sensations the urban environment and the machine demanded the evolution of correspondingly novel means of expression to capture them. Their oft-repeated maxim was that 'there can be no modern painting without the starting point of an absolutely modern sensation'.[4]

To evoke a sense of speed or dynamism – the very essence of modernity for the Futurists – became the movement's central artistic goal and the evolution of its pictorial vocabulary developed in tandem with their deepening research into this

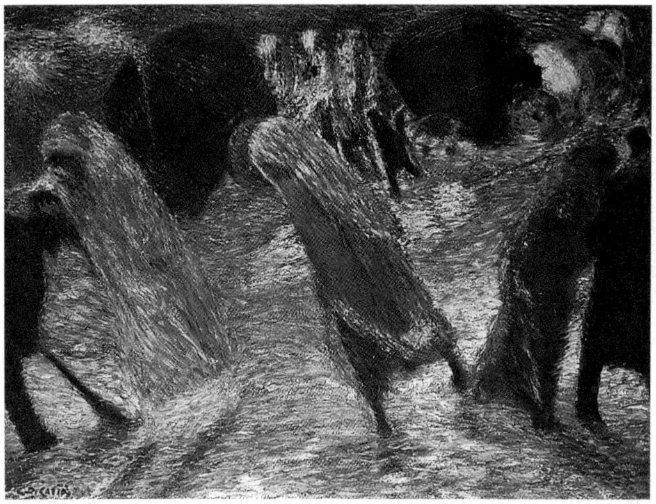

problem. Initially, the painters continued to employ the Divisionist technique with which Balla, Boccioni and Severini in particular had been experimenting for several years. At that time considered the most avant-garde school of painting within Italy, Divisionism was the Italian variant of French Impressionism, utilising as it did a similar combination of small dabs or dashes of colour juxtaposed in such a way as to blend in the eye of the spectator when viewed from a distance. In their 'Technical Manifesto' of 1910, the Futurists observed how objects seem to lose their sense of definition and take on more fluid profiles when seen in movement. Using Divisionism's broken brushstrokes, they vividly illustrated this phenomenon in their works, dissolving the contours of objects to give a convincing idea of blurred motion and flux [fig. 2]. Experimental photography also suggested solutions, particularly the work of the Frenchman Etienne-Jules Marey, who succeeded in capturing several of the infinite number of sequential stages from which actions and movements are constituted on a single photographic plate [fig. 3]. Subsequently, following a visit to Paris in late 1911, Cubist principles were swiftly assimilated and employed to render a more 'intellectual' evocation of movement. The Futurists quickly realised that Cubism's simultaneous incorporation of several different viewpoints into a single image could be adapted to express motion by enabling the artist to record changes in the position of a moving object or figure.

Works reflecting all of the above aesthetics and influences were displayed in the exhibition with which the Futurists made their Parisian début in February 1912 and which travelled to London the following month. However, Marinetti's first appearance in the English capital had taken place two years earlier, the Futurist leader having promoted his fledgling movement with a lecture at the Lyceum Club in which he alternately blasted and blessed various aspects of British culture and society in much the same way as the Vorticists were to do in their own manifesto of 1914. Such public appearances formed part of Marinetti's aggressive and revolutionary approach to cultural exchange. In contrast to schools of painting such as Cubism or Impressionism, which coalesced into movements over time, and whose names were derogatory appellations applied to them by hostile critics, Futurism was a movement proudly defined as such by its founder in a blaze of publicity, with a predetermined, detailed agenda that its creations were intended to reflect and promote. The urgency of this agenda demanded maximum attention and this Marinetti achieved through the continuous conveyance of artists and exhibitions around the globe, the distribution of a never-ending stream of inflammatory manifestos and widespread press coverage, assured by means of riotous 'Futurist evenings' and performances. Profoundly Futurist tactics, they proved that 'living culture could participate in the speed and mobility of the modern world'.[5] Dubbed 'the caffeine of Europe' for his tireless proselytising, Marinetti single-handedly discredited the tired cliché of the misunderstood artist languishing in his garret and called for the emergence of more robust, dynamic creative spirits, whose works would not only passively reflect the contemporary world, but engage with, influence and shape it. In its most practical sense, this concept led to Futurism's intervention in almost every sphere of human creativity, from interior design to dancing, from photography to fashion. In line with the movement's worship of technology and hatred of tradition, for instance, Futurist architecture was intended both to resemble gigantic machinery and to be ephemeral.

In many ways it was entirely natural that the call of Futurism should have produced an echo from the British avant-garde. In the early years of the twentieth century, artists of both countries were united in a common struggle against stagnant and reactionary cultural establishments. Futurism's complaint that Italy's self-appointed 'guardians of old aesthetic laws' were ignoring those 'artists who have not yet had twenty years of struggle and suffering behind them, but [who] are still producing works destined to honour their fatherland' would have struck a chord with those many young British artists who, having trained in Paris, had returned home to find their work meet with incomprehension and derision.[6] Likewise, Futurism's exposure of 'the false claims to belong to the future put forward by the secessionists and the independents, who have installed new academies no less trite and attached to routine than the preceding ones',[7] could have been written about the New English Art Club (NEAC). Having challenged the conservatism of the Royal Academy since the late nineteenth century, the NEAC had itself grown conservative by

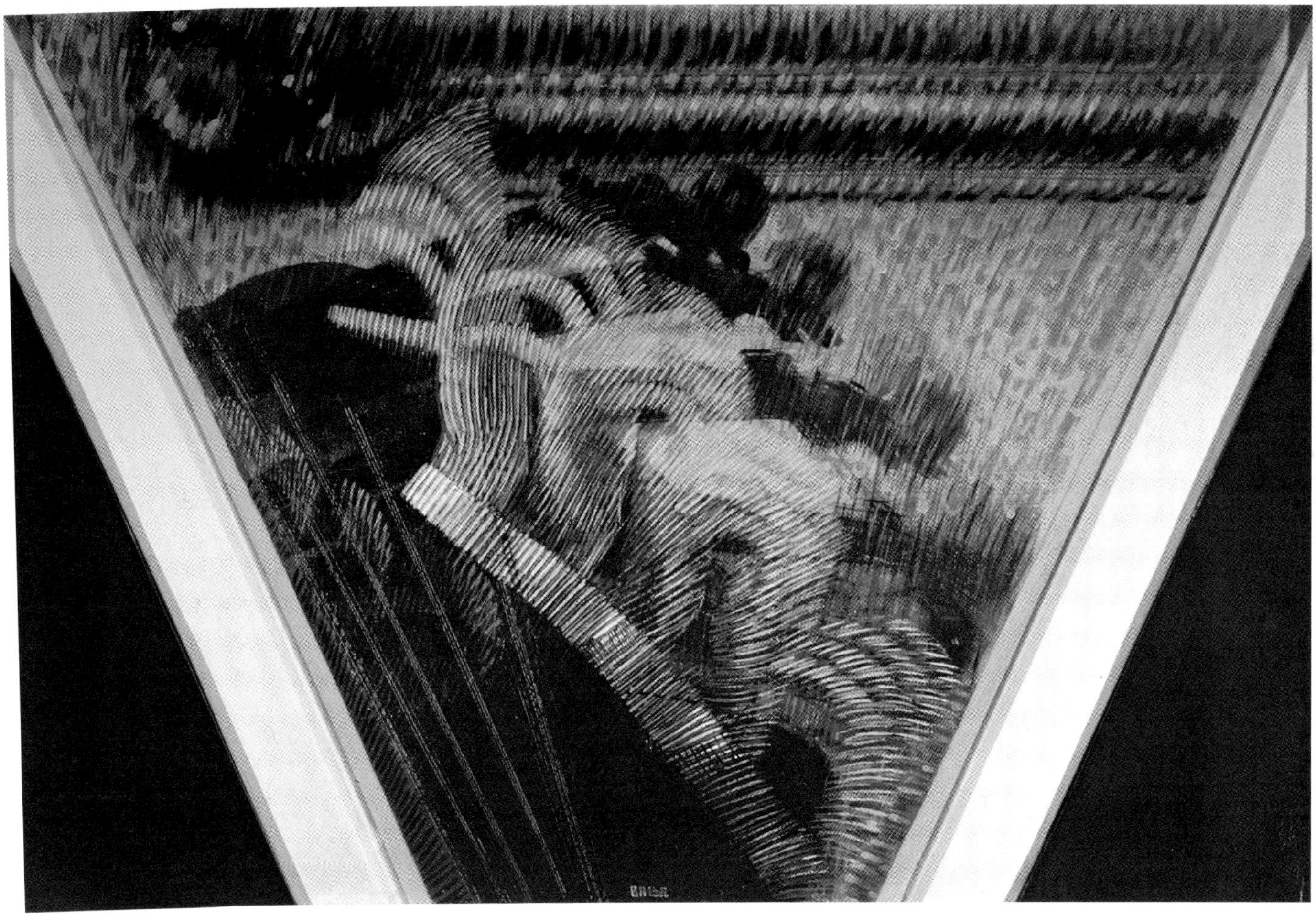

FIG. 3
GIACOMO BALLA
The Hand of the Violinist
1912
oil on canvas
56 x 78.3 cm
Estorick Collection, London

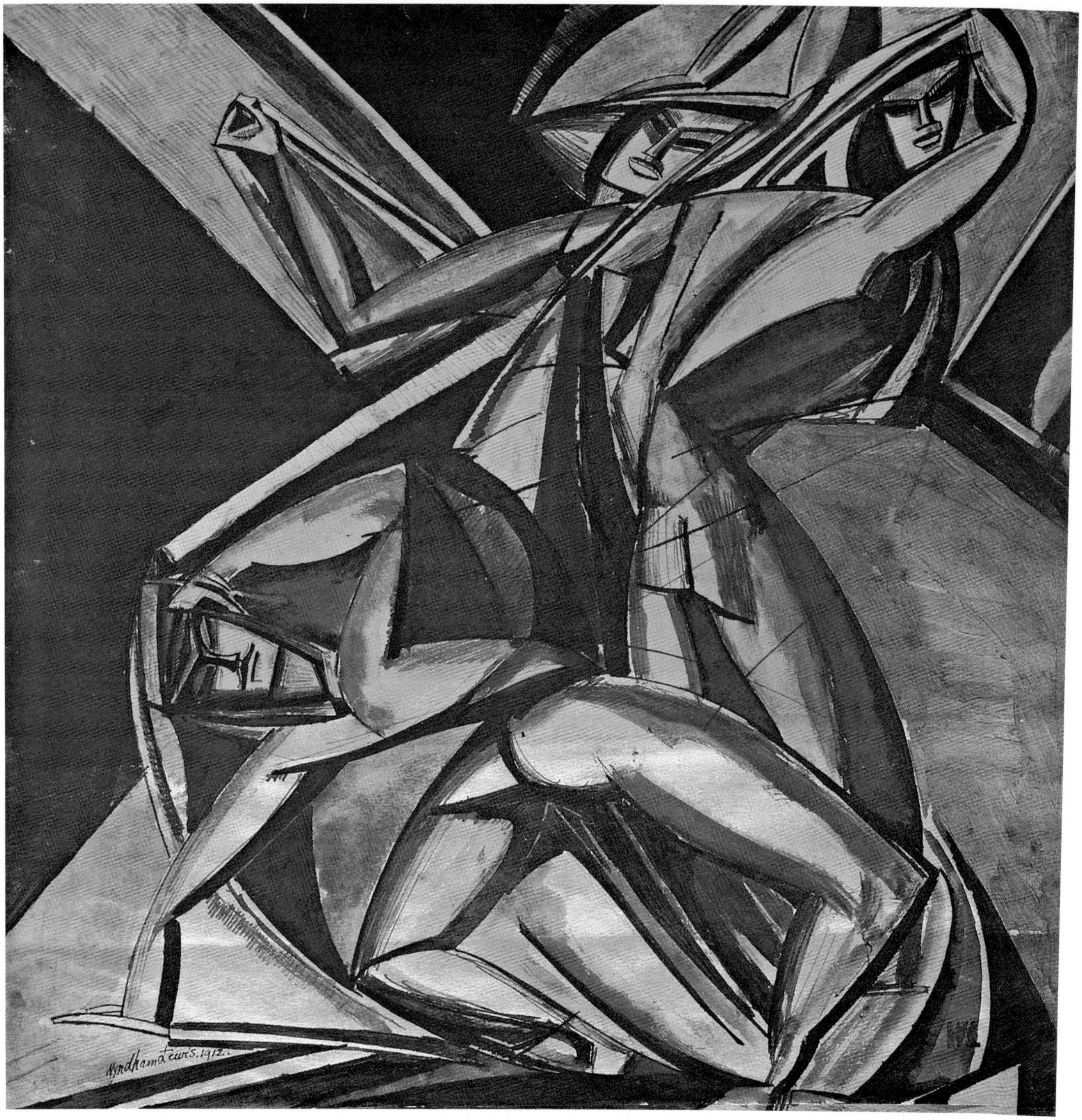
Wyndham Lewis. 1912.

FIG. 4
WYNDHAM LEWIS
The Dancers
1912
pencil, black ink and watercolour on buff paper
30.1 × 29.2 cm
Manchester City Galleries

the end of the Edwardian era, partly in response to the shock of the two Post-Impressionist exhibitions of 1910 and 1912, organised by the critic Roger Fry. Indeed, the 1914 manifesto 'Vital English Art', written by Marinetti and the English Futurist C. R. W. Nevinson, contained a direct attack on 'the sham revolutionaries of the New English Art Club, who, having destroyed the prestige of the Royal Academy, now show themselves grossly hostile to the later movements of the advance guard'.[8] In both countries there was a general ignorance about contemporary artistic trends. Indeed, Impressionism was still being derided in the British press as late as 1905. In short, a broadly equivalent cultural status quo made the British avant-garde especially receptive to the revolutionary rhetoric of its Italian counterpart.

Almost all of those artists who were later to make up the Vorticist group had been associated with Roger Fry's circle from around 1910. At the time, Fry was one of the most influential figures in British artistic culture owing to his evangelical attitude towards modernism. It was thus of no small consequence that in 1912, a few months after the Futurists had unleashed their paintings on an unsuspecting British public at the Sackville Gallery, works by Frederick Etchells and Lewis were included in the second of Fry's landmark Post-Impressionist exhibitions. At this time, Lewis's work may perhaps best be described as a dynamic blend of primitivism, Cubism and Futurism, but infused with that particular severity and angularity which was to be so characteristic of the Vorticist style [fig. 4] [pl. 49]. In the spring of 1913 these two artists, along with Edward Wadsworth and Cuthbert Hamilton, were to participate in Fry's applied arts venture, the Omega Workshops, a project which cast the critic in the role of a latter-day William Morris, overseeing an Arts and Crafts movement for the modern era. By late autumn, the infamously surly Lewis had fallen out with Fry after the latter poached a commission for the Ideal Home Exhibition which its organisers had originally intended for Lewis and the painter Spencer Gore. Taking Wadsworth, Hamilton and Etchells with him, Lewis resolved to set up in opposition to what he termed Fry's 'curtain and pincushion factory in Fitzroy Square'.[9] However, as Karin Orchard has observed, the quarrel with Fry was merely a 'pretext' and the real basis for this secession from the Omega Workshops was a fundamental conflict of aesthetics.[10] In Lewis's eyes, the comparison of Fry's initiative with its nineteenth-century predecessor had become increasingly pertinent, whilst his own work and that of his faction was developing in a more aggressively modernistic direction. The dinner that Lewis organised with Nevinson in honour of Marinetti's return to London in November 1913 was symbolic of this shift in affiliation. In March of the following year, Lewis established the Rebel Art Centre as a platform for the art and ideas of his circle, the ranks of which were swollen by Jessica Dismorr, William Roberts, Helen Saunders and Henri Gaudier-Brzeska.

Futurist activity in London had steadily increased since Marinetti's lecture of 1910, and was to peak in 1914. Following the Sackville Gallery exhibition and Severini's one-man show at the Marlborough Gallery in 1913, London was subjected to an all-out Futurist assault in 1914 with a second group exhibition at the Doré Gallery, a dozen concert performances featuring Russolo's *intonarumori* (or 'noise intoners') at the Coliseum and a barrage of lectures and 'words in freedom' poetry recitals by the movement's leader. As stated, the spirit of Marinetti's vigorous and confrontational campaign against traditionalism had captured the imagination of the more progressive sectors of the British avant-garde, which wholeheartedly endorsed and embraced it. Despite this, however, Nevinson was to be Marinetti's only fully-fledged 'conquest' – works such as *The Arrival* [fig. 9] reflecting his Futurist orthodoxy – and his attempt to co-opt the Rebel Art Centre into the Futurist movement against its will was to backfire spectacularly. On 30 May 1914, Lewis published an article in *The New Weekly* lauding Marinetti as 'Man of the Week'. Within a month, however, he had severed all links with the leader of Futurism.

Eager to carve a niche for his group in the contemporary British art scene – and to assert his authority over it – Lewis was furious when, in June 1914, the aforementioned (and 'unauthorised') manifesto 'Vital English Art' appeared in the press. In it, Nevinson and Marinetti effectively presented the Rebel Art Centre as nothing more than an English outpost of Italian Futurism, thereby denying it an independent identity and undermining Lewis's leadership aspirations. Like the Russian artists Larionov and Khlebnikov, Lewis had no intention of allowing his group's distinct brand of modernism to be perceived as a pale imitation of Futurism in the way that the Italian movement had itself initially been dismissed as 'the inferior cousin of Cubism'.[11] Having promptly and publicly disavowed any links with Marinetti's movement, the artists associated with the Centre set about defining and promoting their own. Baptised 'Vorticism' by Ezra Pound, the American poet and associate of Lewis, it was to quickly supplant the role of the Rebel Art Centre. Ironically, the weapons which Futurism had deployed against its enemies to such great effect – unified action, polemical journals and manifestos and the introduction of 'the fisticuff into the artistic battle' – were now those used by the Vorticists to attack and divorce themselves from Marinetti's movement.[12] Along with Lewis, Richard Aldington, Malcolm Arbuthnot, Lawrence Atkinson, Gaudier-Brzeska, Dismorr, Hamilton, Pound, Roberts, Saunders and Wadsworth may be considered 'true' Vorticists by virtue of being signatories of the movement's manifesto, which was published in the first number of its official organ, *Blast*, in July 1914. Although closely associated with Vorticism, David Bomberg and the sculptor Jacob Epstein never actually joined the movement.

The break with Futurism was not, as has been suggested, simply due to 'snobbish hostility',[13] nor to Lewis's personal ambition, although this would obviously have been a contributing factor. In order to properly account for it, one should not overlook the genuine aesthetic differences that frustrated relations between the two movements, notwithstanding the existence of a certain amount of common ground.

Blast confirmed Vorticism's commitment to the industrial era, as an extract from the first manifesto's famous 'Blast' and 'Bless' lists makes clear:

> BLESS ALL PORTS.
> PORTS, RESTLESS MACHINES of
> scooped out basins
> heavy insect dredgers
> monotonous cranes
> stations
> lighthouses, blazing
> through the frosty
> starlight, cutting the
> storm like a cake [fig. 4][14]

However, the Vorticists did not intend their work to engage with, or reflect, the industrial era through its subject matter, but rather through its employment of a specific visual vocabulary whose formal qualities – precision, hard-edged forcefulness, clean lines, geometrical severity – were inherently expressive of mechanical values, quite independently of any figurative associations. Indeed, the Vorticists ridiculed Futurism's emphasis upon subject matter – which Lewis scornfully ascribed to the Italians' excitement at the belated industrialisation of their country – nicknaming the movement 'Automobilism'.[15] One can also interpret the mechanistic associations of Vorticism's pictorial vocabulary as the deliberate antithesis of the soft, 'organic' qualities of early Futurism's Divisionist brushstrokes – and of that style's 'passéist' nineteenth-century overtones.

The aesthetic implications of the machine identified by the Vorticists were, then, far removed from those perceived by the Futurists whose works, in their rhapsodic evocation of 'our whirling life of steel, of pride, of fever and of speed',[16] focussed on quite different aspects, and represented a late flowering of the romantic spirit that was diametrically opposed to the cool classicism of the Vorticists. Initially used in the context of a description of the lively London cultural scene, the image of the vortex – conflated with that of the eye of a storm – was adopted by the movement as being symbolic of its art's sober, yet highly charged character. According to Pound: 'The vortex is the point of maximum energy ... Futurism is the disgorging spray of a vortex with no drive behind it, *dispersal*.'[17]

Generally speaking, it is easier to gain a sense of Vorticist aesthetics by looking at the movement's works than by examining its written statements, for in contrast to the clarity of Futurist manifestos those of Vorticism are far more oblique, cryptic and metaphorical. This is nowhere more apparent than in Lewis's exposition of the movement's classical aesthetics:

> BLESS the HAIRDRESSER.
> He attacks Mother Nature for a small fee.
> Hourly he ploughs heads for sixpence,
> Scours chins and lips for threepence.
> He makes systematic mercenary war on this
> WILDNESS.
> He trims aimless and retrograde growths
> into CLEAN ARCHED SHAPES and
> ANGULAR PLOTS.[18]

It is interesting to note that Futurism – which, unlike Vorticism, did not perish in the squalor of the First World War, but survived into the mid-1940s – was to later reflect aesthetic tendencies resonant of Vorticism, although this was never directly acknowledged. The 1922 manifesto 'Mechanical Art',

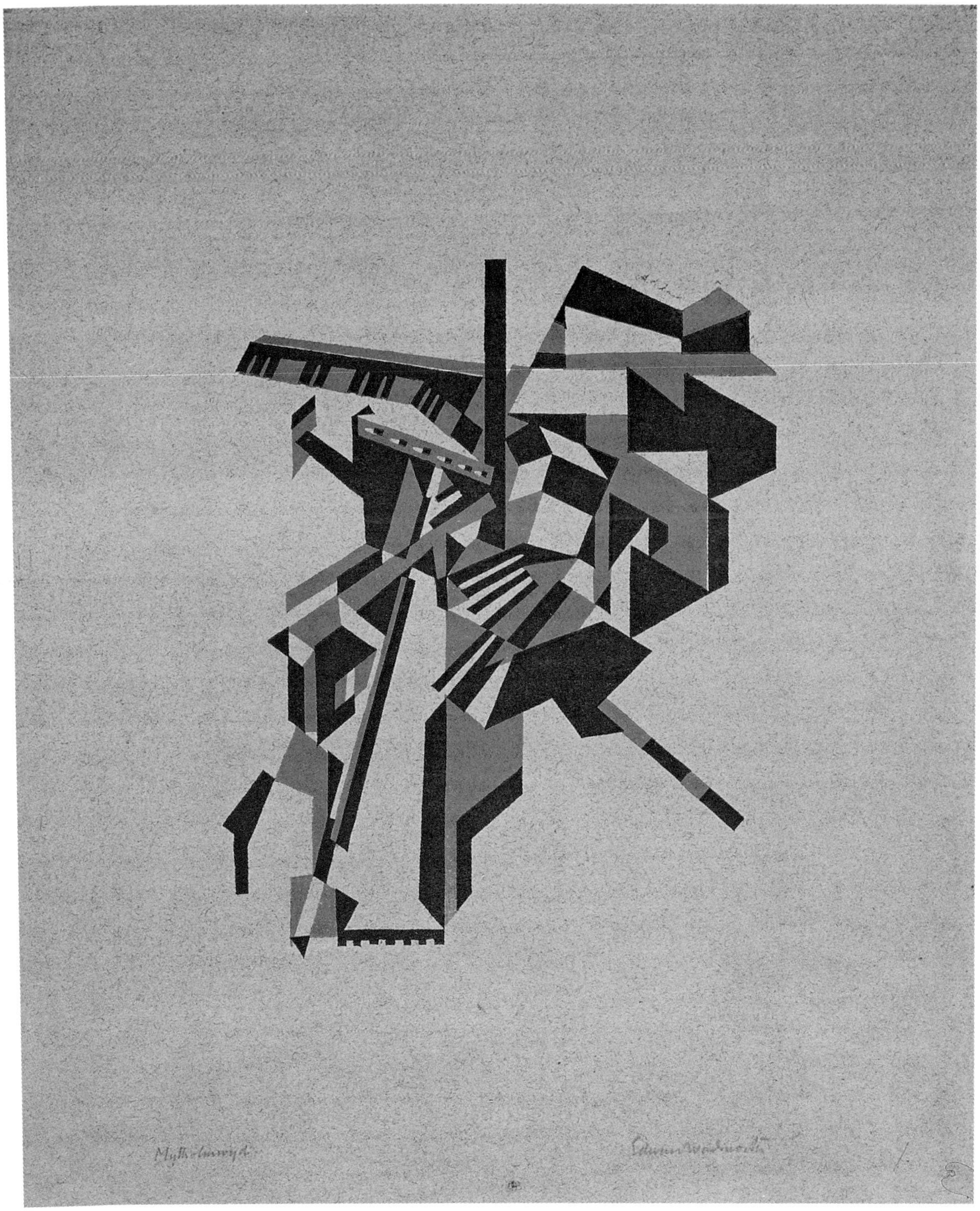

1
EDWARD WADSWORTH
Mytholmroyd
*c.*1914
two-colour woodcut
38 × 30.4 cm
The Whitworth Art Gallery,
The University of Manchester

FIG. 5
EDWARD WADSWORTH
RMS Mauretania in dazzle camouflage on the River Mersey
1918
photograph
Alex Hollweg

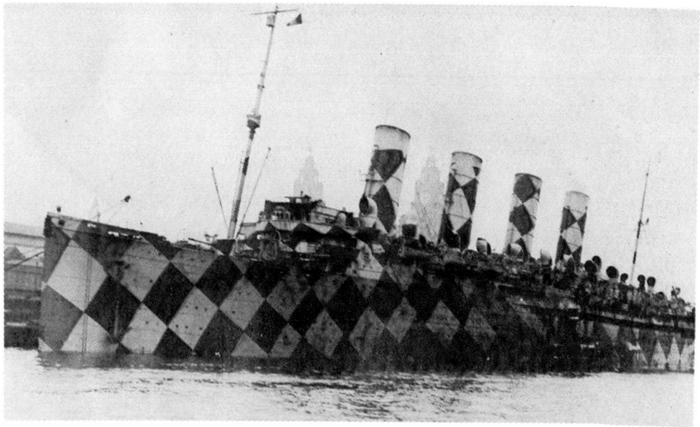

written by the second-generation Futurist painters Enrico Prampolini, Ivo Pannaggi and Vinicio Paladini, codified this new direction, whilst an accompanying text by Paladini elucidated the specific visual characteristics of such art:

> No longer the atmosphere ... of Manet, Renoir or Medardo [Rosso], the marvellous liquefaction of forms in the ether, but rather geometry and solidification, leading to the creation of a unique and indestructible architecture.
>
> Thought and calculation ... rigid and metallic art, *classical* art![19]

This tendency in Futurist art of the 1920s to view the machine less as a source of spatial disruption and explosive dynamism, and more as a 'model of formal purity and exactitude',[20] is generally attributed to the contemporary influence of *L'Esprit Nouveau*, French Purism and the aesthetics of De Stijl. It is worth noting, however, that the issue of the Futurist journal *Noi* devoted to mechanical art, in which the aforementioned manifesto appeared, also carried a reproduction of a Vorticist work by Wadsworth entitled *Mechanical Construction*. Certainly, of all the Vorticists, Wadsworth's work was closest to that produced under the Futurist banner during the twenties: works such as *Mytholmroyd* [pl. 1] were very similar to the ink drawings of Prampolini and Fillia and the paintings of De Pistoris and Angelo Maino. Works such as Bomberg's *Ju-Jitsu* [pl. 16] and *In the Hold* (Tate Britain) are also similar to Futurist 'mechanical art' of the 1920s. Interestingly, Wadsworth's name surfaces again in one of the last Futurist manifestos, written by Marinetti and the painter Tullio Crali in 1942. 'Plastic Illusionism: The Perfection of the Earth' called on Futurist artists to contribute to the war effort by devising ingenious camouflage techniques to disorientate enemy aircraft. It recognised Wadsworth and Nevinson as pioneers in this field, referring to the development of 'dazzle' camouflage during the First World War [figs. 5, 13 and 14] [pls. 26 and 44].[21]

Vorticism had emerged shortly before the outbreak of the First World War and the conflict was to rob the movement of its momentum by fragmenting the group and claiming the lives of certain of its supporters, such as the sculptor Gaudier-Brzeska (killed in 1915) and the philosopher/journalist T. E. Hulme (killed in 1917). Additionally, many artists, including Lewis, Nevinson and Roberts, became involved in official war artists' programmes, the requirements of which – and the sheer wretchedness of the subject matter – demanded a more humanistic, less abstract approach, diluting the aesthetic radicalism of the pre-war era [pls. 19, 20 and 21]. A second, less abrasive edition of *Blast* was issued in July 1915, one month after the opening at the Doré Gallery of what proved to be the only genuine Vorticist exhibition to be held on British soil during the movement's lifespan. It turned out to be a retrospective. Arguably a more 'mature', thoughtful response to the industrial age than Futurism had ever been, or indeed ever was to be, Vorticism had been cut down in its prime.

Notes

1. F. Spalding, *British Art Since 1900* (London, 1986), p. 7.
2. Ibid.
3. F. T. Marinetti, 'The Founding and Manifesto of Futurism', in *Let's Murder the Moonshine: Selected Writings*, ed. by R. W. Flint (Los Angeles, 1991), pp. 47–52 (p. 51).
4. U. Boccioni and others, 'The Exhibitors to the Public', in *Futurist Manifestos*, ed. by U. Apollonio (Boston, 2001), pp. 45–50 (p. 46).
5. C. Tisdall and A. Bozzolla, *Futurism* (London, 1977), p. 14.
6. U. Boccioni and others, 'Manifesto of the Futurist Painters', in *Futurist Manifestos*, pp. 24–27 (p. 26).
7. U. Boccioni and others, 'Futurist Painting: Technical Manifesto', in *Futurist Manifestos*, pp. 27–31 (p. 30).
8. *Observer*, 7 June 1914. Reprinted in *Futurism & Futurisms*, ed. by P. Hulten (London, 1987), p. 529.
9. Quoted in C. Harrison, *English Art and Modernism 1900–1939*, 2nd edn. (New Haven and London, 1994), p. 100.
10. K. Orchard, '"A Laugh Like a Bomb": The History and the Ideas of the Vorticists', in *Blast: Vorticism 1914–1918*, ed. by P. Edwards (Aldershot, 2000), pp. 14–23 (p. 15).
11. C. Tisdall and A. Bozzolla, p. 58.

12. F. T. Marinetti, *Guerra sola igiene del mondo* (Milan, 1915), p. 5. For the Vorticists' disruptive antics, see Michael Walsh's essay in this catalogue.

13. R. W. Flint, introduction to *Let's Murder the Moonshine*, p. 26.

14. W. Lewis, 'Manifesto – I', *Blast*, ed. by W. Lewis (London, 1914; repr. Santa Rosa, 2002), pp. 9–28 (p. 23).

15. 'Long Live the Vortex!', *Blast*, pp. 7–8 (p. 8). See the exchange between Marinetti and Lewis, recounted in W. Lewis, *Blasting and Bombardiering*, rev. edn. (London and New York, 1982), p. 34: 'You Wops insist too much on the Machine. You're always on about these driving-belts, you are always exploding about internal combustion. We've had machines here in England for a donkey's years. They're no novelty to *us*.' The Industrial Revolution had begun in England during the eighteenth century. By contrast, industrialisation only significantly developed in Italy during the tail-end of the nineteenth century. Even then, cautions Martin Clark, 'one should not exaggerate. Italy in 1914 was still *'Italietta'*, an agricultural economy, and her most important industry was still cotton; it was the First World War that provided the real stimulus to the engineering industries.' M. Clark, *Modern Italy 1871–1995*, 2nd edn. (Harlow, 1996), p. 119.

16. U. Boccioni and others, 'Futurist Painting: Technical Manifesto', p. 30.

17. E. Pound, 'Vortex', *Blast*, pp. 153–54 (p. 153).

18. W. Lewis, 'Manifesto – I', p. 25.

19. V. Paladini, 'Estetica meccanica', *Noi*, 2nd series, I, no. 2 (May 1923), p. 2 (Paladini's italics).

20. E. Crispolti, 'Second Futurism', in *Italian Art in the 20th Century: Painting and Sculpture 1900–1988*, ed. by E. Braun (Munich and London, 1989), pp. 165–71 (p. 167).

21. Even so, Marinetti and Crali were unable to resist making the claim that the vocabulary of this technique ultimately derived from Futurist aesthetics: 'We Futurist aeropoets admire Michelangelo because he dreamed of sculpting the mountains. On the eve of the Great War the English Futurists Nevinson and Wadsvorth [sic], stimulated by the aeropoetic lectures delivered by Marinetti in London's Dore Gallery [sic] … created the first illusory camouflage designs for battleships, employing the force-lines and plastic dynamism of Boccioni and Balla.' Reproduced in *Crali aeropittore futurista*, ed. by C. Rebeschini (Milan, 1994), p. 80.

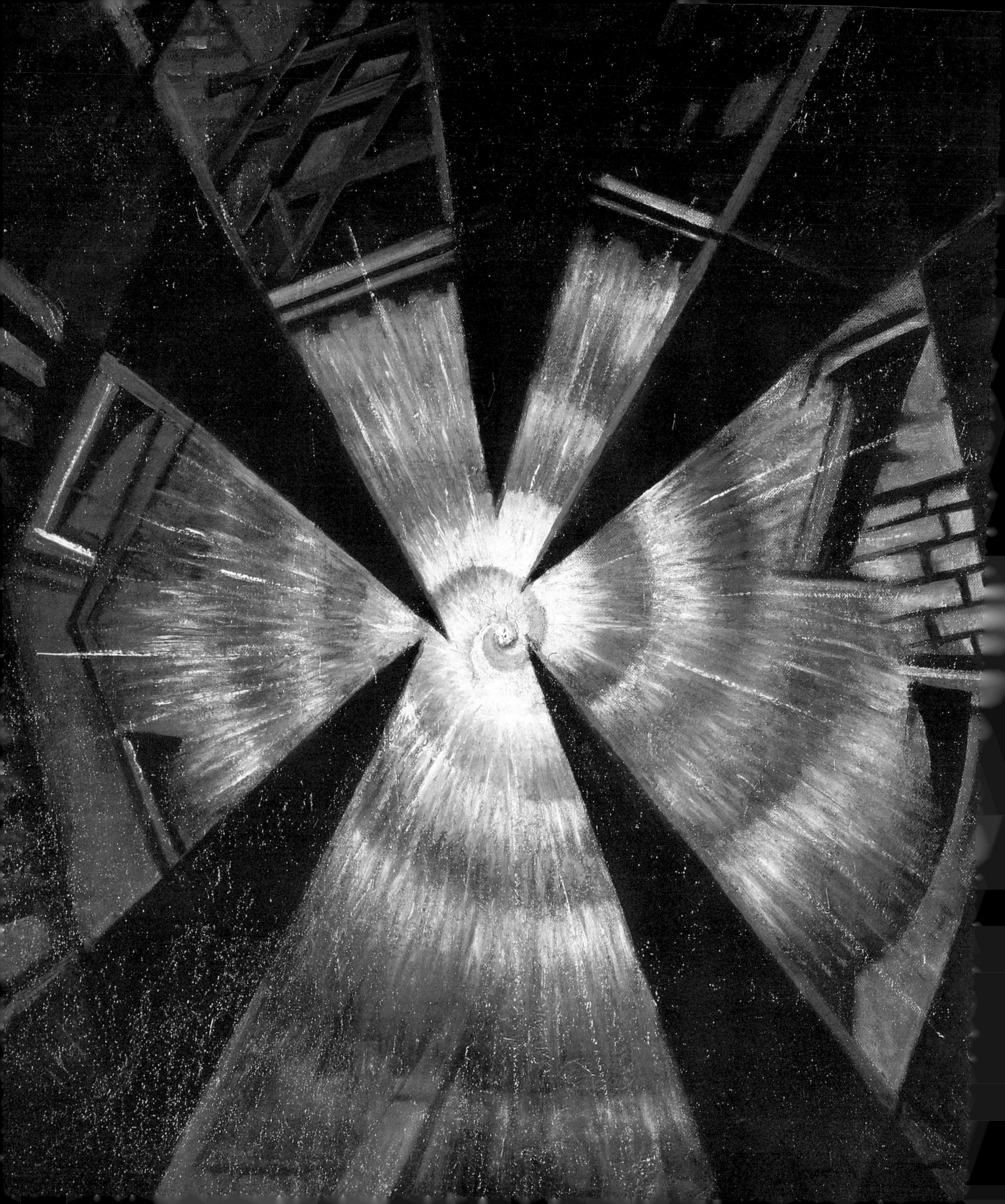

'THE EMINENT ENGLISH FUTURIST'

C.R.W. Nevinson and English Futurism in Peace and War

Michael J. K. Walsh
Department of Archaeology and Art History
Eastern Mediterranean University
Cyprus

> Arriving in London in 1912, he [Marinetti] found the most industrially and scientifically advanced nation in the world, the country of H. G. Wells, overrun with some of its most backward and house trained poets and painters. Two years later they were breaking up his lectures on a British Futurist programme they claimed was more futuristic than that of the Futurists.[1]

It was inevitable that Futurism should come to London, and when it did it was equally inevitable that C. R. W. Nevinson should be the English artist who associated his name most closely with it.[2] The son of a suffragette mother and a war-correspondent father, raised in an intellectual and international household in Hampstead, the young Slade graduate searching for direction within the modernist experimentation of pre-war London found the extravagant rhetoric of the original Futurist manifesto irresistible. Anathema to the establishment, it propounded the merits of danger, energy, fearlessness, courage, audacity, speed (the newest form of beauty), war (the world's only hygiene), militarism, patriotism, scorn for women and an absolute contempt for the past. Futurism, he would have felt, was modern art for a modern era, in a city where the youth had exhausted its patience for the strictures of its Victorian inheritance.

Nevinson's mother, Margaret, reported on a lecture Marinetti gave in 1910, unaware that her own son would head the movement's British chapter within a few years. She wrote in *The Vote*: 'The members of the society are young men in revolt at the worship of the past. They are determined to destroy it, and erect upon its ashes the Temple of the future. War seems to be the chief tenet in the gospel of Futurism: war upon the classical in art, literature, music.'[3]

Nevinson's father, the war journalist, writer and political activist Henry Wood Nevinson, also admired some aspects of Marinetti's work, following

> a never-to-be-forgotten occasion in the Balkan Wars, when the Italian had found himself cooped up in a train full of journalists for a whole day, a golden opportunity for him. He made the most of it by reciting for hours on end various Italian poems and expounding the theory of Italian Futurism to an audience which could not get away.[4]

FIG. 6
C. R. W. NEVINSON
Bursting Shell (detail)
1915
oil on canvas
76.2 × 55.9 cm
Tate, London

FIG. 7
C. R. W. NEVINSON
The Departure of the Train de Luxe
1913
Whereabouts unknown
Photograph Tate Archive

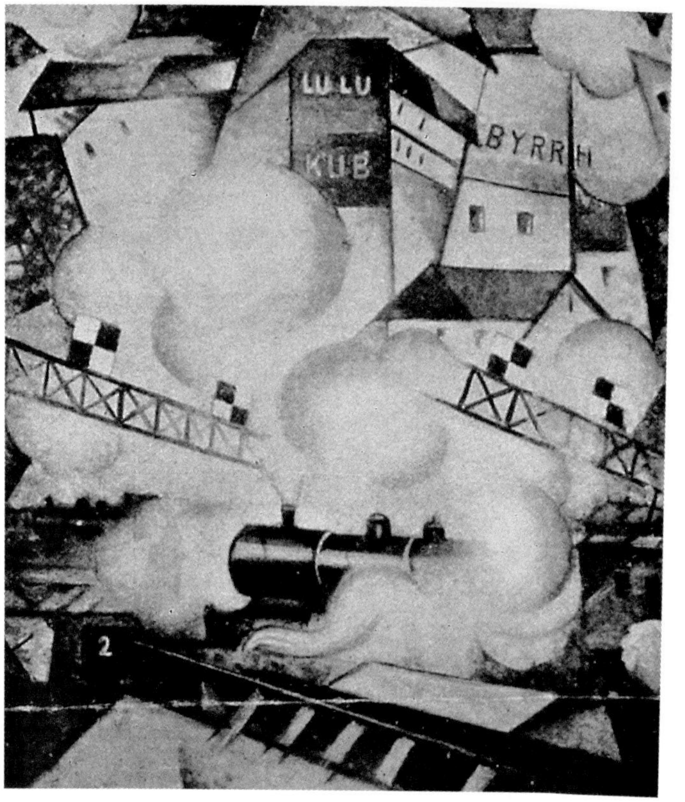

FIG. 8
C. R. W. Nevinson in front of his painting 'Tum-Tiddly-Um-Tum-Pom-Pom'
from *The Western Daily Mail,* 15 May 1914
Photograph Tate Archive

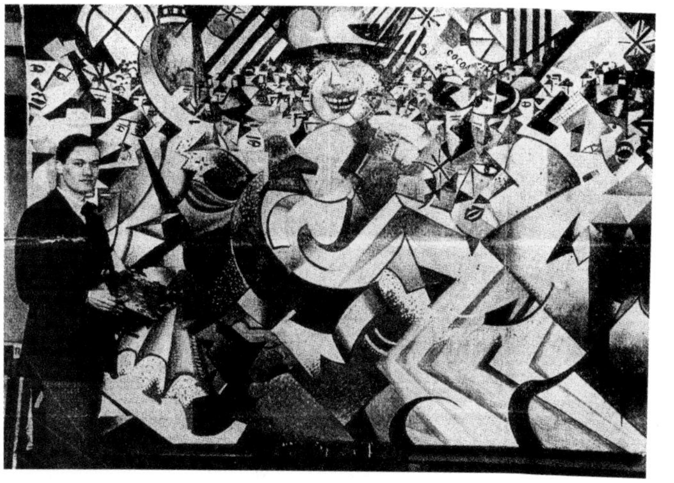

Thus, while *The Times* categorically stated that 'the anarchical extravagance of the Futurists must deprive the movement of the sympathy of all reasonable men',[5] the Nevinson household seems to have been more accommodating.[6]

In April 1913, Nevinson formed a crucial friendship with the Italian Futurist Gino Severini, who wrote enthusiastically to Marinetti:

> I have to tell you about a young painter whose name is Nevinson. I met him during my exhibition, and he introduced me to other young artists, who, with him, all became convinced Futurists. ... Nevinson will thus introduce himself to you on my behalf; he writes to me enthusiastically about Futurism and will put himself at your service for any purpose that you may deem useful.[7]

On two occasions Severini dined with the Nevinsons in Hampstead, where he 'talked Futurism in French'.[8] Nevinson, in return, attended his one-man show at the Marlborough Gallery, entitled 'The Futurist Painter Severini Exhibits His Latest Works'. Nevinson's art and theories on modernism thus began their alignment with the Italian's, and at 'The Post-Impressionist and Futurist Exhibition' at the Doré Gallery in October 1913, in the prestigious continental company of Cézanne, Van Gogh, Matisse, Delaunay, Picasso, Marc *et al.*, he ventured his first Futurist canvas into the public domain. *The Departure of the Train de Luxe* [fig. 7] was the most modern interpretation of an industrial scene yet undertaken by Nevinson and Frank Rutter appreciatively called it 'the first English Futurist picture'.[9] This was a definite move towards modernising the presentation of the contemporary theme in the mode of Severini's *Nord-Sud* (1912). It also marked a definitive shift forward from his Slade output, which had also gravitated around urban themes, though conducted in a mode reminiscent of the French Impressionists of the 1880s.[10]

Both artists attempted to capture the sensation of motion in a modern, industrial context, introducing a kinetic element to the painting through truncated words and interlocking planes to create this fourth dimension of movement in space and time. Simultaneity was generated by the superimposition of multiple views of the moving train, as versions of the same event in sequence, but superimposed onto the canvas in one frozen moment. It was a brave, if faltering, first step. Nevinson had also

FIG. 9
C. R. W. NEVINSON
The Arrival
1914
oil on canvas
76.2 x 63.5 cm
Tate, London

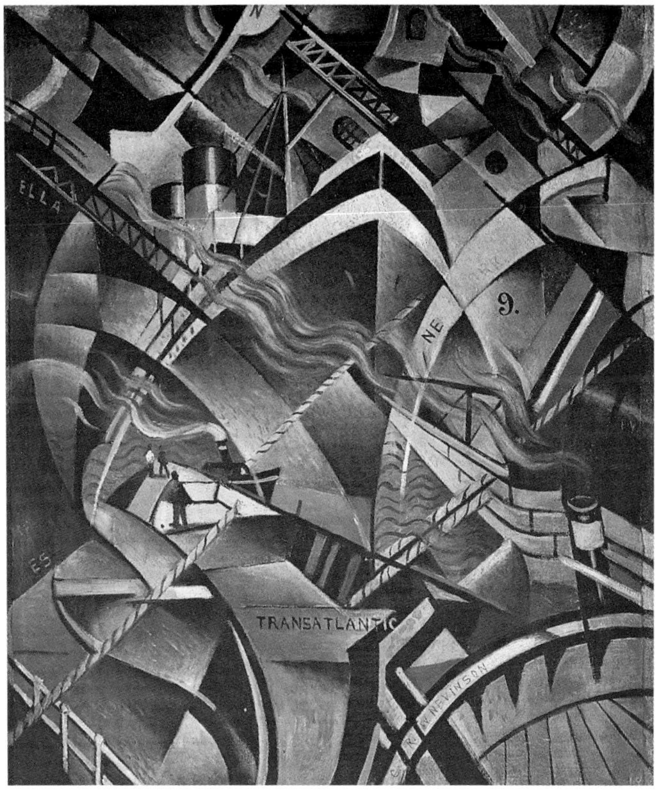

been particularly taken by another painting of Severini's, *Pan-Pan at the Monico*, which later formed the foundation for his own *At the Dance Hall* [pl. 6]. Severini had declared that he was trying to capture 'light and ambience [which] act simultaneously on the forms in movement',[11] and both Severini's and Nevinson's scenes revelled in the noise and movement of music, fashion and dance as experienced in modern-day Paris and London. Stylised figures, forms and colours conveyed the dynamism of the experience, rather than creating an accurate visual representation of it.

Whether or not Nevinson instigated Marinetti's return to London in 1913, as he claimed in his autobiography *Paint and Prejudice*, is uncertain. Nonetheless, on 18 November 1913, a committee of rebel artists including Frederick Etchells, William Roberts, Wyndham Lewis and Nevinson organised a dinner in Marinetti's honour at the Florence Restaurant on Rupert Street. Though Lewis would later call Marinetti 'the intellectual Cromwell of our time' and acknowledge that 'England has need of these foreign auxiliaries to put her energies to rights and restore order',[12] he did not wish to see the Italian dominate the emergent English avant-garde. Nevinson, too, saw the dangers and wrote to Lewis after the dinner: 'I had quite a great deal of difficulty in preventing Marinetti from again expounding and proposing his philanthropic desire to present us to Europe and be our continental guide.'[13]

Though Nevinson was now referring to the rebel English painters as the 'Blast Group', the press tended to make the association more directly with Futurism, particularly when Nevinson and Marinetti finally came together publicly at the Doré Gallery in April 1914 to perform *The Siege of Adrianople*. The poem, already familiar to H. W. Nevinson from his encounter on the Balkan train journey, was enhanced by Marinetti striking wood with a hammer, while Nevinson responded with 'two big drums in a distant room [which] produced the boom of cannon, when I told him to do so over the telephone'.[14] At this time Marinetti also dined at the Nevinson household where Henry recorded, perhaps disappointedly, that he was 'quite tame and sensible'.[15] There Marinetti saw and approved of Nevinson's most daring Futurist composition to date, *Tum-Tiddly-Um-Tum-Pom-Pom* [fig. 8], in which the artist had attempted to capture the dynamism of a bank holiday on Hampstead Heath rather than creating a static representation of the day, place and time. There were stylistic links to Severini and Boccioni in truncated figures, musical references, words and numbers, and the sequins in Severini's composition were echoed by the confetti in Nevinson's. T. E. Hulme declared it Nevinson's 'best picture',[16] but fellow Rebel Art Centre member Henri Gaudier-Brzeska did not share the enthusiasm, calling it 'union jacks, lace stockings and other tommy rot'.[17]

The most significant alliance between Marinetti and Nevinson was in their joint declaration of 'Vital English Art: Futurist Manifesto' in early June 1914. The document began in Marinetti's voice:

> I am an Italian Futurist poet, and a passionate admirer of England. I wish, however, to cure English Art of that most grave of all maladies – passéism. I have the right to speak plainly and without compromise, and together with my friend Nevinson, an English Futurist painter, to give the signal for battle.

The manifesto then went on to attack worship of tradition,

effeminacy, decorativeness, sentimentality, snobs, the New English Art Club, the King, sham revolutionaries, indifference, the 'right of the ignorant to discuss ... Art', 'passéist filth' and the 'mania for immortality'. It demanded an English art which would be 'strong, virile and anti-sentimental', characterised by optimism, heroism, creativity, excitement and genius, with physical and moral courage. It concluded:

> So we call upon the English public to support, defend, and glorify the genius of the great Futurist painters or pioneers and advance forces of Vital English Art – Atkinson, Bomberg, Epstein, Etchells, Hamilton, Nevinson, Roberts, Wadsworth, Wyndham Lewis.
> *F. T. Marinetti* – Italian Futurist Movement (Milan)
> *C. R. W. Nevinson* – Art Rebel [sic] Centre (London)

The main analogy in the manifesto was that of English art as a sick patient and the promise of antidotes which would bring to it, through a revolutionary purge, hygiene and purity. Typically Futurist, it was eye-catching, offensive and personal; but curiously the manifesto also signalled the beginning of the end for Futurism in London. Presented by Marinetti alone it might have been dismissed as 'a spirited display of fireworks',[18] but the fact that Nevinson co-signed it, thrusting himself to the forefront of the avant-garde, caused an irreparable rift with his rebel peers. Not only had he used the Rebel Art Centre address, as if it were the London branch of Futurism, but had also named, as signatories, other artists, none of whom had been consulted about its content.

This schism became apparent in the mutiny at the Doré Gallery on 12 June 1914, where Nevinson, emerging from Marinetti's shadow, delivered a lecture on the disgrace of immortality in art and how the United States viewed England as 'a little old woman with a past'. He then listed enemies of progressive art which included the 'backwoods of Chelsea', the 'barbarians of the West End' and those who painted in the style of Blake, Constable and Turner.[19] The polemics of the evening, however, came not from the stage but from the audience, who had had enough of Italian bombast and arrogance. Lewis recorded, 'I assembled in Greek Street a determined band of miscellaneous anti-futurists. ... There were about ten of us.'[20] The artists whose names had been used in the manifesto, together with Hulme and Gaudier-Brzeska, heckled the speakers, let off fireworks and generally disrupted the evening violently. The next day Nevinson wrote to Lewis: 'I regret having been the cause of so much trouble & expense to the "Rebel" Art Centre on account of my "irresponsibility" regarding the Manifesto that Marinetti & myself drew up.' His tone, however, became progressively more personal to the point where he attributed the problems 'entirely and absolutely [to] the Delusions of your highly suspicious neuresthenic mind.' Nevinson identified the crux of the problem in his conclusion stating, 'neither you nor the others have in the past objected to your names being used by Marinetti, but when my name appears also then you adopt your narrow minded and pompous tone. There lies the cause of the trouble.'[21]

To the press Nevinson was now 'the eminent English Futurist',[22] while Lewis was doing everything possible to disassociate both himself and his peers from the movement – indeed to compete against it. In his autobiography, *Blasting and Bombardiering*, Lewis recalled a conversation with Marinetti in which he laid national claim to the origins of Futurism, telling him: 'you Wops insist too much on the Machine ... We've had machines here in England for a donkey's years. They're no novelty to *us*.'[23]

Lewis, with the newly formed Vorticists, wanted to exercise a classical, perhaps mature, control over the phenomenon of modernity in a structural, geometric and precise way, implying a reverence for, but not a novel fascination with, the modern industrial era. Another letter from Nevinson to Lewis showed that there was now little hope of reconciliation between the two men or their groups. He wrote: 'As a Futurist and not a Vorticist I have no doubt I shall change and evolve what ideas I possess. I know this to be a great source of trouble to you as I notice a continuous complaint in your articles on "automobilism" that the Futurists are not doing exactly what they were doing two years ago.'[24]

Through his absolute association with the movement, Nevinson was becoming its sole defender against contemporary national hostility, to the point that the *Yorkshire Observer* anticipated 'Mr Nevinson will have the distinction of Abdiel – "Faithful among the faithless, only he"'.[25]

Perhaps the zenith of Nevinson's peace-time Futurist experimentation is *The Arrival* [fig. 9] whose associations with the work of the French Futurist painter Felix Delmarle are more than coincidental. While sharing a studio with Severini in Paris, Delmarle painted two depictions of a similar theme, both called *The Port*.

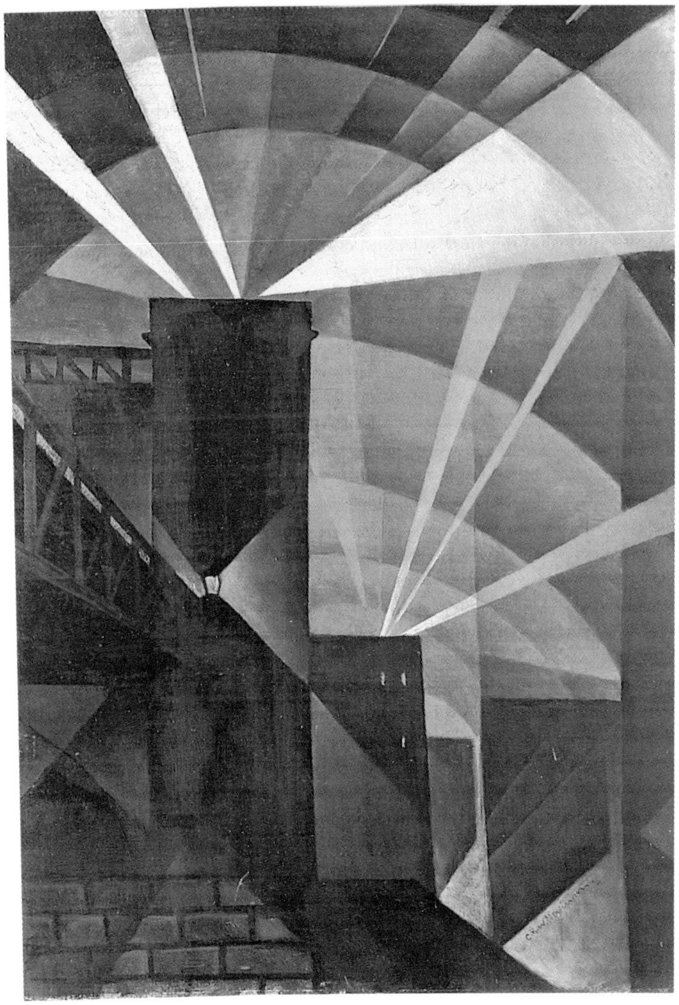

FIG. 10
C. R. W. NEVINSON
The First Searchlights at Charing Cross
1914
oil on canvas
60.9 × 40.6 cm
Leeds Museums and Galleries (City Art Gallery)

Nevinson would have seen these, and a similar work by Russolo, as significant templates for his own future compositions.[26] The subject matter – the arrival in port of a transatlantic steamer – satisfied Futurist ideology (indeed the Futurists had sought tickets on the *Titanic* in 1912), as did the technique which fragmented the picture plane into a simultaneity of time and movement. Attempting to evoke 'universal dynamism' in order to capture what the Futurists described in their 1910 'Technical Manifesto' of Futurist painting as 'our whirling life of steel, of pride, of fever and of speed',[27] the entirety of events surrounding the arrival of the ship, from the cacophony of noises, to the cranes and notices of the dockside, all compositionally rooted by the towering hull of the vessel, would have been the *raison d'être* of Nevinson's painting. The spectator was hurled into the centre of the composition to become part of the event, not an impartial and distant observer of it, in a scene where conventional comprehensions of space and time were distorted, perhaps confounded, into a single vision of the event in its entirety. Accordingly, *The Star* observed, 'it resembles a Channel steamer after a violent collision with the pier'.[28]

When war came in August 1914, Nevinson believed the real Futurist hour had arrived with a conflict tailor-made for it. There was no other vocabulary as relevant, in his opinion, to create depictions of modern war, and modern depictions of war. By November 1914 Nevinson, therefore, unlike Severini and the other Futurists, was uniformed and at the Front as a Red Cross ambulance driver on the Ypres Salient. On his return he proclaimed: 'This war will be a violent incentive to Futurism, for we believe that there is no beauty except in strife, no masterpiece without aggressiveness.'[29] In private, however, he had deep concerns as his father's journal reveals: 'Rich[ard] much disturbed about the war + the Futurist support of its horror. Declares he will abandon Futurism + and will call his new movement Mentalist.'[30] But Nevinson persevered, publicly at least, and *did* take Futurism to the Front.

Nevinson's first experiments with 'war Futurism' were conducted in London, either before his departure for Belgium, or on his return in January 1915. Searchlights, in their dramatic sweeping searches of the night sky, emphasized the rivalry between man and machine, creating aesthetic and ethical juxtapositions (and contradictions) of warfare within the pastoral context of a Whistlerian 'nocturne'. At the Friday Club exhibition in

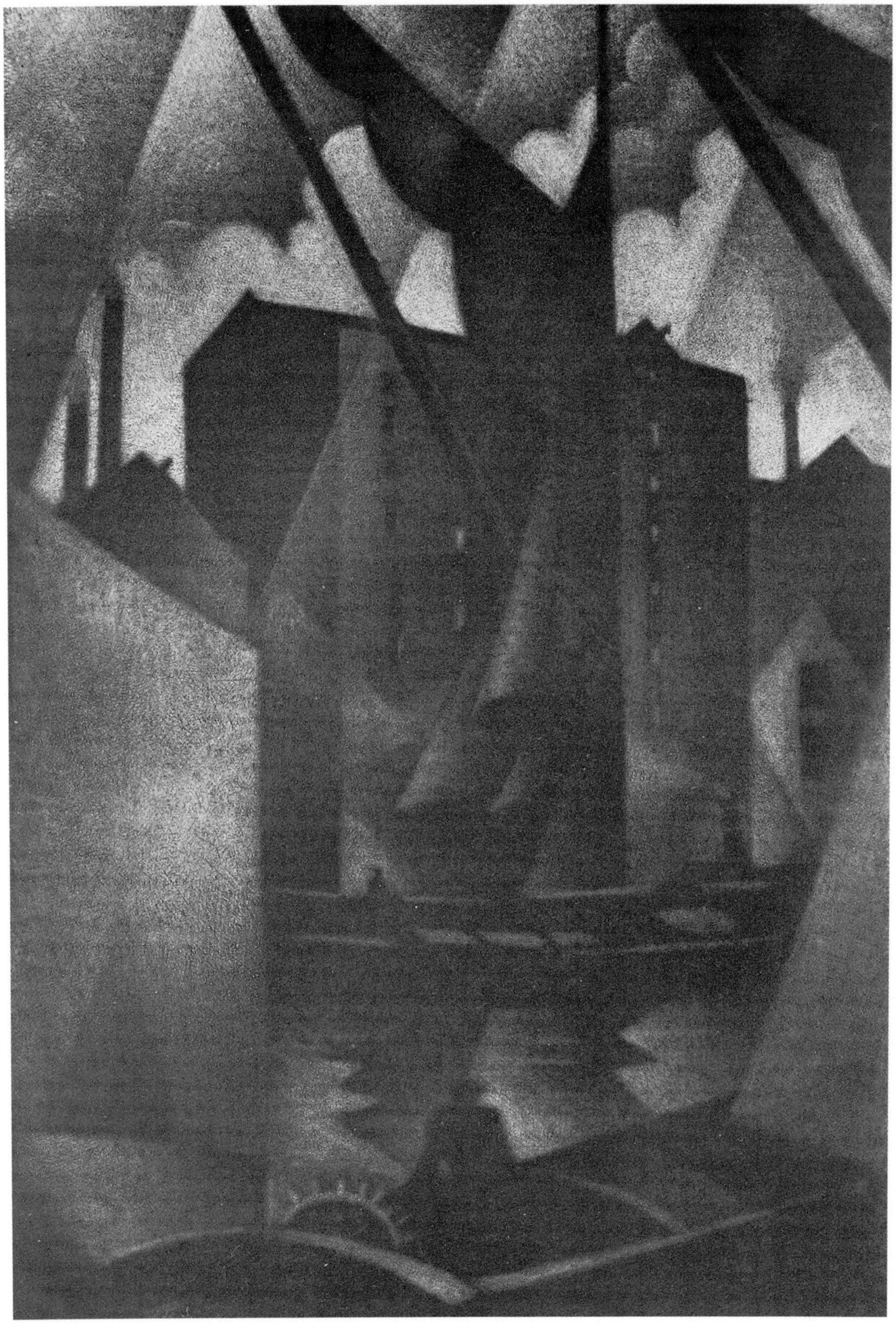

2
C. R. W. NEVINSON
Southwark
1918
mezzotint
22.5 × 15 cm
The British Museum

February 1915, Nevinson cautiously unveiled his first experiment, *First Searchlights at Charing Cross* [fig. 10] – a depiction from Hungerford Bridge of a London 'nightscape' during a threatened air raid. In appearance it boasted the Futurist hallmarks of geometric rectangles, triangles and arcs of light, intersecting to steer the composition away from conventional narrative functions. In subject matter Nevinson was demonstrating that a facet of modernist art, and the modernity of modern war, could co-exist very comfortably. Even Nevinson's new rival Wyndham Lewis complimented the work, declaring: 'Mr Nevinson's *Searchlights*, the best picture there, is perhaps too, the best he has painted'.[31]

In this pursuit of novelty, originality and dynamism, Nevinson turned wholeheartedly to embrace aviation, and from this came *A Taube Pursued by Commander Samson* [pl. 25].[32] Commander Samson himself was the perfect Marinettian character,[33] and with him came the extension of conflict, and Futurist passion, into nature's last preserve of normality, the sky. Nevinson, and his mode of painting, was equal to the task and accordingly *The Sunday Times* enthused: 'If all Futurists gave us such beauty of colour and conveyed movement with such imaginative power as Mr Nevinson shows us in these aeroplanes rushing through space, we should have no quarrel with them.'[34]

The *Evening Standard* looked positively on the modern 'language' employed by the artist, commenting that his work was treated with 'a force and convincingness that no realistic snapshot could equal ... It is the best flying picture that has yet been done.'[35]

But this was principally a ground war and so the force and sensation of a *Bursting Shell* [fig. 6] proved to be an irresistible theme for England's only remaining Futurist. In his shattered compositional representation of an experience with which he was now familiar, Nevinson expressed the force inherent in the instant of the destructive moment. The viewer, through this kaleidoscopic lens, was thrust into the whirling heart of the vortex, where urban motifs such as bricks and walls recalled the wholesale destruction of towns such as Ypres. P. G. Konody called it 'Futurism, pure and simple',[36] and praised the composition for being both novel and innovative, comprehensible to most yet not regressive in terms of art theory. The mixed critical response, however, no doubt warned Nevinson that it represented a high-water mark for the degree of Futurist 'abstraction' that would be acceptable to the increasingly conservative war-time public and critic alike.

Marching Men (*Returning to the Trenches*) [pl. 24], therefore, retreated a modicum from the extremities of an ultra-Futurist vocabulary. Now Nevinson's combatants, the *poilus*, were moulded together into one semi-abstract unit where rhythmic repetitions suggested metaphorical associations with the military machine, devoid of sentiment and human feeling, grinding towards impending conflict – but neither Futurist glory, nor Allied victory. The soldiers are not recognisable individuals; they betray no rank, expression, or any recognisable feature other than that they are French. Although the *Daily Express* published a version of the painting with the heading 'Will these pictures help the Germans?',[37] critics such as Konody were sympathetic:

> His *Returning to the Trenches* is really an uncommonly interesting picture, in which he has found an extremely expressive formula for the rhythmic marching of a body of French infantrymen fully armed and laden with all the paraphernalia for a prolonged stay in the trenches. While avoiding anything like literal representation of objects, he leaves the spectator in no manner of doubt concerning the meaning of every touch of the brush.[38]

Elsewhere he was singled out for more high praise: 'Mr Nevinson, the English disciple of this movement [Futurism], is a very oasis of intellectual clearness among a babel of artistic gibberish.'[39]

Perhaps under perceived pressures from the Official War Artists Scheme, or through eventual disenchantment with the Futurist glorification of machinery and industrialised conflict, Nevinson's painting began to retreat definitively from its Futurist roots after 1916. The last two years of the Great War saw only glimmers of his extreme pre-war and early war affiliations in compositions such as *The Bomber* [pl. 22]. Within weeks of the Armistice, in an article entitled 'Are Futurists Mad?', he openly declared: 'I have now given up Futurism and am devoting my time to legitimate art'.[40] For Nevinson, this legitimacy lay in the positive modernity of New York City, where technology worked for the betterment of mankind as opposed to the destruction wrought at its hands in Europe. Remembering Marinetti's arrival in London in 1910, Nevinson planned a similar Futurist-style attack on the USA which backfired spectacularly, not least when he declared that Americans were 'splendid painters, but no artists'. He distanced his potential audience further by saying that 'it was with horror that I found artists in America a thing apart and of little importance'. He put the final seal on his fate by stating: 'The impression I have thus far gained of the American public is one of mental sterility.'[41] New York, it transpired, had no need to be woken up – and so Charles Lewis Hind was hardly overstating the facts when he wrote, 'it is something, at the age of thirty-one, to be among the most discussed, most successful, most promising, most admired and most hated British artists'.[42]

Nevinson would return to neither the United States nor Futurism again. Writing his autobiography nearly twenty years later, he mused on his Futurist association: 'In retrospect it certainly would seem that some of us were already preparing our technique to express the horror, the cruelty, and the violence which were to be our destiny.'[43] He concluded, however: 'it is a black thought for me to look back and see that I was associated with Italian Futurism, which ended in Fascism'. Fallen into the wrong hands, and in a context of unprecedented mass destruction, he sighed, 'what a fate for an intellectual idea!'.[44]

Notes

1. P. Hamilton, *The Role of Futurism, Dada and Surrealism in the Construction of British Modernism, 1910–1940* (Ph.D. diss. University of Oxford, 1987), p. 58.
2. For a full study of Futurism in London and the Nevinson family association with it, see M. J. K. Walsh, *C. R. W. Nevinson: This Cult of Violence* (New Haven and London, 2002).
3. *The Vote*, 31 December 1910. 7311.1-2, Nevinson Press Cuttings Collection, Tate Gallery Archive (Hereafter: T.G.A.).
4. C. R. W. Nevinson, *Paint and Prejudice* (London, 1937), p. 57.
5. *The Times*, 21 March 1912, p. 2.
6. Professor Angela V. John is currently finishing her text on the Nevinson family and this should be published next year under the title *Rebel Correspondent: H. W. Nevinson, War, Journalism and Justice.*
7. A. Hanson, *Severini Futurista: 1912–1917* (London, 1995), p. 158.
8. H. W. Nevinson, Journals (MSS Eng. Misc. e.610-628), e.617/4, 21 April 1913. Bodleian Library, Oxford University. (Hereafter: H.W.N. Journals).
9. Cited in R. Cork, *Vorticism and Abstract Art in the First Machine Age* (London, 1976), p. 243.
10. See M. J. K. Walsh, 'Nevinson at the Slade: Carrington, Gertler and Art', *Apollo* (October, 2001), p. 27.
11. G. Severini, *The Futurist Painter Severini Exhibits His Latest Works,* (Marlborough Gallery, London, April 1913), p. 1.
12. W. Lewis, 'Man of the Week: Marinetti', *The New Weekly*, 30 May 1914, p. 329.
13. Nevinson to W. Lewis, 19 November 1913, Department of Rare Books, Wyndham Lewis collection (no. 4612, box 128), Karl A. Kroch Library, Cornell University (Hereafter: Cornell).
14. *Marinetti: Selected Writings*, ed. by R. W. Flint (London, 1972), p. 147.
15. H.W.N. Journals. e.618/2, 3 May 1914.
16. T. E. Hulme, 'Modern Art III: The London Group', *The New Age*, 26 March 1914. 7311.2A-23, T.G.A.
17. H. Gaudier-Brzeska, 'Allied Artists Associations Ltd', *The Egoist*, 15 June 1914. 7311.2A-56, T.G.A.
18. J. Rothenstein, *Modern English Painters* 2 (London, 1956), p. 131.
19. 'The Futurists Again', *Manchester Courier*, 13 June 1914. 7311.2A-43, T.G.A.
20. W. Lewis, *Blasting and Bombardiering* (London, 1937), p. 33.
21. Nevinson to W. Lewis, 13 June 1914. Cornell.
22. G. K. Chesterton, *The Illustrated London News*, 11 July 1914. 7311.2A-67, T.G.A.
23. W. Lewis, *Blasting and Bombardiering*, p. 35.
24. Nevinson to W. Lewis, 13 July 1914. Cornell.
25. *Yorkshire Observer*, 15 June 1914. 7311.2A-44, T.G.A.
26. M. J. K. Walsh, *C. R. W. Nevinson: This Cult of Violence*, p. 83.
27. Cited in C. Harrison, *English Art and Modernism 1900–1939* (London, 1981), p. 87.
28. 'Shocking Pictures Designed to Jolt the Senses: Cubist Reproductions in Regent Street', *The Star* (undated). 7311.2A-24, T.G.A.
29. *Daily Express*, 25 February 1915. 7311.2A-85, T.G.A.
30. H.W.N. Journals. e. 616/3, 25 October 1914.
31. *Blast: War Number* (London, 1915), p. 77.
32. A Taube is a German monoplane, the name being derived from the German word for 'dove'.
33. Charles R. Samson (1883–1931) was one of the great pioneers in pre-war and wartime aviation.
34. *Sunday Times*, 21 March 1915, p. 15.
35. J. M., *Evening Standard and St. James Gazette*, 16 March 1915. 7311.2A-120, T.G.A.
36. P. G. Konody, *Modern War by C. R. W. Nevinson* (London, 1917), p. 28.
37. *Daily Express*, 25 February 1915. 7311.2A-85, T.G.A.
38. *The Observer*, 14 March 1915. 7311.2A-95, T.G.A.
39. 'The Unconscious Humorists', *Evening News*, 13 March 1915, p. 7.
40. 'Are Futurists Mad?', *Daily Express*, 21 January 1919. 7311.3A-592, T.G.A.
41. *The New York Sun*, 17 May 1919. 7311.4-784, T.G.A.
42. C. Lewis Hind, 'An Appreciation', *The Old World and the New* (Bourgeois Galleries, 10 November – 4 December, 1920), p. 4.
43. C. R. W. Nevinson, *Paint and Prejudice*, p. 64.
44. Ibid., p. 66.

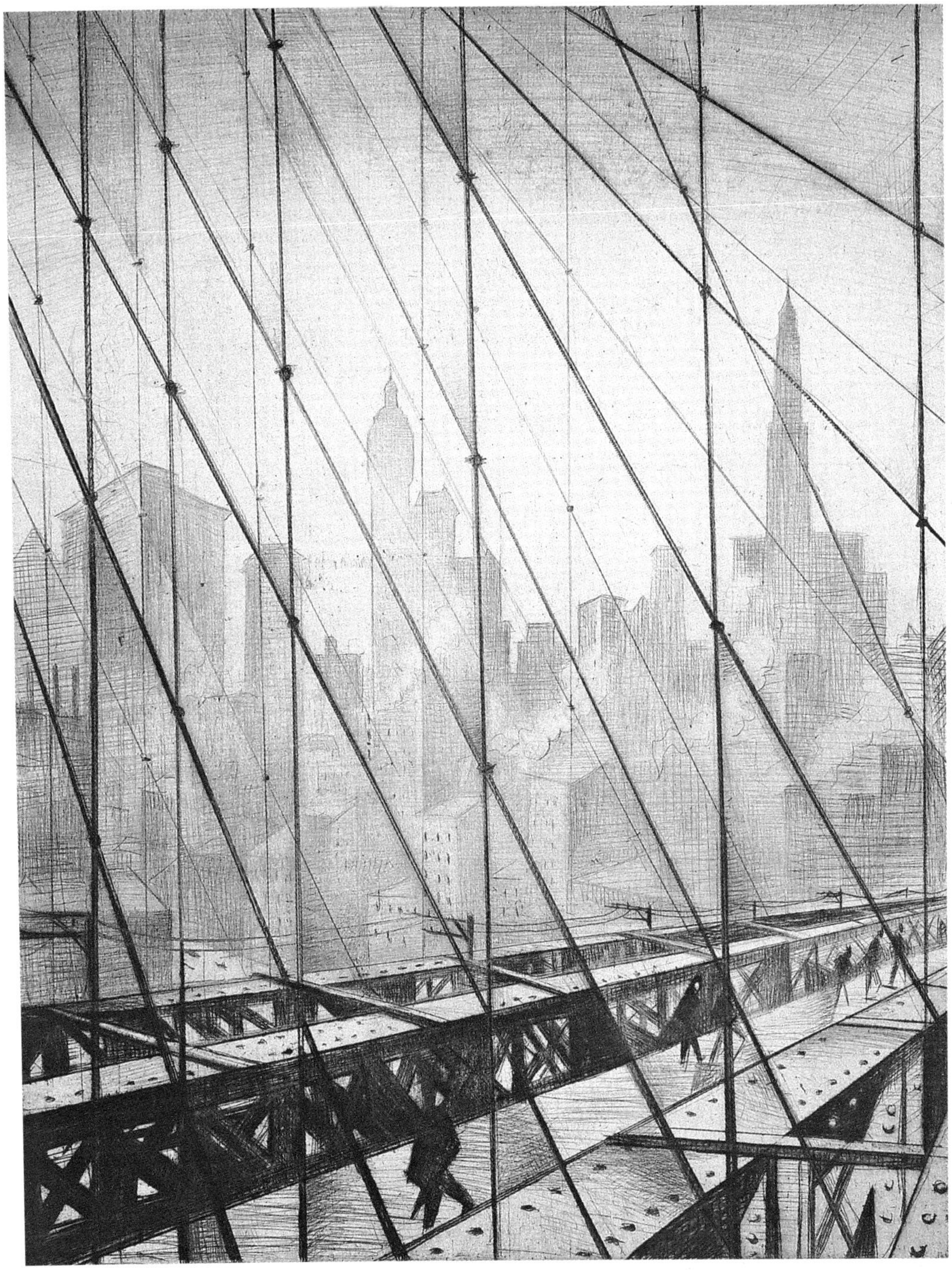

FIG. 11
C. R. W. NEVINSON
Looking through Brooklyn Bridge
1920–21
drypoint
23.5 × 17.5 cm
The Whitworth Art Gallery,
The University of Manchester

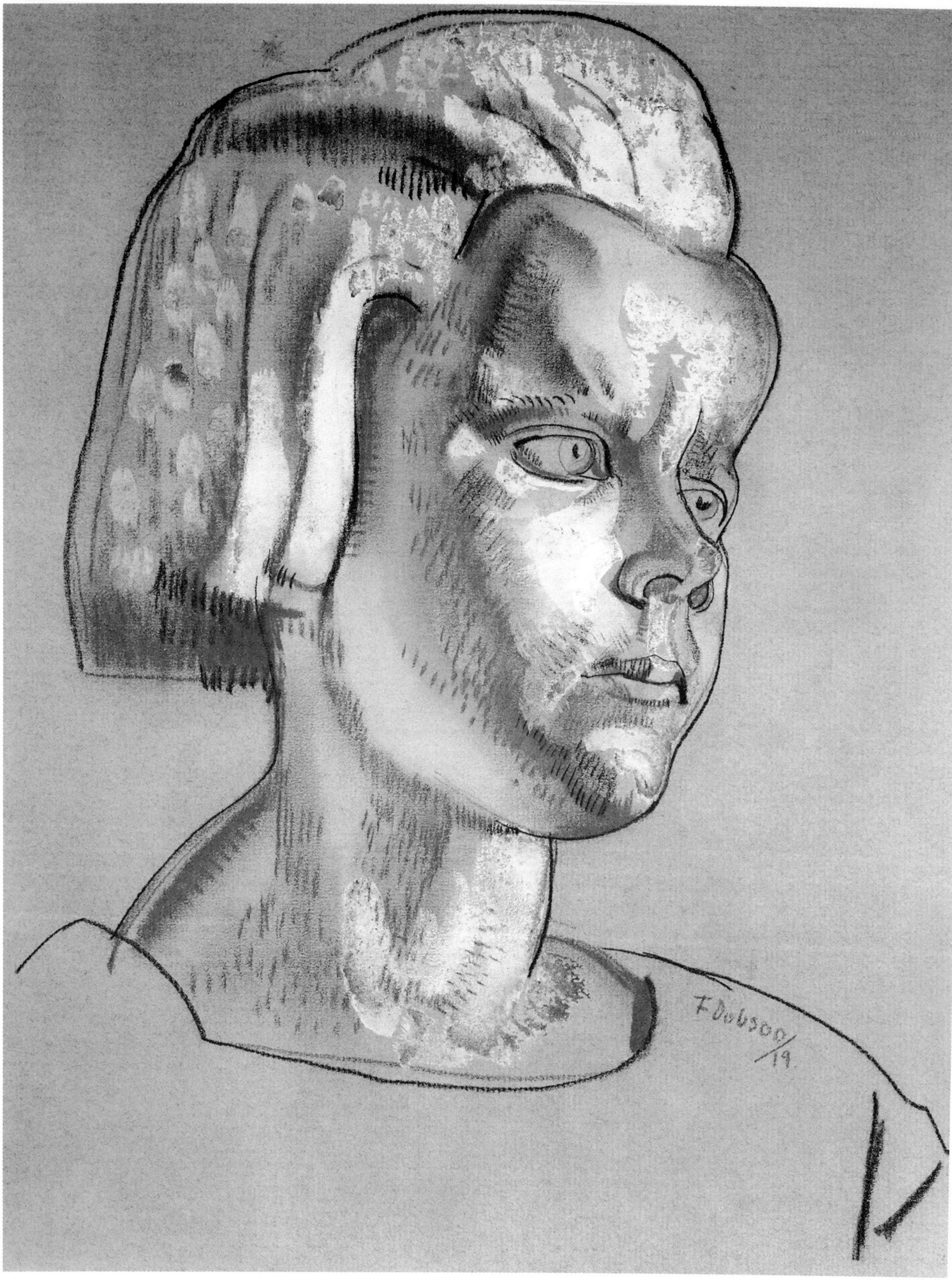
F Dobson/19

TAKING HEAVEN BY VIOLENCE

Futurism and Vorticism as seen by the British Press c.1912–20

Jonathan Black

FIG. 12
FRANK DOBSON
Portrait of a Girl
1919
red and black chalk on paper
31.5 × 24.1 cm
The Whitworth Art Gallery,
The University of Manchester

Futurism was never likely to be accorded much respect in Great Britain in the years leading up to the First World War. Claims made by avant-garde Italian artists that their country had the potential to be at the forefront of industrial and technological progress rang hollow in British ears. With its enormous Empire, its standing as the world's first fully industrialised nation and well-deserved reputation as the globe's most imposing naval power, Britain was stronger economically and militarily. Italy was commonly perceived in Britain as a young, untested and relatively backward country, unified as recently as 1861. Furthermore, it did not possess an impressive track record for winning victories on the colonial battlefield. For example, in September 1911 Italy declared war on the Ottoman Empire and invaded Libya. A swift and comprehensive victory over the 'sick man of Europe' was confidently predicted in Rome. However, by the time the Futurists' first joint exhibition was held in London's Sackville Gallery six months later, Italian forces were still bogged down fighting a bitter guerrilla war in the desert outside Tripoli. Italy's war in Libya was not well regarded by many English commentators, pundits and journalists. For example, in May 1912, the war correspondent Francis McCullagh published a scathing attack on the martial prowess of Italian troops in Libya, describing the average Italian soldier as either a 'poltroon' or a 'mutineer'.[1] Meanwhile, Italy was condemned as:

> the militant suffragette of the nations. She breaks diplomatic, international and strategic laws as Miss Christabel Pankhurst breaks windows and then raises an ear-splitting, hysterical yell if anybody ventures to criticise her ... She goes cruising in the Mediterranean, with her fleet, exactly as Mrs Pankhurst goes cruising in the Strand with her hammer.[2]

McCullagh then proceeded to connect Italy's Libyan campaign with Marinetti and the Futurists and, particularly, with Marinetti's poem *La Bataille de Tripoli*. This had been inspired by the Battle of Sidi Messri (26 October 1911) and gave the distinct impression that it had been a stunning victory for a technologically advanced Italian army. McCullagh interpreted Marinetti's 'adoration of slaughter' in the poem, as well as his glorification of war as 'the world's only hygiene', as a

> sign of the degeneracy within the Futurist movement ...

> Healthy nations take it for granted that their soldiers have ordinary male courage. It is only morbid and cowardly degenerates who go into paroxysms of excitement and sing wild poems when they see an artillerist pointing a canon at an enemy three miles off and unable to reply.

He added that an English audience would not be surprised to learn that during the battle Italian troops had, in actual fact, 'run like deer before the Arabs and the result of the whole engagement was an Italian retreat'.[3]

A good degree of the contempt McCullagh felt for Futurist bellicosity and for Italian pretensions to modernity is evident within initial British press reactions to the March 1912 Futurist exhibition in London. The *Daily Express*, for example, was outraged by the exhibits and by the content of the 'Founding Manifesto of Futurism' reproduced in the exhibition catalogue. The main review of the Sackville Gallery exhibition was headlined 'Picture Gallery of a Madhouse. Crazy Dreams Put on Canvas'. The display, as a whole, was likened to 'the picture gallery of a lunatic asylum, where the inmates have been allowed to visualise their mad imaginings'.[4] Not for the first time, Futurist artists were accused of being criminally insane and 'hysterical'. In addition, their work was often described as 'anarchistic': anarchism was a political philosophy frequently associated with Italians. A March 1912 editorial, for example, in *The Manchester Evening News*, detected a connection between 'Futurist paintings' on show in London and a recent attempt by an anarchist to assassinate King Vittorio Emanuele III in Rome. The piece confidently concluded that 'Italy, with its hot-blooded and hysterical subjects, has a particularly bad record for … assassinations'.[5]

The Times was dismissively condescending in its response to what it had seen at the Sackville Gallery, describing the exhibition catalogue as containing a manifesto in which:

> the Italian painters explain their aims and tell us that they have succeeded in them … The worst of it is that the more intelligible the pictures, the more commonplace they appear … Signor Boccioni, in his *Modern Idol* [pl. 7], has painted a perfectly commonplace picture of a very ugly woman, and he does not make it any less commonplace by his effects of light any more than a bad actor becomes a good one when limelights play upon him.

The review conveyed a distinct impression that there was something rather Italian about the grandiose and exaggerated character of the language used by Marinetti and his cohorts.[6]

Meanwhile, the *Manchester Guardian* seemed unsure as to when Futurism had actually started – stating that the movement was about 'two years old' – or who had been its founder. Marinetti's name is not mentioned once. However, the review conceded the movement's art was 'novelty without cutting all adrift'. In particular, Severini's *Pan-Pan at the Monico* was admired for conveying the 'bustle and hubbub created by the Tsigane dancers, the champagne-drinking crowd and the clashing of colour and laughter. The sharp, strange lights split up shapes and local colour. Black lips, yellow noses and azure patches appear in confusion.' Despite the 'outlandish' and 'hysterical' nature of some of the exhibits, others were undoubtedly impressive and the reviewer concluded, 'one can see a Future in Futurism'.[7] However, Frank Rutter (1876–1933), in the *Sunday Times*, was more representative of those English critics – with some awareness of recent stylistic developments on the continent – in arguing that the Futurists were not as stylistically innovative as they liked to claim. Rutter acknowledged, 'all London is talking of the Italian Futurist Painters at the Sackville Gallery'. Yet he emphasised, 'all their little novelties have already been paraded in Paris, by men as able and abler than themselves'. The Futurists might well repudiate Impressionism in their manifestos. However, he argued, they 'make use, often ill-advised, of divisionist technique and all their intelligible works are, more or less, impressions of actualities'.[8]

Two years later, Futurism, as a label for comical eye-catching novelty, was very much *en vogue* in London. In March 1914, for example, the music critics of the *Daily Express* noted the presence of 'a good many Futurists scattered among the audience' at a performance of Stravinsky's 'Fireworks' at the Queen's Hall, conducted by Sir Henry Wood. The conductor was, apparently, much distracted by 'one young man in the gallery, dangling his legs so as to show to the best advantage a pair of very Futuristic socks. They were bright yellow and ornamented with cubes of vivid colours. I was so dazzled, I could only distinguish green, blue, vermilion and pink.'[9] If Futurist socks possessed a certain charm, there was still considerable antipathy, especially among the papers one would today describe as 'tabloids', to the work on display at the second Futurist exhibition in London. This opened

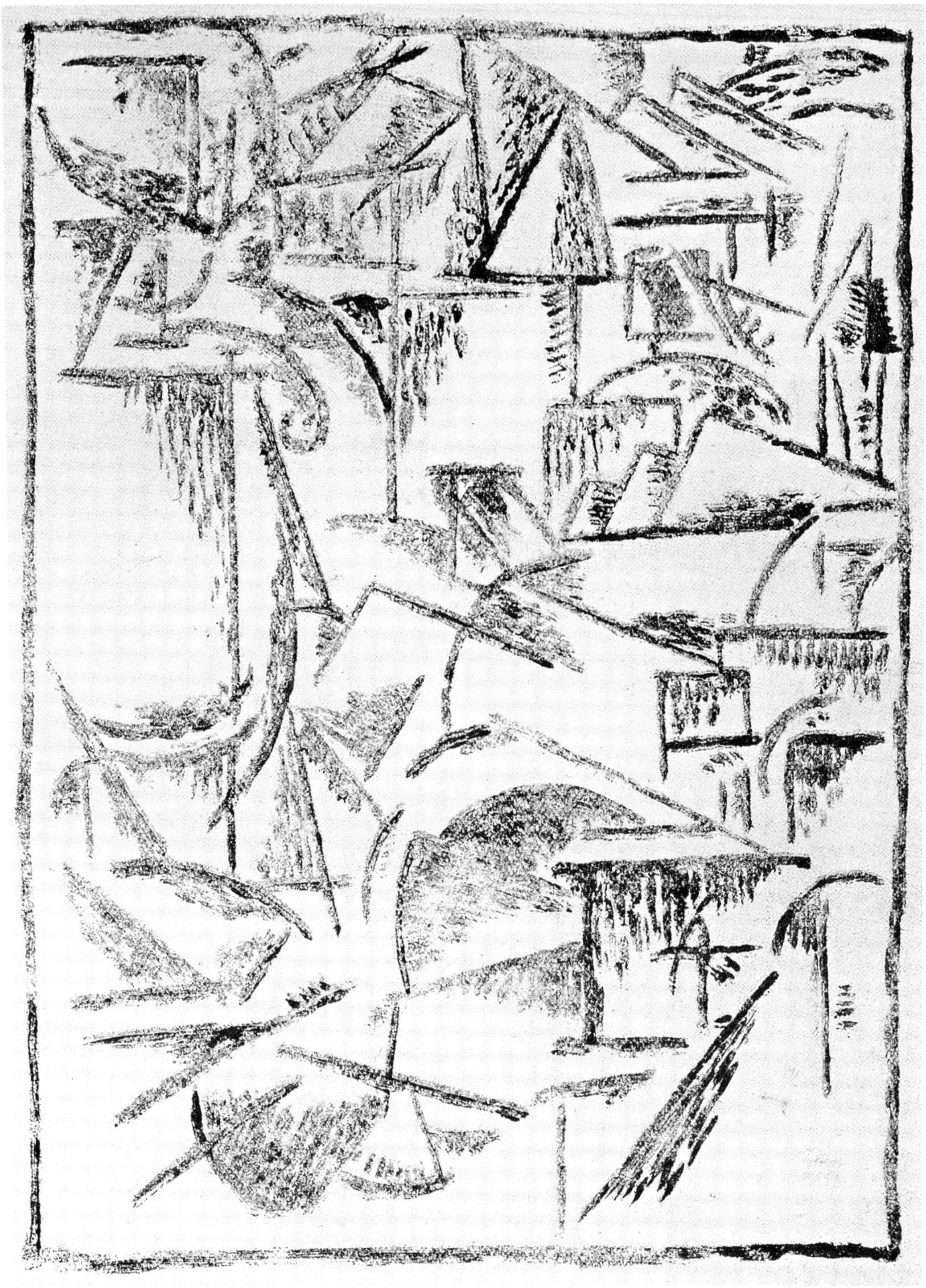

3
ARDEGNO SOFFICI
Landscape
*c.*1913–14
woodcut
26 × 18 cm
Estorick Collection, London

at the Doré Gallery towards the end of April 1914. The *Daily Express* described the exhibits collectively as 'Lunacy Masquerading as Art' and was scornfully dismissive of Futurist attempts at sculpture, such as Marinetti's *Self-Portrait*. The reviewer wrote: 'Suspended from the ceiling of the large room at the Doré Galleries is a weird-looking object, not unlike a gigantic long-limbed insect or the armature intended for a clay model of a dancing or running figure.' He wondered what the innocuous watercolours of 'Mr. Percy French' and the poignant evocations of 'the Old West' by C. M. Russell 'the Cowboy Artist' had done to deserve being on display in the same gallery as the 'tumultuous' and 'anarchistic' Futurists.[10]

Arthur Clutton-Brock (1868–1924), art critic of *The Times*, was much exercised by Boccioni's *ensembles plastiques*. He felt the most glaring problem with Boccioni's sculptures was that they were so 'commonplace'. In the case of *Woman-Window-Balcony*, he noted:

> some parts of the woman's head are easily recognisable and it is no better than the ordinary effigy of a provincial mayor … these abstract forms remind one of the abstract forms of *art nouveau* more than of anything else and that is why, perhaps, the public is rather taken with them and with Futurist art in general. Nearly all of it, however unintelligible, is based upon quite familiar and vulgar design and is common, both in colour and execution.

However, Clutton-Brock was impressed by the work of two Futurists who had not exhibited in London before. In his opinion 'the best artist in the present exhibition [was] Mr Soffici' [pl. 3] because his *Pictorial Syntheses* clearly demonstrated that he 'understood the fundamentals of Cubism'. Meanwhile, he was attracted by Balla's 'abstract designs' [pl. 5] because, like recent work by Picasso, they possessed 'a logic for the eye like that of a scientific diagram'.[11] It is interesting that Clutton-Brock deplored the fact that 'the public is interested in the Futurists because they explain themselves so volubly and so often' and hoped the 'current crop' of 'young English artists' would not emulate their 'mania' for publishing their 'childish outpourings'.[12] Ironically, within two months of his writing this, such a group of younger artists published *Blast* with the very intention of provoking the cultural establishment of which Clutton-Brock was such a prominent member.

However, just as Clutton-Brock was prepared to concede that some Futurists were producing more aesthetically impressive work than others, Frank Rutter argued the exhibition at the Doré Gallery supplied definite proof for

> Futurism passing on and developing into something else … the representative element and with it [the expression of] movement has disappeared from the majority of the exhibits … this second exhibition is dominated by the work of Balla … because his paintings, however small, stand out for the sheer beauty and splendour of their colour and design.[13]

Thus, in the minds of some leading cultural opinion formers, Futurism finally seemed to be acquiring a certain degree of artistic credibility, even respectability. The more populist papers carried many articles extolling the virtues of 'Futurist clothes for men' and 'Futurist interior design',[14] and even 'Futurist food'.[15] Yet such coverage also suggests the speed with which Futurism was toned down and debased to the level of 'life-style' accessory. Indeed, almost inevitably, the English mania for anthropomorphism was able to adroitly domesticate and trivialise the most controversial avant-garde art movement of the day. In June 1914, the *Daily Express* reported that 'the Futurist cat is the latest thing in freak ornament' as a selection of porcelain and ceramic 'Futurist cats', designed by a Louis Wain, had recently gone on display in the shop windows of Messrs. Max Emmanuel & Co., Shoe Lane, London EC4. Priced at one shilling a piece, designs tempting the adventurous 'Futurist shopper' included: 'The Lucky Futurist Cat … [with] meow-meow notes printed on the animals porcelain body – a weird sort of music which it would be quite impossible for any but a futurist musician to read.'[16]

Only a couple of days before reporting on the emergence of the feline Futurist table ornament, the *Daily Express* carried a story entitled 'The Coming Blast', stating that *Blast*, 'the quarterly, which Mr Wyndham Lewis is to edit', was soon to be published. The article noted the new magazine was described as 'The Manifesto of the Vorticists, The English Parallel Movement to Cubism and Expressionism, Imagism in Poetry, Death Blow to Impressionism and Futurism and all the Refuse of Naïf Science'. The piece concluded: 'So, Mr. Wyndham Lewis is a Vorticist. That is clear. It is also clear that he is quite friendly to the cubists.' In addition, while he may have damned the Futurists, Lewis was evidently happy to take a 'leaf' from their 'book of tricks' by publishing his own 'explosive ... attention-grabbing' manifesto.[17] The same newspaper noted that on the same day that *Blast* was published (2 July 1914) manifestos were now deemed rather *vieux jeu* (old hat) by the most 'advanced artists' and predicted 'it will not be long, I hear, before [a] 'Counter Blast' is out [which will] be ruthless in its exposure of the corrupt intellectuality of *Blast!*'[18] Evidently, there were so many 'isms' already jostling for the public's attention that yet another one would find it extremely difficult to generate the notoriety required to give it the necessary cachet with the minority who took avant-garde art seriously.

Indeed, despite the fact that the first issue of *Blast* conspicuously 'blessed' three leading art critics and cultural pundits – Charles Lewis Hind, Frank Rutter and Paul Konody (the latter being art critic for the *Observer* and the *Daily Mail*) – it generated relatively little coverage. If anything, the reaction was decidedly luke-warm and underwhelmed. Even the 'blessed' Konody wrote that 'without Marinetti *Blast* would have been inconceivable. The Manifesto is based on those of the Italian Futurists but is far behind them as regards force, literary form, wit and original thought.' *Blast* was, furthermore, a 'strange mixture of seriousness and facetiousness, common sense and absurdity. Much of it reads like the production of naughty boys who are impelled by a love of mischief.'[19] In that sense, perhaps, *Blast* should be appreciated more as an anticipation of the scatological publications, in 1916 and 1917, of the Zurich Dadaists rather than as attempt merely to ape a format the Futurists had very much made their own.

Elsewhere, *Blast* was somewhat casually, and dismissively, identified as a manifestation of Futurism. Two days after its publication, the author G. K. Chesterton opined that 'the paradox of Futurism is that it has no future. It is sterile and suicidal.'[20] Towards the end of July, as a World War threatened, the *English Review* breathed a sigh of relief that *Blast* had signally failed to rouse the multitude. The *Review* took it as an encouraging sign that 'the hideous Futurist craze for sensationalism is happily passing'.[21]

As it transpired, the war effectively pushed the debate as to the merits of Futurism and Vorticism from the news. When a number of artists, including C. R. W. Nevinson, Wyndham Lewis and Edward Wadsworth, exhibited together early in 1915 with the Friday Club and the London Group, many observers expressed surprise at the continued existence of any artists wishing to uphold the banners of pre-war Futurism and Vorticism. Clutton-Brock, for example, referred to the qualified Futurist style of Nevinson's *The First Searchlights at Charing Cross* [fig. 10] as 'the fashion of the year before' and, since it was a style so closely associated with pre-war frivolities, hardly suitable for the grim realties of wartime.[22] In March 1915, reviewing the London Group, Clutton-Brock went so far as to accuse Lewis, Wadsworth and William Roberts of pursuing 'Junkerism in Art', interpreting their brand of geometric abstraction as unpatriotic because he regarded such work as the direct debased product of militaristic German philosophy.[23]

It was also widely noted that the Vorticists, as well as many of like-mind among the artists exhibiting with the London Group, were not yet in uniform. After attending the private view of the London Group, the *Manchester Guardian's* London correspondent commented sarcastically:

> The London Group was a rallying place for all that was wild and even desperate in the new generation of artist. It was expressed, outwardly, by the wearing of side-whiskers, gipsy beards, jerseys, dungarees, by long hair in men and short hair in women. In those days it was easy to feel defiant and superior. The enemy was convention. Nowadays, there is another enemy and it is difficult to be wild and desperate and defiant and to be superior. To be young and healthy-looking and to still wear civilian clothes, however unusual, does not suggest that one is a daring and remarkable person ... it is difficult, at the moment, to see any art as daring and as strange.[24]

Another newspaper, at the other end of the political spectrum, acknowledged that Futurism now seemed almost respectable when compared to what the Vorticists were creating: 'There was a time, not so very long ago, when the experiments of the Italian Futurists evoked boisterous hilarity and were considered the last step towards madness.' However, after his spell at the front Marinetti's English disciple, C. R. W. Nevinson, constituted 'a very oasis of intellectual clearness amidst a babble of artistic gibberish' at the London Group in works such as *Marching Men (Returning to the Trenches)* [pl. 24].[25] However, by the time of the one and only Vorticism exhibition in June 1915, a few

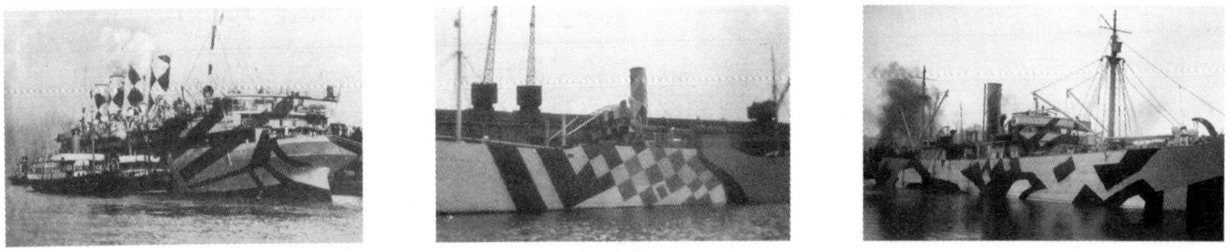

FIG. 13
EDWARD WADSWORTH
British Merchant Ships in Dazzle Camouflage at Bristol and Liverpool
1918
photographs
Alex Hollweg

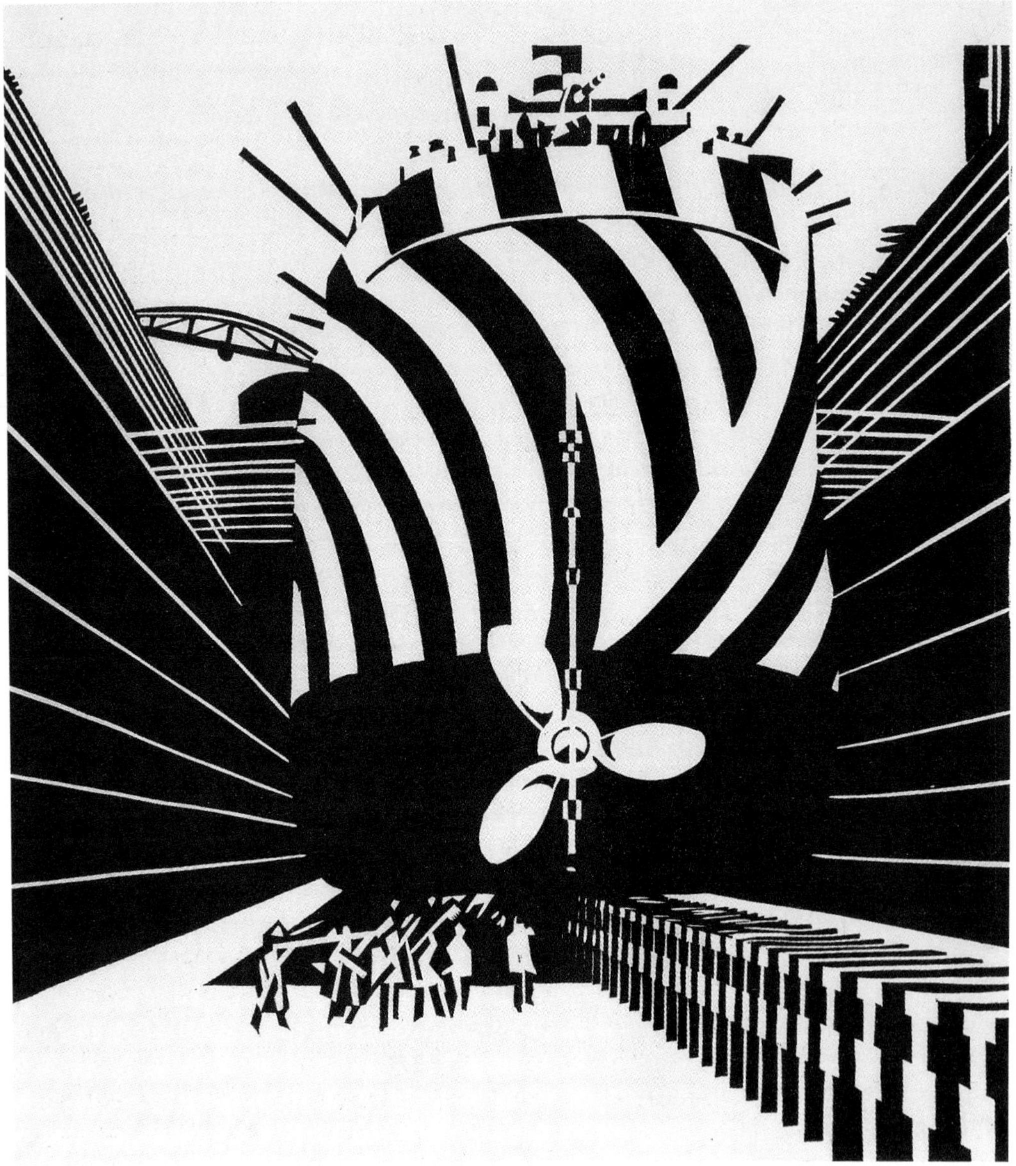

FIG. 14
EDWARD WADSWORTH
Drydocked for Scaling and Painting
1918
woodcut
22.4 × 20.8 cm
David Thomson

FIG. 15
EDWARD WADSWORTH
Granite Quarries, Darby Hill, Oldbury
1919
pen and ink on paper
25.5 × 36.2 cm
The Whitworth Art Gallery,
The University of Manchester

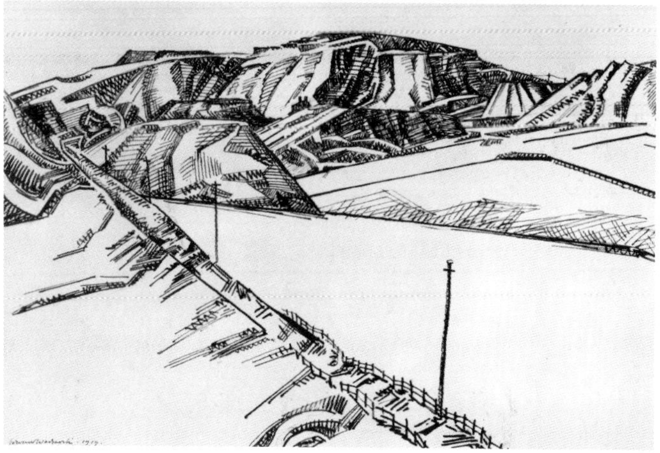

observers began to differentiate between Futurism and Vorticism, identifying the latter as making a worthy effort to symbolically evoke a world dominated by the machine through a form of sharp-edged, geometrical minimalism. Though decidedly conservative and orthodox in taste, *The Athenaeum*, for example, found itself rather attracted by Vorticist art. The work of Lewis or Wadsworth was admiringly described as 'virtually rectilinear, the small, sharp curve occasionally introduced as a kind of knot being used not for purposes of transition but rather to envenom the clash of opposing forms'.[26] In *The Sunday Times*, Frank Rutter wrote that the Vorticist exhibition was proof that the war had not killed off 'all the … revolutionary art movements' and that Vorticism could 'no longer be hailed as a novelty'. In his opinion, Lewis was 'clearly … the ablest of the Vorticists' because his designs resembled diagrams explaining the course of a battle on the Western Front. Lewis's 'abstract patterns' were as disciplined as 'military forces on a battlefield'. Rutter was among the first to correctly surmise that Vorticism had 'undoubtedly, been influenced by Kandinsky, the pioneer of Expressionism' and therefore could claim a wider European lineage beyond Italian Futurism.[27]

Just over a month after Rutter's admiring review of the Vorticist exhibition, Lewis published the second and, as it transpired, last issue of *Blast*. In it Lewis gloated: 'the War will take Marinetti's occupation of platform-boomer away … The War has, for the moment, exhausted interest in booming and banging.'[28] However, Lewis did not anticipate that the war's continuing and ever more horrific carnage would also make the vast majority of the population entirely lose interest in Vorticism. The publication of *Blast: War Number* received scant attention in the British press as it was understandably preoccupied with coverage of the titanic struggle on the Eastern Front between Germany and Austria-Hungary on the one hand and Britain's ally, Imperial Russia, on the other. At the same time, the British casualty rate on the Western Front, after unsuccessful offensives at Aubers Ridge in May 1915 and at Festubert in June to July 1915, was climbing vertiginously.

The terrible drain on British manpower led, in January 1916, to the conscription of all single men aged between eighteen and forty-one years. With some reluctance the Vorticists decided to pre-empt the compulsory call-up and to enter the military, independent as ever, on their own terms. Early in 1916 Wadsworth joined the Royal Naval Volunteer Reserve and served with Naval Intelligence in the Eastern Mediterranean for a year. On returning to England, in the autumn of 1917, he worked on the camouflaging of troop and merchant ships in Bristol and Liverpool, applying decorative schemes devised by Norman Wilkinson which would, it was hoped, mislead and confuse U-Boat commanders attempting to judge the course and speed of a ship through their periscopes [fig. 5, 13 and 14] [pls. 26 and 44]. In March 1916, Lewis and Roberts enlisted in the Royal Artillery. Lewis eventually became a Lieutenant in the Royal Garrison Artillery and Robert a gunner in the Royal Field Artillery. Roberts spent nearly two hellish years on the Western Front (August 1916 to April 1918) while Lewis served the best part of five months in the much-shelled vicinity of Ypres. Bomberg enlisted in the Royal Engineers. The talented Helen Saunders, who had by 1915 formulated her own compelling variation of Vorticism infused by the anxiety-charged rhythms of wartime [fig. 17] [pl. 10 and 11], went to work in a Government office for the best part of two years (1916–18).[29]

By late 1917 Lewis and Roberts were, understandably, keen to find some form of employment as official war artists. They were eventually offered positions by the Canadian War Records Scheme and then by the British Ministry of Information. Both took care to give the impression that they would not be painting Vorticist evocations of front-line life. Roberts, writing to his wife, admitted he would be happy to compromise his independence as an artist if it meant him leaving the Front where his existence was 'so absolutely monotonous … every day lived to order, the only excitement being to dodge and duck for your bloody, miserable life'.[30] Lewis visited the Front, as a war artist, in January 1918, while Roberts followed in August 1918. The war art they exhibited in Britain in 1919 helped considerably to revive their reputations and served to make their past association with Vorticism almost respectable. In his foreword to the catalogue of his February 1919 'Guns' exhibition, Lewis sardonically acknowledged that many visitors would doubtless be surprised by how intelligible his images of war were. He wrote:

> The public, surprised at finding eyes and noses in this exhibition, will begin by the reflection that the artist has conceded Nature, and abandoned those vexing diagrams by

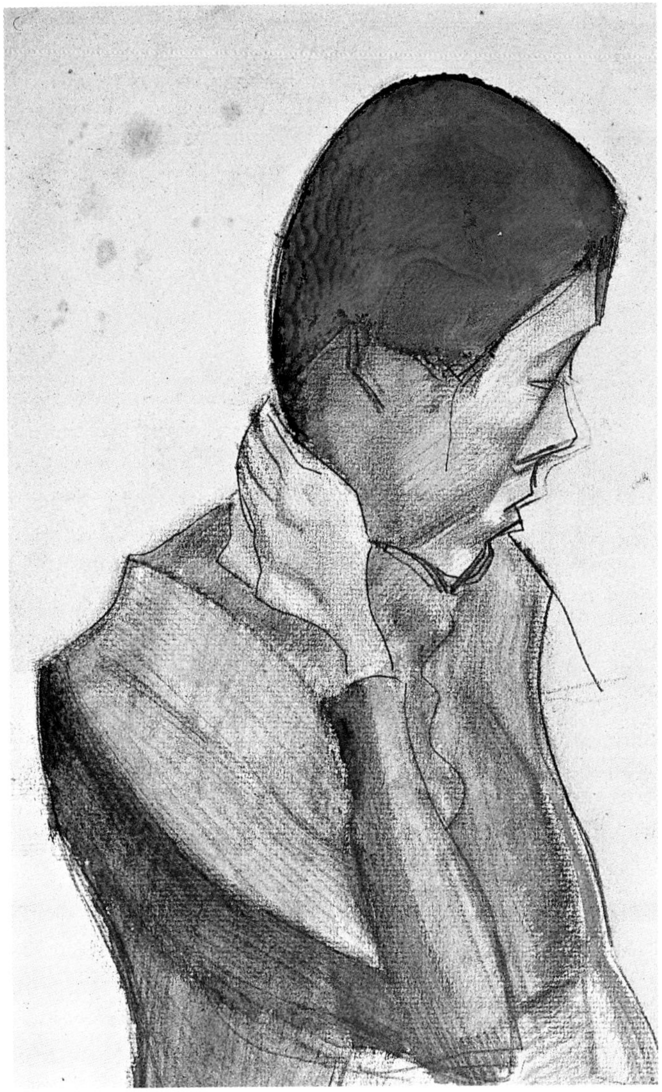

FIG. 16
WYNDHAM LEWIS
Portrait of Helen Saunders
c.1914
pencil and watercolour on paper
28.5 × 18 cm
Private collection

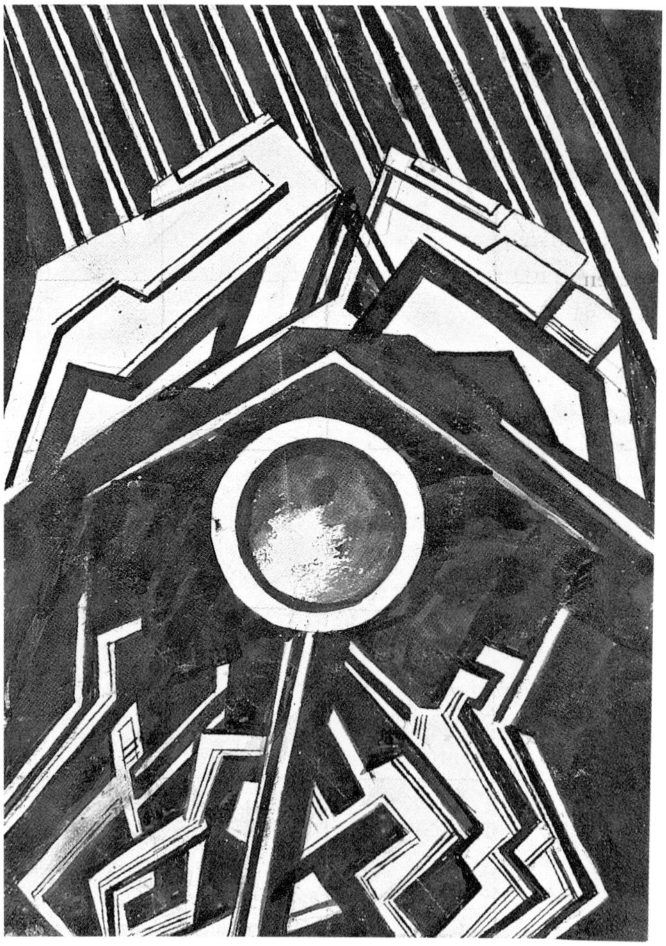

FIG. 17
HELEN SAUNDERS
Vorticist Composition
c.1915
pen and indian ink on paper
25.5 × 17.5 cm
Private collection

which he puzzled and annoyed. Experimentation is waived: I have tried to do with the pencil and brush what storytellers like Chekov and Stendhal did in their books.[31]

In *The Times*, Clutton-Brock noted Lewis was now, commendably, more interested in art from Italy that was far older than Futurism. In his catalogue foreword Lewis praised the battle paintings of Paulo Uccello (1397–1475). Clutton-Brock also suspected Lewis had studied closely the work of another Italian Renaissance artist, Cosimo Tura (*c.*1431–95). He felt that by combining this interest with his pre-war avant-garde work, Lewis had created a convincing vision of the First World War battlefield and the dominance exercised over it by the machine in the form of the artillery piece [pl. 19]. Clutton-Brock wrote:

> [Lewis's] figures, his ground, his very explosions, look as if they were made of iron, like Tura's … Machinery seems to be the reality of his world; everything works with the force and rhythm of a machine. It might be a satire on the manner in which war turns men into machines, or on our mechanical conception of life and way of living.

Lewis thus offered a very bleak observation on the nature of modern warfare and the civilisation which made its mass industrialised slaughter possible.[32]

When the works commissioned from Lewis [pl. 19] and Roberts [pl. 20] by the Ministry of Information were exhibited at the Royal Academy in December 1919 a surprising number of critics – who before the war had poured scorn on Futurism and Vorticism – congratulated them for having discovered convincing pictorial formulas that persuasively conveyed the reality of modern war on the Western Front. Visiting the Royal Academy in December 1919, the war correspondent Harry Tomlinson heard an art critic exclaim on standing in front of a work by Lewis: 'It disturbs me … It is so discordant and worrying.' On reflection, Tomlinson remarked: 'Of course it was disturbing … It was scene of the Ypres Salient. What did he expect? A box of chocolates?'[33] Frank Rutter, evidently, was not the critic who had recoiled from Lewis's war art. In December 1919, he described the 'pictures of the younger artists' on show at the Royal Academy as 'more stimulating, more intensely felt, more significant'. He was impressed by the attitude displayed by artists such as Lewis, Bomberg [pl. 18] and Roberts [pl. 21]. He wrote:

> We didn't like the war. You made us go through with it. You ask us to make pictures out of our experience. Very well, we do so, but not to please you; we shall paint them to express what we feel about the whole business and if you don't like our attitude and method of expression, then have a war of your own and paint your own pictures of it.[34]

Rutter wondered, given the success of their war art at the Royal Academy, whether the Vorticists would attempt to revive their art movement through its rabble-rousing publication *Blast*. However, post-1918, conditions were far from favourable for the return of a rejuvenated Vorticism. Retrenchment in the arts was everywhere as Picasso rediscovered, and sought to reproduce, the incisive, pure draughtsmanship of Ingres. Other artists in Paris responded eagerly to Apollinaire's 1917 'call to order', urging a return to more traditional styles in art. Meanwhile, as the war had fragmented Vorticism, it had also taken its toll on Futurism. By the end of hostilities, for example, Boccioni was dead, Severini had defected to the 'call to order' cause in France and Marinetti was more interested in the post-war political future of Italy than in artistic matters. Indeed, Marinetti founded an extreme nationalist Futurist Political Party and, in March 1919, was present at the meeting in Milan that led to the creation of the Fascist movement.[35]

Early in September 1919 Lewis wrote to the American collector John Quinn that he hoped to publish a third issue of *Blast* in a couple of months time.[36] Nothing came of these plans as Lewis was, as usual, in dire financial straits and there simply was no money for the venture. However, he did succeed in coaxing nine other artists to exhibit together, in March 1920, as the enigmatically titled 'Group X' in London. On the whole, 'Group X' was given a friendly welcome. One exception was Paul Konody who now interpreted the group's 'motivating principle' as 'Cubism rather than Futurism'. However, he did not deem this to be an encouraging development as he interpreted Cubism as an integral part of an ethos which had made the First World War possible. He commented: 'To saddle Cubism with the crimes of the war may seem severe, but it is certainly an art which effectively presaged the achievements of air raids.' Indeed, Cuthbert Hamilton's *The Glass Factory* and *Reconstruction* [pl. 32] lay 'shivered and shattered as after a Zeppelin night raid'.[37] Frank Rutter was far more impressed by the collective efforts of 'Group

X'. He saw its members moving away from Futurism and Vorticism and towards a very promising 'new sort of realism'. The 'rectangular forms', for example, in Roberts' *Athletes Exercising in a Gymnasium* [pl. 29] exposed 'the Vorticist foundation on which this realism is based'. Rutter added he had previously detected this encouraging trend towards an energised realism in the prints and drawings of the Black Country that Wadsworth had exhibited in January 1920 [pls. 27 and 43]. He now believed, more than ever, that the artist was doing the nation a service in forcefully confronting the visitor to the Mansard Gallery with the fact that 'factories, chimneys and slag heaps' and the uninhibited exploitation of nature [fig. 15] constituted 'the base on which our modern civilisation is built'.[38] Rutter was also very taken, as were other commentators, with Dobson's 'exquisite' drawings of the nude [pl. 35] and with his 'powerfully metallic' portraits [fig. 12]. In their 'deliberate archaism and sense of humour', his carvings and works in metal [fig. 18] suggested Dobson would blossom into a 'sculptor of great and original powers'.

Rutter justly acknowledged that the exhibition was 'largely the outcome' of Lewis's 'irrepressible energy and zeal' and suspected British avant-garde art would suffer if he withdrew from its ranks. He described Lewis as 'one of the most brilliant and original draughtsman of his generation and a creative designer of the most fertile invention. There is no soothing syrup in his art.'[39] It all seemed very promising but if Lewis's 'irrepressible energy' brought 'Group X' together, it was also largely responsible for its rapid disintegration after the close of the exhibition towards the end of April 1920. His compulsive need to move swiftly on from one amorous conquest to another had already alienated Helen Saunders, to the extent she felt she could not participate in 'Group X', and prompted a spurned Jessica Dismorr to have a nervous breakdown.[40] Roberts did not care to continually be thought of as Lewis's most youthful acolyte, Wadsworth grew tired of loaning Lewis money he knew would never be repaid, while Dobson wanted to avoid being labelled the new Vorticist sculptor. Etchells was more interested in architecture than painting and eventually became a practising architect. John Turnbull fell out with the mercurial Lewis and disappeared altogether, leaving no trace. The following year, reviewing Lewis's 'Tyros and Portraits' exhibition at the Leicester Galleries, Clutton-Brock reflected that, in a similar fashion to the Futurists, Lewis and the Vorticists had always attempted to rudely capture the popular imagination as if to 'take the Kingdom of Heaven by violence'.[41] After ten years of experimentation he believed most serious critics might, grudgingly, appreciate their efforts to enliven and energise contemporary art. Clutton-Brock regretted, however, that the British public were not so appreciative and, as it transpired, correctly predicted it would not respond positively to such attention-seeking tactics for many years to come.

Notes

1. F. McCullagh, *Italy's War For A Desert: Some Experiences of a War-Correspondent with the Italians in Tripoli* (London, 1912), p. 168.
2. Ibid. p. xxiv.
3. Ibid. pp. 397–98.
4. *Daily Express*, 1 March 1912, p. 2.
5. *Manchester Evening News*, 15 March 1912, p. 3.
6. *The Times*, 1 March 1912, p. 1.
7. *Manchester Guardian*, 1 March 1912, p. 6.
8. *Sunday Times*, 10 March 1912, p. 19.
9. *Daily Express*, 2 March 1914, p. 6.
10. *Daily Express*, 30 April 1914, p. 4.
11. *The Times*, 9 May 1914, p. 6.
12. Ibid.
13. *Sunday Times*, 24 May 1914, p. 7.
14. *London Life*, 4 April 1914, p. 6.
15. *Daily Mail*, 16 March 1914, p. 4.
16. *Daily Express*, 13 June 1914, p. 6.
17. *Daily Express*, 11 June 1914, p. 4.
18. *Daily Express*, 2 July 1914, p. 4.
19. *The Observer*, 5 July 1914, p. 12.
20. *T. P.'s Weekly*, 4 July 1914, p. 24.
21. *English Review*, 23 July 1914, p. 5.
22. *The Times*, 11 February 1915, p. 12.
23. *The Times*, 10 March 1915, p. 11.
24. *Manchester Guardian*, 13 March 1915, p. 8.
25. *Evening News*, 13 March 1915, p. 7.
26. *The Athenaeum*, 19 June 1915, p. 566.
27. *Sunday Times*, 19 June 1915, p. 15.
28. Quoted in C. Harrison, *English Art and Modernism: 1900–1939* (London, 1994), p. 126.
29. B. Peppin, *Helen Saunders: 1885–1963* (Ashmolean Museum, University of Oxford, 1996), p. 39.
30. R. Cork, 'Machine Age Apocalypse and Pastoral', in *British Art in the 20th Century*, ed. by A. Causey (London, 1987), p. 69.
31. W. Michel, *Wyndham Lewis: Paintings and Drawings* (London, 1971), pp. 433–34.
32. *The Times*, 11 February 1919, p. 13.
33. *The Star*, 16 December 1919, p. 9.
34. *Arts Gazette*, 20 December 1919, p. 14.

35. N. Farrell, *Mussolini: A New Life* (London, 2003), p. 80.
36. D. P. Corbett, *The Modernity of English Art: 1914–1939* (Manchester, 1997), p. 129.
37. *Daily Mail*, 29 March 1920, p. 10.
38. *Sunday Times*, 28 March 1920, p. 7.
39. Ibid.
40. B. Peppin, pp. 16 and 39.
41. *The Times*, 14 April 1921, p. 8.

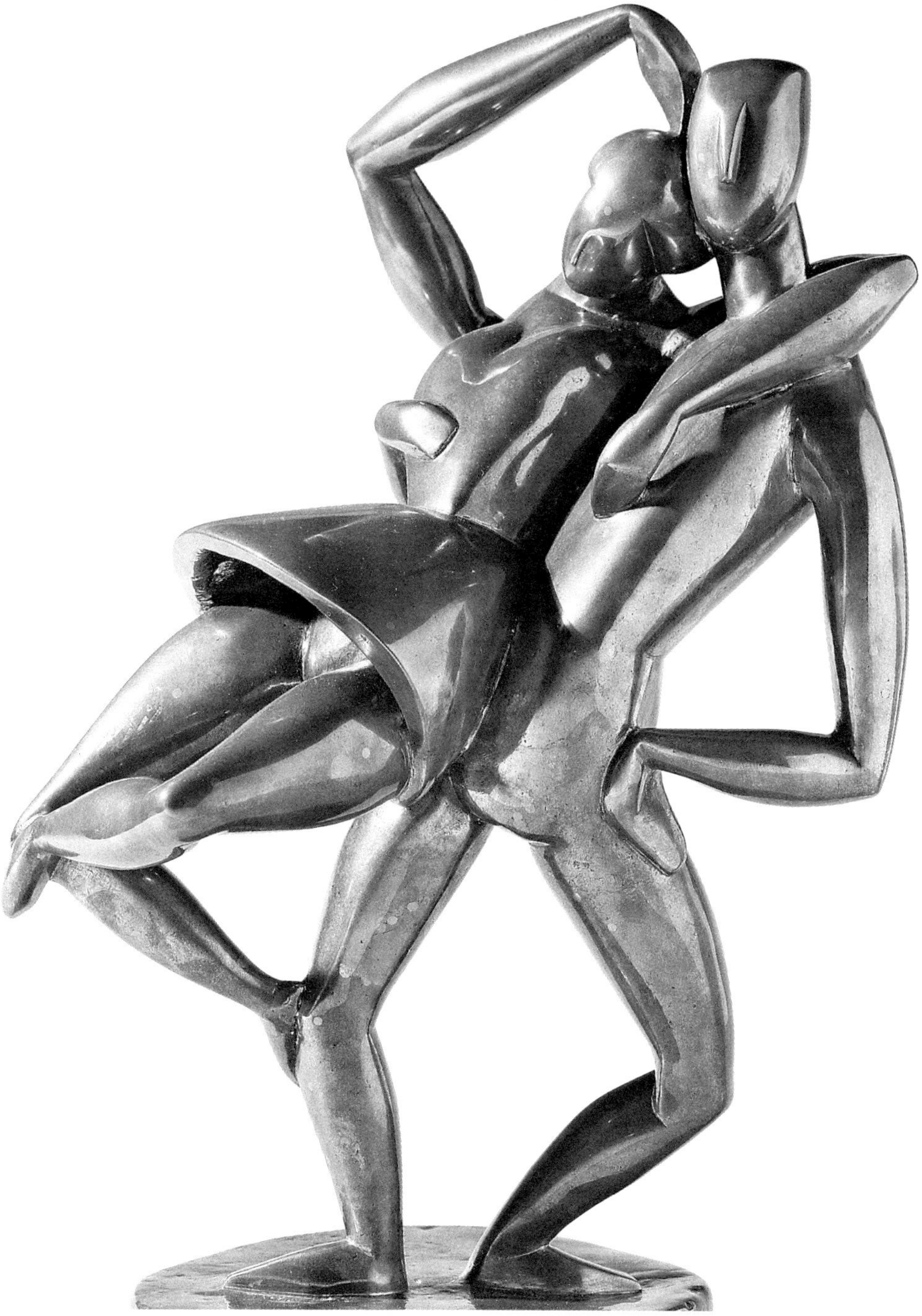

FIG. 18
FRANK DOBSON
The Dancers
1919
bronze
40.7 cm high
Fine Art Society plc, London

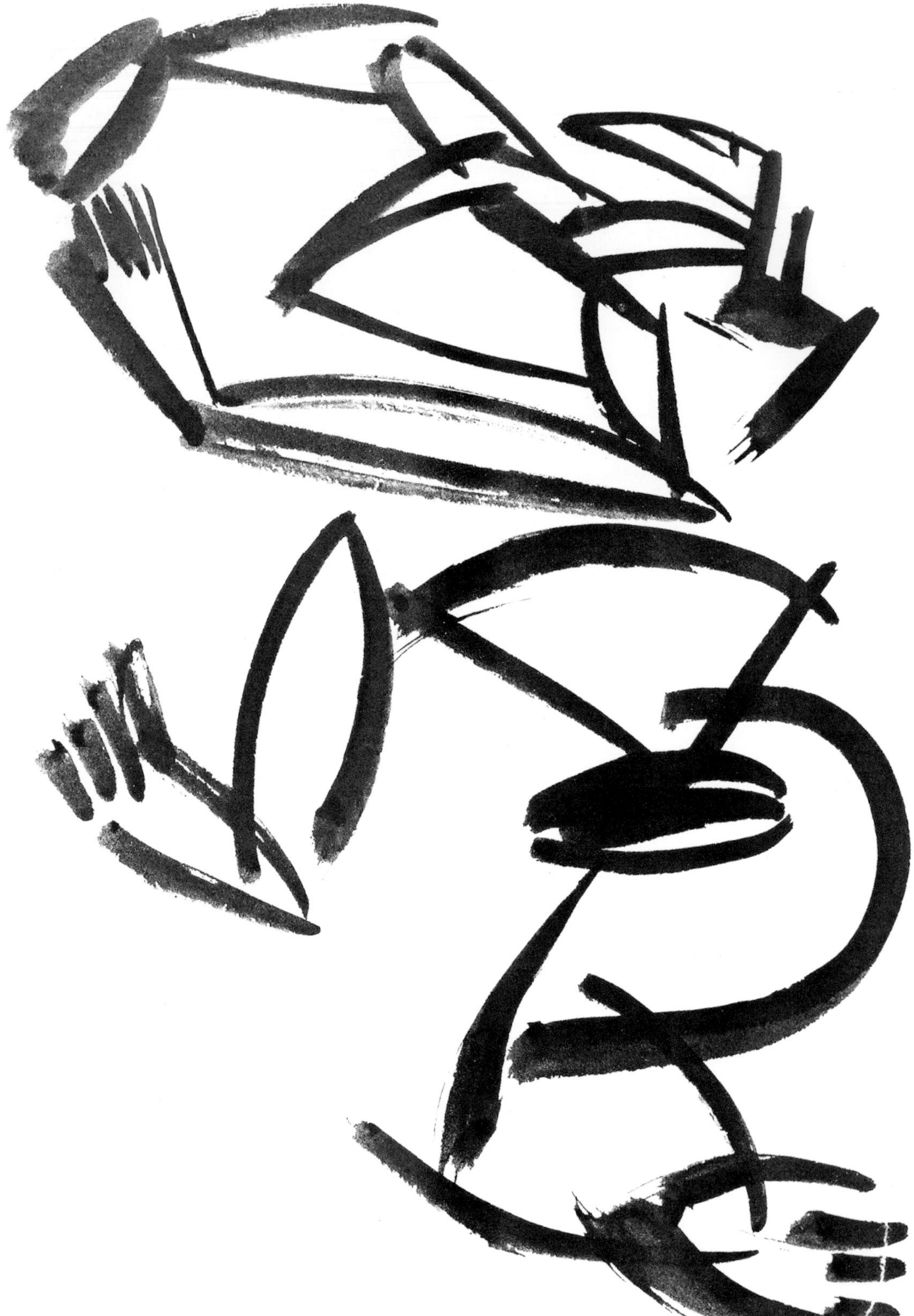

ORNAMENTS, TALISMANS AND TOYS

The Hand-held Sculptures of Henri Gaudier-Brzeska

Jonathan Wood
Henry Moore Institute, Leeds

When Umberto Boccioni was killed in 1916, his death was announced on the front cover of *L'Italia Futurista*, with a short statement by the Futurist leader Filippo Tommaso Marinetti.[1] Immediately below, and occupying over half of the page, was a line drawing by Giacomo Balla entitled *The Italian Fist of Boccioni*. This was Futurist obituary at its most ebullient: Boccioni may be dead, but his genius, energy and achievements live on. Boccioni's fist was now not only a dynamic icon of avant-garde agency, but also a symbol of Italian military strength.

This was not, however, the first or indeed the last time that Balla would use this image. He had first started on it a year earlier when the artist was still alive, and had executed a handful of drawings entitled *Boccioni's Fist* in pencil and red crayon. (It was with the announcement of Boccioni's death that Balla momentarily changed the title to emphasise the artist's nationality.) Most significantly, he had also made that year, from cardboard and wood, a large, red-painted sculpture with the same title [fig. 20]. This image became the letterhead on the Futurist movement's stationary and was printed beside the slogan 'Marciare, Non Marcire!' ('March, Don't Rot!'). Later, after the war, it was used for a poster advertising an exhibition of Balla's work at Bragaglia's Gallery (October 1918) and then on the poster for the 'Exhibition of the Paintings of the Italian Futurists' at the Galérie Reinhardt in Paris (May 1921). Balla even used a large, red cardboard fist, kept in his studio, for his Futurist performances.[2]

At the centre of these images, Balla's sculpture *Boccioni's Fist* is a work that reveals a great deal about the subjects and avant-garde strategies of the Futurist homage. First, it was a tribute not only from one artist to another, but also to a sculptor whose 'Manifesto of Futurist Sculpture' promoted the use of non-precious materials such as cardboard. It was also, however, a celebration of an avant-garde collaboration that breaks down artistic categories such as 'sculptor', 'painter' and 'graphic designer': *Boccioni's Fist*, across this group of images, is Balla's fist, three-dimensionally and on paper, graphically and typographically. This conceit consolidates their mutual Futurist practice and their togetherness as avant-garde colleagues. Second, *Boccioni's Fist* is a double-image: as well as being a fist, it is also an image of an entire body and, in turn, a specific tribute to Boccioni's famous

FIG. 19
HENRI GAUDIER-BRZESKA
Dancing Woman
1914
ink and brush on paper
22.7 × 14 cm
Musée des Beaux Arts, Orléans

FIG. 20
GIACOMO BALLA
Boccioni's Fist
*c.*1915/1956
brass (originally made of cardboard and wood painted red)
80 × 75 × 33 cm
Hirschhorn Museum of Art, Washington DC

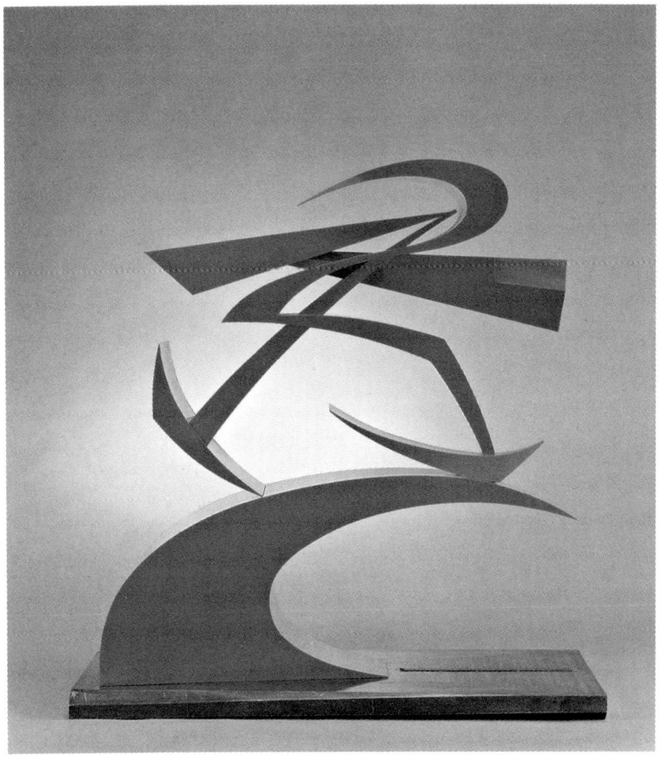

sculpture of 1913, *Unique Forms of Continuity in Space*. Balla's abstract forms suggest the streamlined and aerodynamic limbs of a figure, striding fist first and from right to left, on top of a moving crest. It is also a subtle form of portraiture and, as such, recalls Marinetti's own (now lost) wooden *Self-Portrait (Dynamic Combination of Objects)* (1914), which took the form of a running stick figure with its arms in the air.[3] The red of *Boccioni's Fist* is also very resonant of Marinetti, who wrote in 1915: 'We are red and love red: eyes and cheeks reddened by reflections from the fireboxes of locomotives.'[4] Finally, Balla's sculpture is a telling reminder of the important status and function of the hand in Futurist art and thought, in which it acts as a metonymic register for cultural meaning and as the dynamic and dramatic point of interaction between subject and object, agent and instrument, man and machine.[5]

Boccioni's Fist (and the issues it raises) now serves as an illuminating, historical comparison with the work and career of the French-born Vorticist sculptor Henri Gaudier-Brzeska. Like Boccioni, Gaudier (who was nine years younger) was killed during the First World War. Like Boccioni, Gaudier wrote about sculpture (in magazines such as *Blast* and *The Egoist*) and like Boccioni, left behind a relatively small sculptural oeuvre that was quickly championed by his avant-garde colleagues after his premature death. Whilst there is not, of course, a 'Gaudier's Fist', that is, a single sculpture which presents such avant-garde ideas, there were often strong formal correspondences, as Gaudier's drawing *Dancing Woman* (1914) demonstrates [fig. 19]. Most importantly, however, there is a group of small-scale, palm-sized sculptures that Gaudier made and circulated amongst the Vorticist group. These are highly evocative of the Vorticist sculptor's hand: designed not just to be looked at, but to be held, handled, played with, worked with, worn and used. Works such as *Médaille* (also known as *Knuckleduster*) (1914), *Doorknocker* [pl. 4], *Ornament Torpille* (now known as *Torpedo Fish*) [fig. 21], *Brass Toy* (also known as *Fish*) (1914), *Toothbrush* (1914), *Charm* (1914) and *Duck* [fig. 22] are regarded as some of Gaudier's most Vorticist works. Although there is detailed and useful information on these as individual works of art in the books and catalogues of Richard Cork, Roger Cole, Jeremy Lewison and Evelyn Silber, they have never been fully considered as a closely related group.[6]

For these objects do indeed constitute a mini-group. 'Of the fist' as well as 'of the hand', evocative of force as well as touch, all were carved directly into stone or brass, a highly unusual carving material which immediately drew attention to the manual, sculptural difficulties entailed in their making. Indeed, their implicit technical achievement alone gave them a special trophy-like status. Gaudier had cut right through metal to make them: many have pierced forms (a fact Gaudier himself was keen to detail as 'perfore', or 'perforated', in his list of works). Gaudier, according to Pound, had 'an apparently inexhaustible manual activity': he would carve into whatever he could get his hands on and many of these small, hand-held works came from the fragmentary offcuts he got from his neighbour Fabrucci.[7] It is far more than this shared source that this group has in common. Their subjects, their obscure iconographies and forms, their geometric/organic abstract designs, their ambiguous categorisation as objects, sculptures and/or ornaments, the deliberately ambivalent and obfuscatory manner in which they could function and were titled, and the circumstances under which they were made, displayed and

FIG. 21
HENRI GAUDIER-BRZESKA
Torpedo Fish
1914
cut bronze
15.9 × 3.8 × 3.2 cm
Kettle's Yard,
University of Cambridge

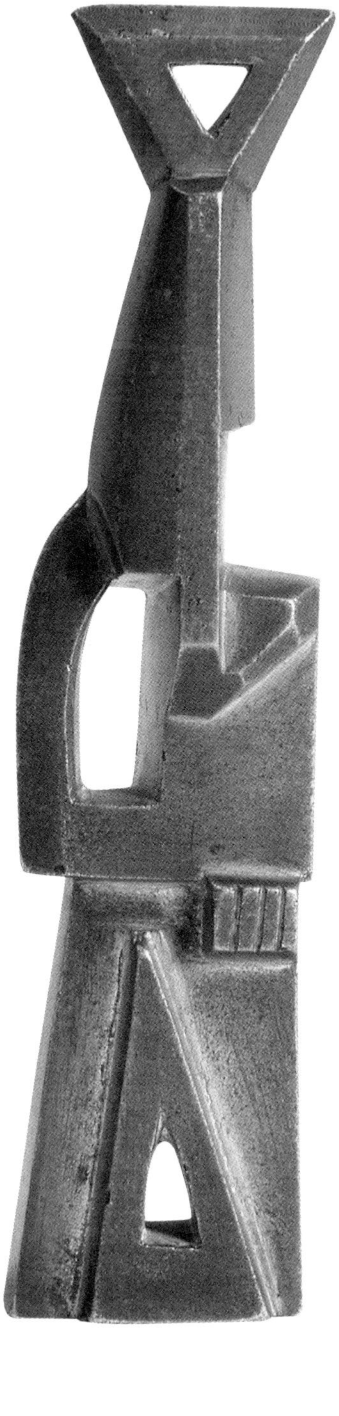

'performed' relate them to one another as a complex and highly informative group of works.

First, they shed interesting light on the peculiar conceptual orientation of what we might loosely call 'Vorticist sculpture'. As with Futurism, the hand is again an important motif of agency, but one that reaches across a wider and less secular range of references, well beyond the Futurist love of speed and dynamism.[8] Indeed Futurism, according to T. E. Hulme, was merely 'the deification of the flux, the last efflorescence of Impressionism' and quite the 'opposite' to Vorticism.[9] The 'Vorticist hand' was a historical and highly interdisciplinary one which embraced not only the mechanised objects and processes of technological modernity (the machine, the gun, the drill), but also notions of craftsmanship (the artisan, the carver, the worker), ideas of magic, animism and 'primitive' agency (talismans, charms, amulets and totemic animalia), physical violence and sport (knuckledusters, boxing, wrestling) [pls. 16, 34 and 45] and erotica and sexual symbolism (fertility symbols, genital imagery, sex toys).

This group of Gaudier's small-scale objects reflect all of these Vorticist preoccupations, often in the same piece. They were all made in 1914 and (soon after Duchamp's initial investigation into the 'readymade') were intended not just to illustrate ideas, but also to activate them: that is, to actually function. For these objects of Gaudier's have a social dimension to them and were principally concerned with the hand. Tellingly, when Epstein reworked *The Rock Drill* [pl. 39] and exhibited it in 1916 as *Torso in Metal from 'The Rock Drill'*, it was not merely the drill that was lost, but crucially the left arm and hand that was holding it. As the preparatory drawings also show, the hand was the point of connection and interaction between the body and the machine.

Second, these objects reveal the ways in which a Frenchman like Gaudier participated socially and intellectually in the Vorticist avant-garde group in London. They demonstrate the ways in which Gaudier disseminated his work amongst Ezra Pound, Wyndham Lewis, Jacob Epstein, T. E. Hulme and others. These works were generated in different ways: some were commissioned, some were given as gifts and tributes, and some were bought (to order or on spec) by women, it is important to note, as well as by men. These were not exclusively 'toys for boys'. As a group, they stand as a form of 'personalia' – synecdocheal objects that were highly evocative of the image and practice of Gaudier himself. They reveal that participating in an

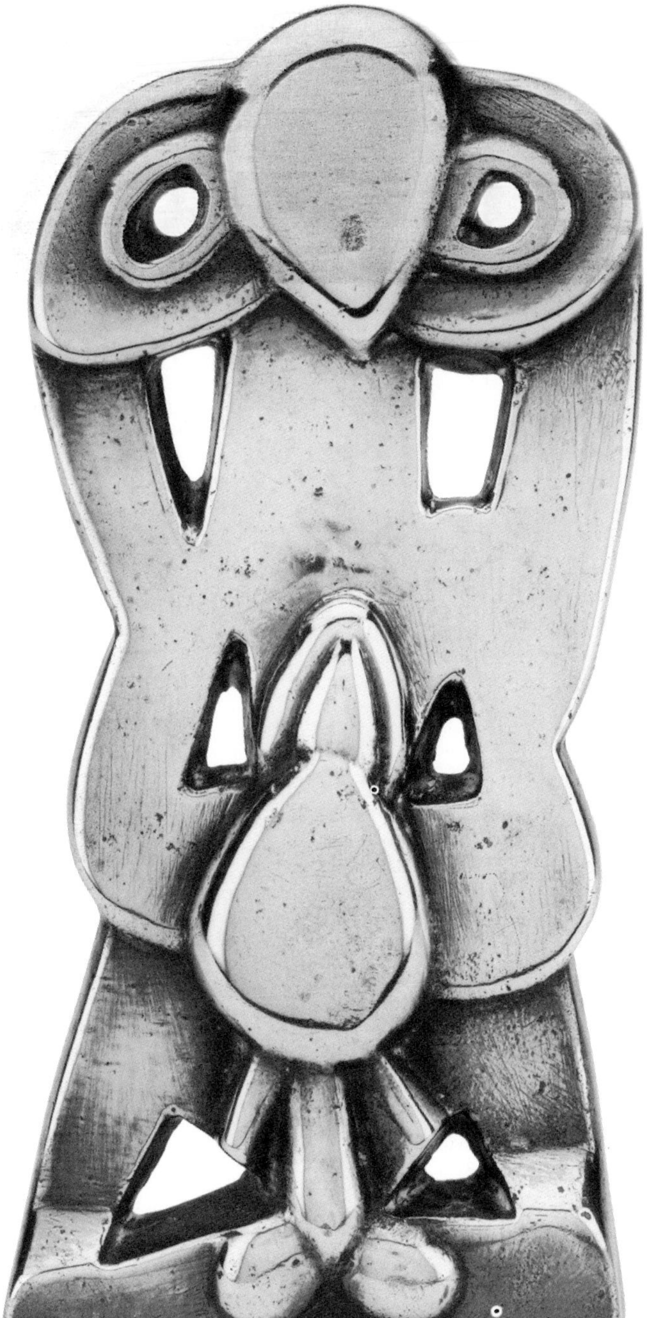

4
HENRI GAUDIER-BRZESKA
Doorknocker
c.1914
brass
17.7 × 18.8 cm
Kettle's Yard, University of Cambridge

FIG. 22
HENRI GAUDIER-BRZESKA
Duck
1914
marble
6.5 × 12 cm
Kettle's Yard, University of Cambridge

FIG. 23
ANON (French)
Doorknocker
19th century
cast iron
17 × 6 cm
Private collection

avant-garde environment signified far more than appearing in group exhibitions, submitting texts for publication and being a manifesto signatory. They allow further insight into the more subtle and complicated ways that Gaudier worked within, and contributed to, the Vorticist group and together provide an important counterpoint to the role historically accredited to Gaudier's single large marble sculpture, the *Hieratic Head of Ezra Pound* (1914).[10]

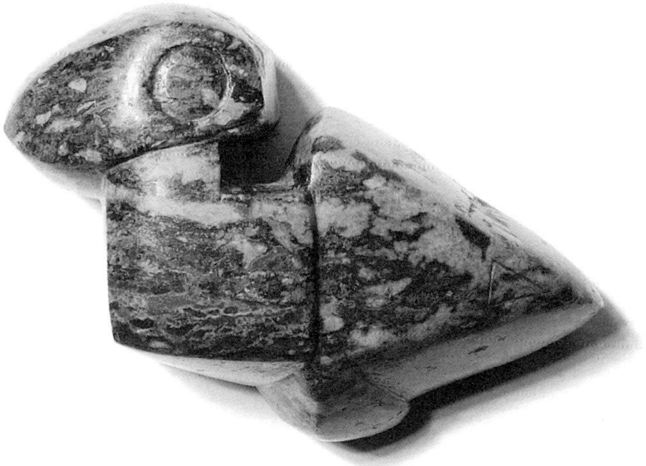

Gaudier's objects lived a double life that folded directly back into his own practice in a self-referential way. These hand-made sculptures were created with hand-made tools: moreover, he resourcefully made the tools – as well as the sculptures – from discarded materials. Sculptures were tools and vice-versa, and they were made of stone as well as metal. *Duck* (1914), carved from marble, is a particularly pertinent example because it does not just look like a duck but, as Lewison has said, 'the sculpture becomes a kind of marble tool. The head of the duck resembles that of a hammer, the tail is reminiscent of a flint tool or arrowhead.'[fig. 22][11] Gaudier's sculpted tools were for thought as much as for action, and the fact that the green stone *Charm* that Pound later bought from Gaudier served to emboss the poet's memoir of the sculptor is a knowing appropriation on behalf of the poet. It gave Pound's book an authentic, authorial and talismanic status as a physical object and, in turn, as a document.

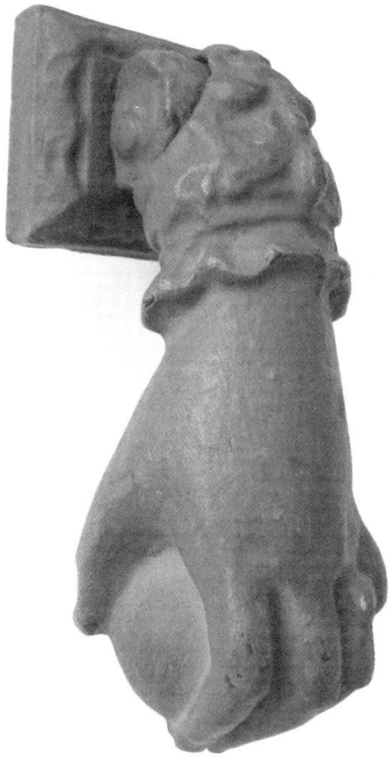

Crucial to the poetry and efficacy of these small objects is the direct relation they had to Gaudier's own body, identity and practice. As Ezra Pound and Horace Brodzky later stated: '[Gaudier] liked to do the whole thing from start to finish: to feel as independent as the savage' and 'would want to pierce his nose with a stick, some four inches long and hang bells on it like a South Sea Islander. He would wish for earrings long and quaint, and he actually carved a large green stone charm in the manner of the Maoris. This he wore suspended from his neck.'[12]

Atavism and non-western references were key here. His hand-held objects were thus 'of' him as much as 'by' him: not crucifixes, St Christopher's medals, or rosary beads, but Vorticist talismans for a non-Christian era which were to be distributed and shared amongst avant-garde colleagues. These were non-linguistic means of communication, and owners of them, thus, became, through them, participatory initiates of Gaudier's practice – friends, as much as collectors of his art. Even Brodzky's negative account reveals this to be a two, not just one-way, process: 'Brzeska would cut a piece of brass for them that would look more like a masonic charm than anything else. He would tell them that it was symbolic of fecundity or virility, or whatever erotic nonsense *he had in his head at the time. That was what they wanted.*' [Jonathan Wood's italics] [13]

In his preview of the 'Allied Artists' Association' at Holland Park in June 1914, Gaudier himself reiterated something of this position, commenting: 'The sculpture I admire is the work of master craftsmen. Every inch of the surface is won at the point of the chisel – every stroke of the hammer is physical and mental effort.' He went on to comment on his own exhibited work and focussed in particular on *Doorknocker* [pl. 4], stating: 'The door-knocker is an instance of an abstract design serving to amplify the value of an object as such. No more cupids riding mermaids, garlands, curtains - stuck anywhere! The technique is unusual; the object is not cast but carved direct out of solid brass. The forms gain in sharpness and rigidity.'[14]

Gaudier's comments are very interesting in the light of the kind of object *Doorknocker* is and how difficult it is to read its asymmetrical forms. Looking at the various studies for door-knockers Gaudier executed, it appears that *Doorknocker* has sexual iconography and shows the forms of a copulating couple.[15] This entirely tallies with Gaudier's rejection of polite, decorative subjects (which he complained could be randomly 'stuck anywhere'): the message here is that sexual intercourse is analogous to knocking on the door and entering a house. Thus, the sexual iconography of 'abstract design' 'amplifies', to use Gaudier's term, the object's meaning. Gaudier's language is telling: *Doorknocker* was also an object that moved and made a noise since it could be activated and (functioning literally as well as metaphorically) has a specific location. *Doorknocker* turns a house or apartment into a knocking shop – or at least a place of extramarital relations. This was more life affecting than Futurist sculpture could be, as Lewis would characteristically have it. He remarked: 'The Futurist statue will move: then it will live a little: but any idiot can do better than that with his good wife, round the corner.'[16] Moreover, as with Gaudier's *Red Stone Dancer* of 1914 (which seems to have one hand too many), there is a deliberate ambiguity between body parts in *Doorknocker*: the hands, for example, double up as breasts. Given that the typical French cast-iron doorknocker of the period represented a female hand holding a ball, it is worth speculating that Gaudier might have had the figurative formulation and the imaginative potential of these ubiquitous objects in mind [fig. 23]. Gaudier's *Doorknocker* was a household object, but unlike the products that were made for Fry's Omega Workshops, it was mischievously loaded with sexual resonance. If Gaudier's group of small-scale works cocked a snook at the ornaments, trinkets and paraphernalia of the luxury and domestic goods market, *Doorknocker* brought new challenges and a new sensibility to the threshold of the bourgeois residence itself.

One residence that was amenable to such ideas was Ethel Kibblewhite's apartment at 67 Frith Street. Kibblewhite was Hulme's partner and Hulme held his Tuesday evening meetings at her Soho flat. As Robert Ferguson has recently described, these salons were lively affairs, full of open and challenging debate and attended by an interesting range of writers, poets, publishers, artists and political thinkers, including (along with Gaudier) A. R. Orage, Ford Maddox Ford, Rupert Brooke, Edward Marsh, Ezra Pound, Richard Aldington, Wyndham Lewis, Walter Sickert, Stanley Spencer, Harriet Harold Monro, Robert Bevan, Harold Gilman, Charles Ginner, Stasia de Karlowska, Spencer Gore and Jacob Epstein.[17] Both Hulme and Kibblewhite owned examples of Gaudier's small-scale sculptures: she owned a small carved metal *Fish* (bought for 10 shillings) and he owned *Ornament Torpille/Torpedo Fish* (bought for £2) and *Médaille/Knuckleduster* (bought for 10 shillings).[18] Others in this group also owned pieces: Lewis (according to Sophie Brzeska's diary) owned a *Médaille/Knuckleduster* and Karlowska (Bevan's Polish wife) owned *Toothbrush* (bought for 10 shillings), which was carved out of bone and then 'smoked' to give it a burnt, used look.[19]

Though it is unlikely that Karlowska ever used her *Toothbrush*, all these pieces entail or evoke an intimate relationship to their owners' bodies. What kind of bodily interaction was thus implied or envisaged, and how did these 'performing objects' function? One fact which is clear, given Pound's and Gaudier's own articles that year in *The Egoist*, is that these objects were not 'caressable' or meant to be stroked lovingly, as late nineteenth century Victorian collectors of statuettes and figurines might have done.[20] These objects were designed to be manipulated and turned around in the hand, a gesture that in turn closely replicated those employed by Gaudier himself in making them. Accordingly, these works have no discernable tops or bottoms, and when they were placed (and later photographed) on the horizontal, they could be positioned a variety of different ways. Indeed, these objects, I think, were not really meant to be placed on display on the level at all, but carried around and secreted about one's person: the fact that many have perforations suggests that they could also hold a string and be worn as pendants. These were mobile sculptures: they were to be held and suspended 'off the ground'. Furthermore, the fact that most were 'fish' (and one a 'duck') poetically emphasised their floating, suspended identities. Ethel Kibblewhite carried her small *Fish* (*Toy*) around in her handbag (as Gaudier suggested) and T. E. Hulme used to take his *Médaille* out of his pocket and out of its leather case and play with it whilst in conversation.[21] These awkward and unusual objects were all, in a sense, 'conversation pieces': objects designed to attract the attention and curiosity of others, and objects to handle whilst talking. In the Vorticist circles of Frith Street, such functions had urgency and relevance: they were far more than just toys 'to fidget with'.[22]

Médaille/Knuckleduster seems to relate to Hulme's interest in Georges Sorel's work on violence, whilst perhaps having a more personal bearing on Hulme's reputation as both a fighter and a womaniser. *Médaille*, meaning medal or pendant, could be both held in the hand and fitted around the fingers. It was both a knuckleduster and according to Kate Lechmere, an object with a specific sexual connotation. She commented: 'The two pieces curving out sideways at the bottom are the woman's parted legs. The central hole is her vagina, and the four holes at the top are the woman's head tossing and turning as she achieves orgasm.'[23] This is most likely more Hulme's appropriation than Gaudier's design: as Lewison has stated, Gaudier may indeed have exhibited a second version of this object under the title *Paperweight* in the Vorticist exhibition at the Doré Gallery in June 1915.[24] When not in 'use', knuckledusters could, it seems, be used to stop a Vorticist writer's notes from blowing away.

Torpedo Fish [fig. 21], which Hulme also owned, is a carved, sharp-edged geometric metal object that has clearly been designed not only to evoke quick thinking, mental agility, hard incisive argument and intellectual clarity, but also to generate it through manual interaction with such an object. Gaudier's small geometric pieces, such as this, were themselves partly inspired by Hulme and by his writing on the new modern, geometric art and (through the work of Wilhelm Worringer) on the function of ornament.[25] These were clearly in part Gaudier's responses to his work. They were, of course sculptural, rather than textual contributions to the debate and function more intuitively and phenomenologically. They thus assert the primacy of the sculpted object: forms generate 'feelings' generate thought. Gaudier incorporates a delicately qualified combination of triangles, circles and clipped edges with smoothed, rounded and organicised angular forms. This geometric/organic combination can be fully appreciated when the object is 'blindly' fingered. The more this metal object is manipulated, the hotter it gets and the more it conducts. They are types of Vorticist stress balls (without the give) that inspire concentration and thought.

Mere ornaments and harmless knick knacks to their 'foes', Gaudier's objects were debating weapons to their Vorticist owners, toys and tools to help them torpedo and blast their opponents' arguments. As the creator of them, Gaudier succeeded in patenting a special role and membership for himself within this avant-garde group. How could any Frith Street Vorticist live without one?

Notes

1. *L'Italia Futurista*, 25 August 1916.
2. For details on these works, see M. Fagiolo, *Balla: The Futurist* (Oxford, 1987), pp. 34–45 and 108–13.
3. This work was reproduced in *The Sketch*, 13 May 1914. See M. W. Martin, *Futurist Art and Theory 1909–1915* (Oxford, 1968), pp. 182–83.
4. F. T. Marinetti, 'We Abjure Our Symbolist Masters, the Last Lovers of the Moon', from *War, the World's Only Hygiene, 1911–1915*, in *Marinetti: Selected Writings*, ed. by R. W. Flint (London, 1971), p. 66.
5. For a recent reading of this subject: C. Poggi, 'Dreams of Metallized Flesh: Futurism and the Masculine Body', *Modernism/Modernity*, vol. 4, no. 3, 1997, pp. 19–43.
6. R. Cole, *Burning to Speak: The life and Art of Henri Gaudier-Brzeska* (London, 1978); R. Cork, *Vorticism and Abstract Art in the First Machine Age*, 2 Vols. (London, 1976); J. Lewison, *Henri Gaudier-Brzeska, Sculptor 1891–1915* (Cambridge, 1983); E. Silber, *Gaudier-Brzeska: Life and Art* (London, 1996).
7. E. Pound, *Gaudier-Brzeska: A Memoir* (1916) (New York, 1970), p. 39.
8. This has been noted elsewhere by R. Mengham in 'From Georges Sorel to *Blast!*', in *The Violent Muse: Violence and the Artistic Imagination in Europe 1910–39*, ed. by J. Howett and R. Mengham (Manchester, 1994), p. 39.
9. T. E. Hulme, 'Modern Art and Its Philosophy', in T. E. Hulme, *Speculations: Essays on Humanism and the Philosophy of Art*, ed. by H. Read (London, 1936), p. 94.
10. For a full account and new interpretation of the status and function of this sculpture, see J. Wood, 'Heads and Tales: Henri Gaudier-Brzeska's *Hieratic Head of Ezra Pound* and the Making of an Avant-Garde Homage', in *Sculpture and the Pursuit of a Modern Ideal in Britain c.1880–1930*, ed. by D. Getsy (Aldershot, forthcoming, 2004).
11. Lewison, p. 51.
12. H. Brodzky, *Henri Gaudier-Brzeska* (London, 1932), p. 56.
13. Ibid. p. 90; E. Pound, p. 40.
14. H. Gaudier-Brzeska, 'Allied Artists' Association Ltd., Holland Park Hall', *The Egoist*, 15 June 1914. Henry Moore Institute Library [HMI].
15. See illustrations in *Henri Gaudier-Brzeska*, ed. by E. Mointe and A. Mousseigne (Toulouse, 1993), pp. 67 and 154.
16. W. Lewis, 'Futurism, Magic and Life', *Blast* (London, 1914), p. 135.
17. R. Ferguson, *The Short Sharp Life of T. E. Hulme* (London, 2002), p. 145.
18. Lewison, pp. 57–58.
19. Ibid. p. 61.
20. H. Gaudier-Brzeska and Ezra Pound, 'Letters', *The Egoist*, 16 March 1914 [HMI].
21. Jacob Epstein recalled: 'Hulme would carry them about in his pocket and handle them while talking' in *Let There Be Sculpture* (London, 1942), p. 61.
22. Lewison, p. 58.
23. Silber , p. 272, quoting Cork's interview with Kate Lechmere.
24. Lewison, p. 58.
25. W. Worringer, *Abstraction and Empathy: A Contribution to the Psychology of Style* (1908), trans. M. Bullock (London, 1963), pp. 51–77.

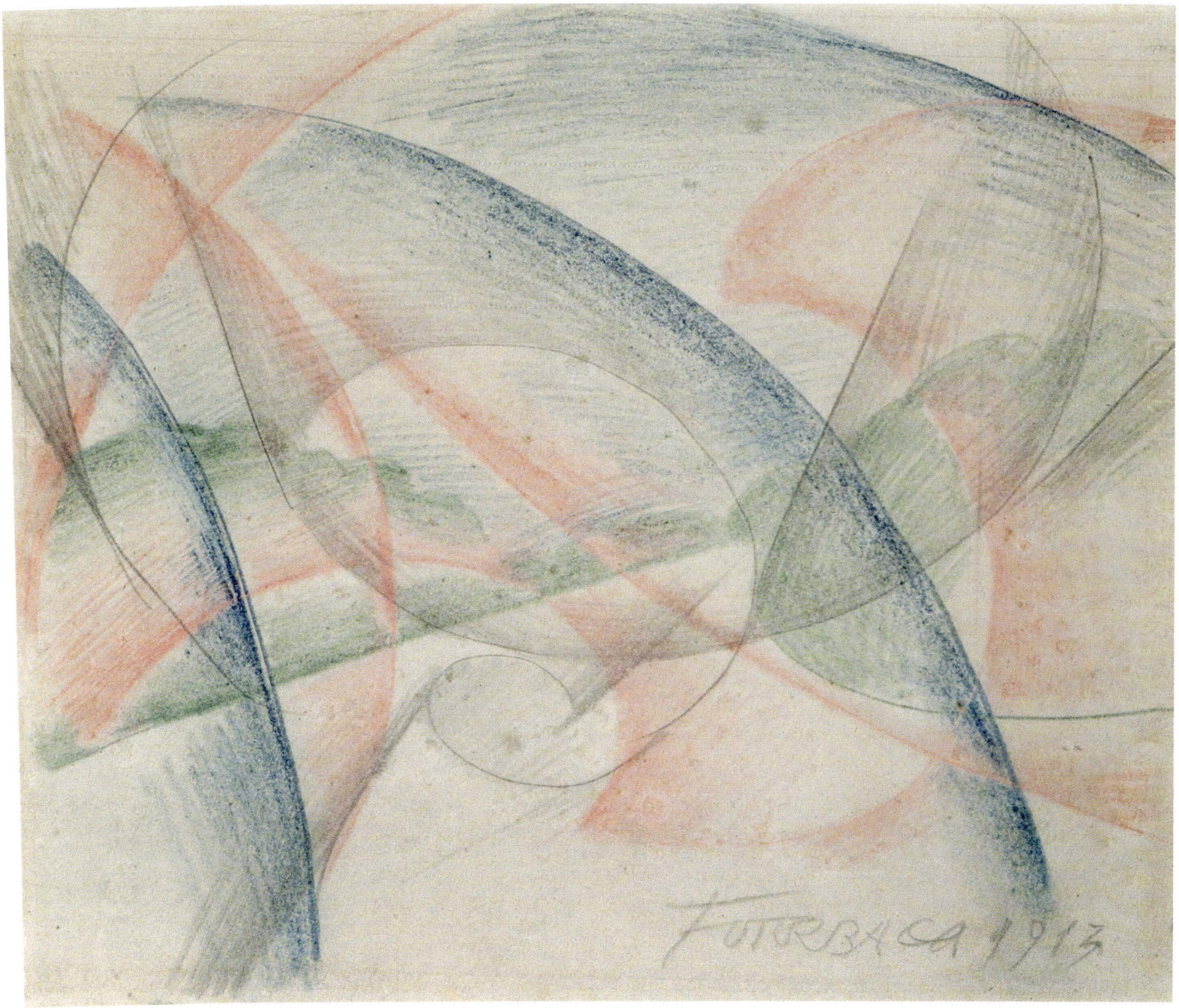

5
GIACOMO BALLA
Speeding Automobile
1913
coloured crayons and pencil on paper
25 × 28.5 cm
Estorick Collection, London

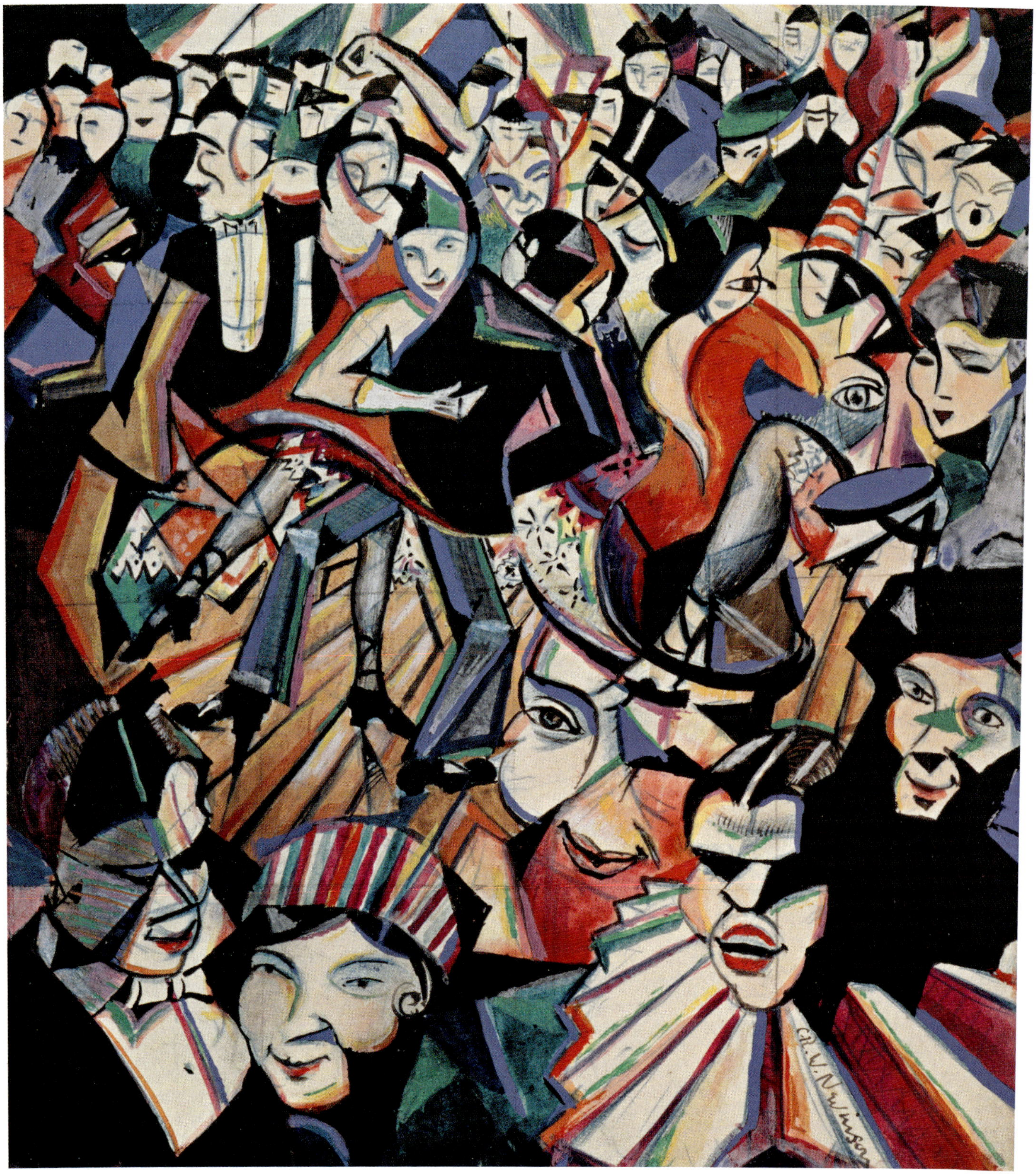
C.R.W. Nevinson

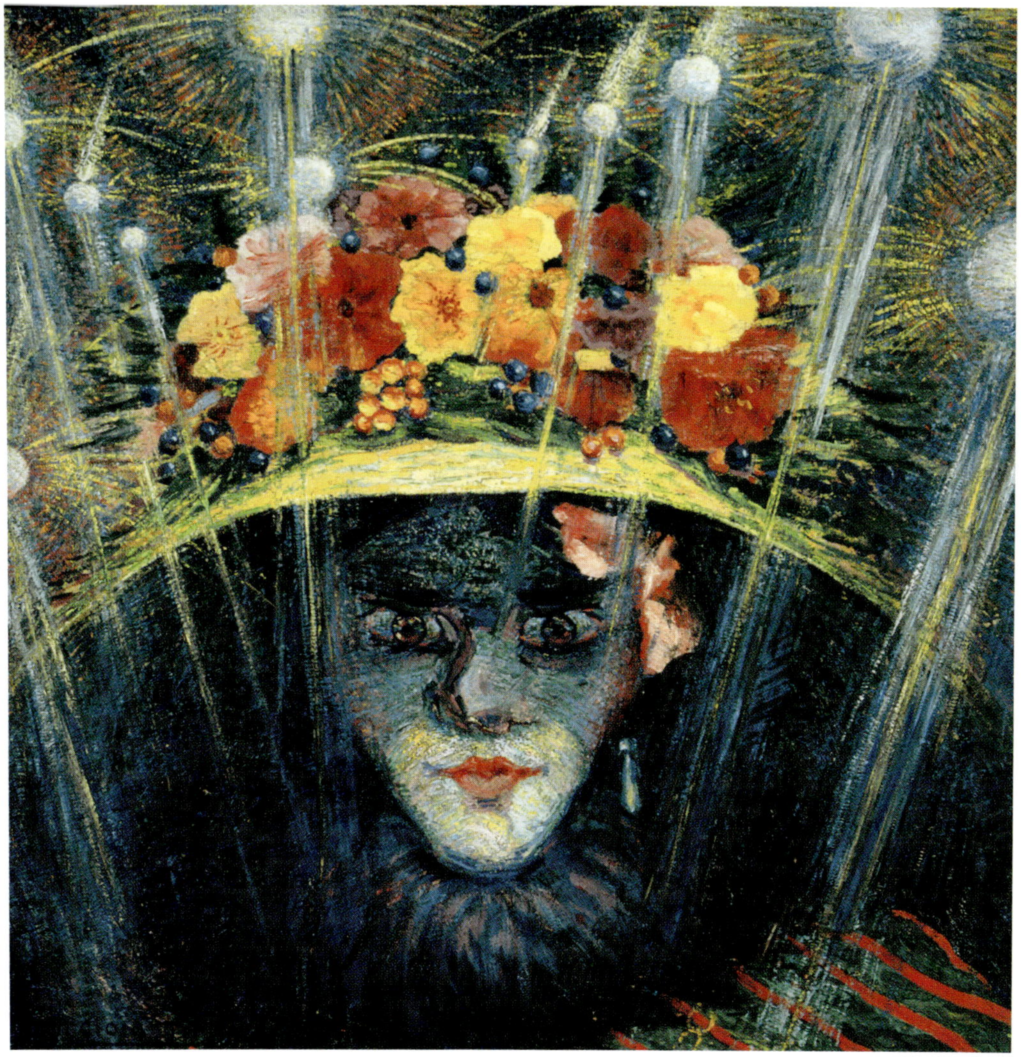

6
C. R. W. NEVINSON
Dance Hall Scene
*c.*1913–14
gouache and pencil on paper
22.2 × 19.7 cm
Tate, London

7
UMBERTO BOCCIONI
Modern Idol
1911
oil on panel
60 × 58.4 cm
Estorick Collection, London

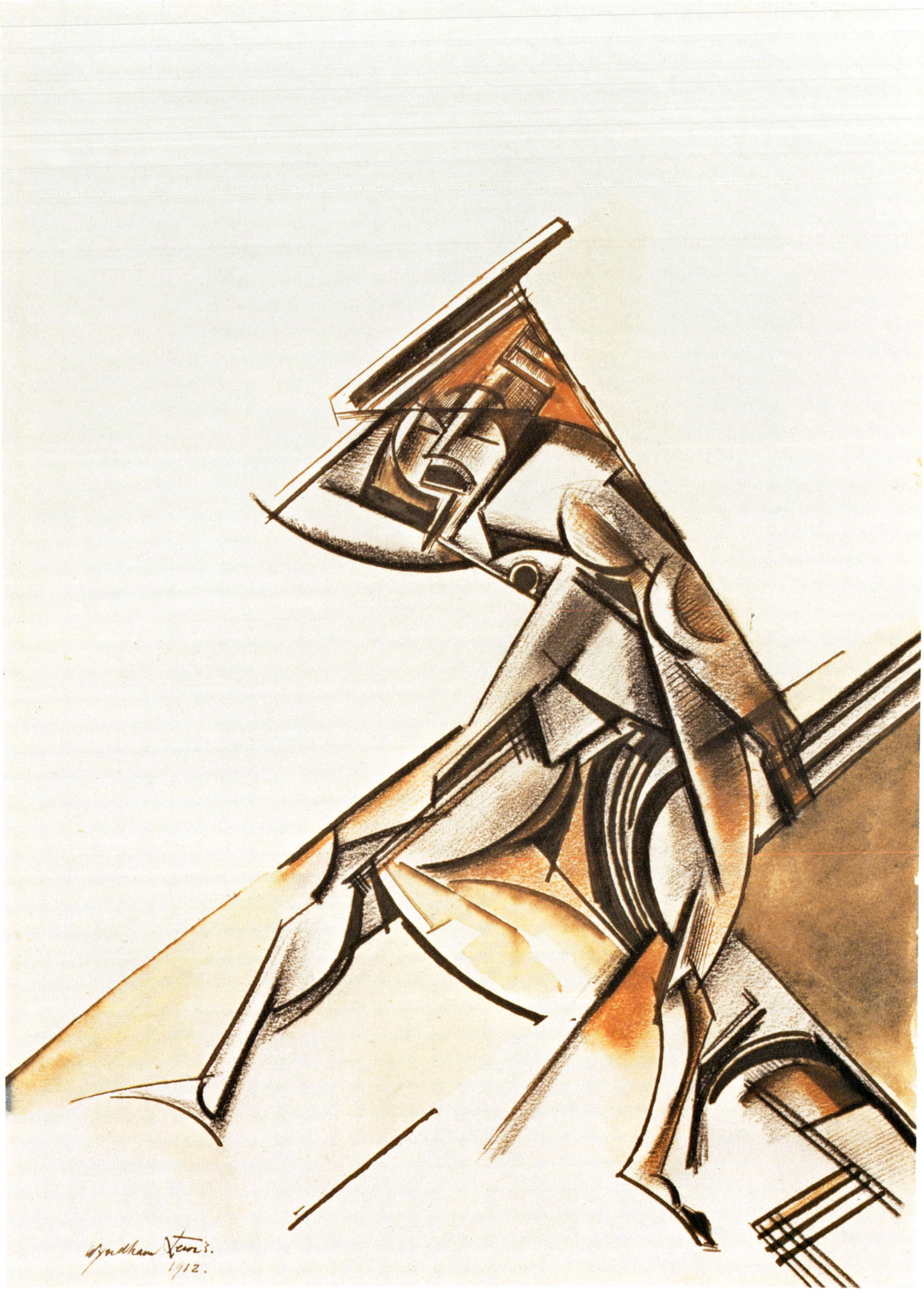

8
WYNDHAM LEWIS
The Vorticist
1912
watercolour, ink and chalk on paper
42.2 × 32.2 cm
Southampton City Art Gallery

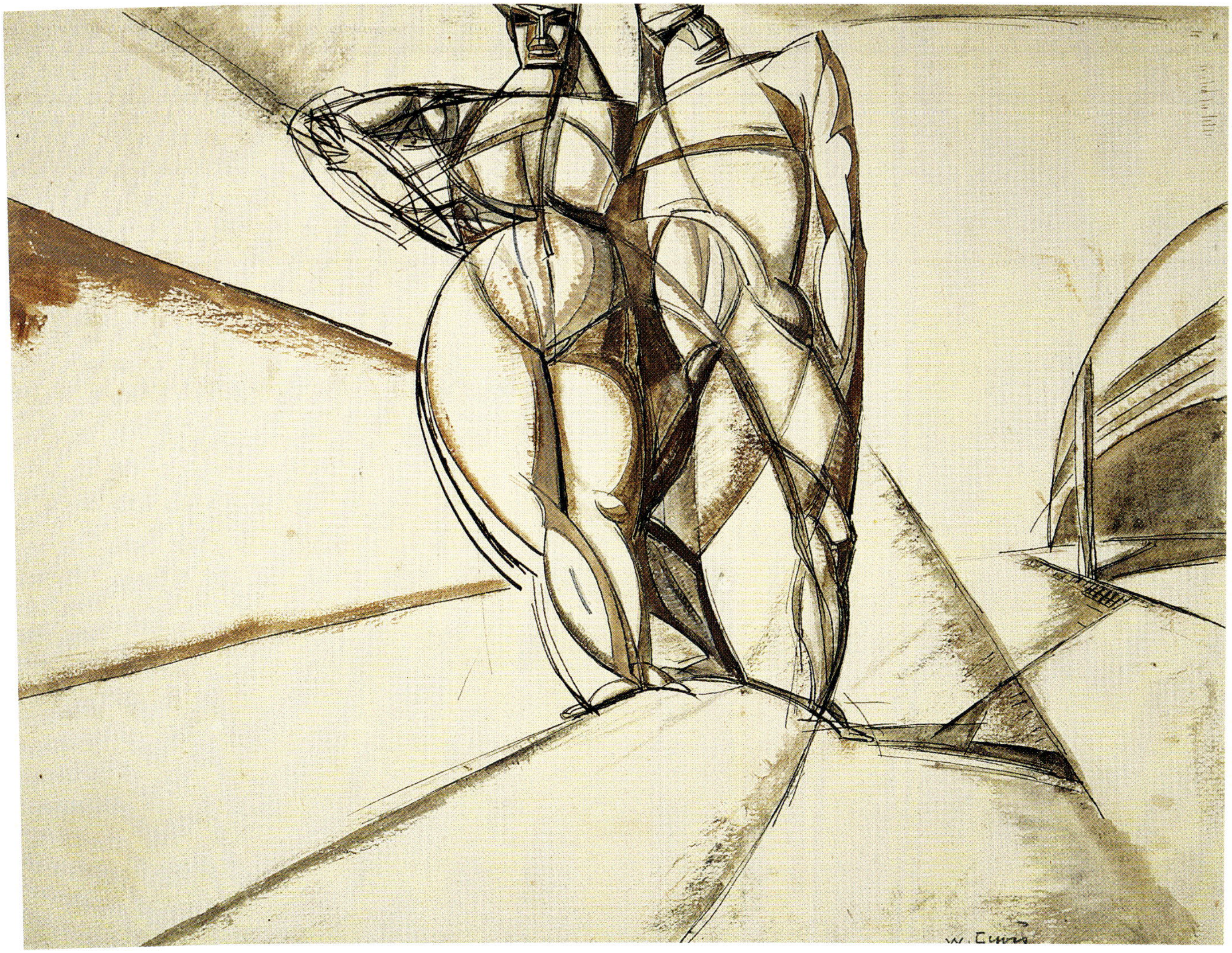

9
WYNDHAM LEWIS
Two Vorticist Figures
*c.*1913–14
ink and watercolour on paper
24.7 × 31.9 cm
The British Museum

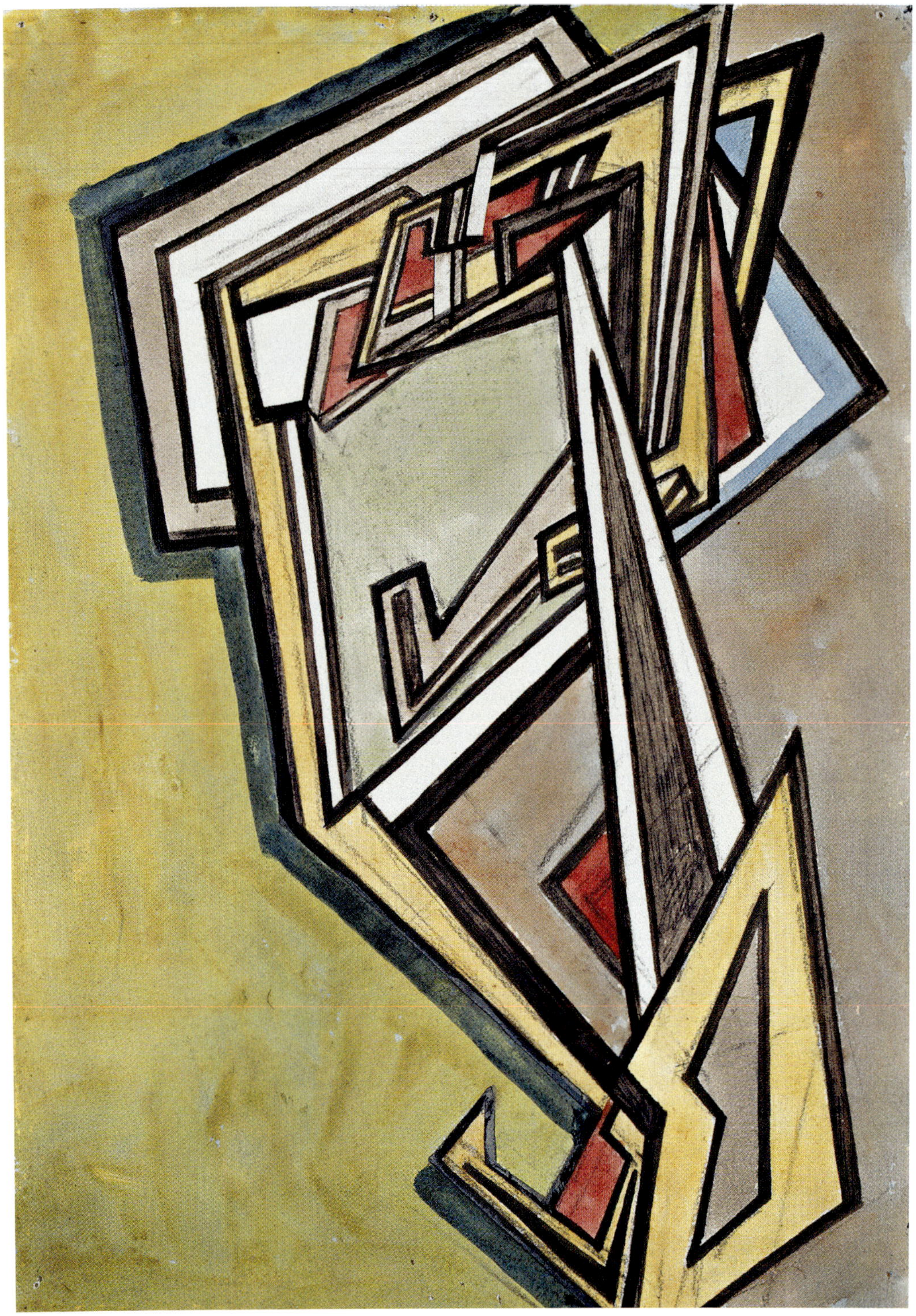

10
HELEN SAUNDERS
Vorticist Composition: Black and Khaki (?)
c.1915
ink and watercolour on paper
25.5 × 18 cm
Private collection

11
HELEN SAUNDERS
Vorticist Composition (Study for 'Cannon'?)
c.1915
ink and watercolour on paper
38 × 30 cm
Private collection

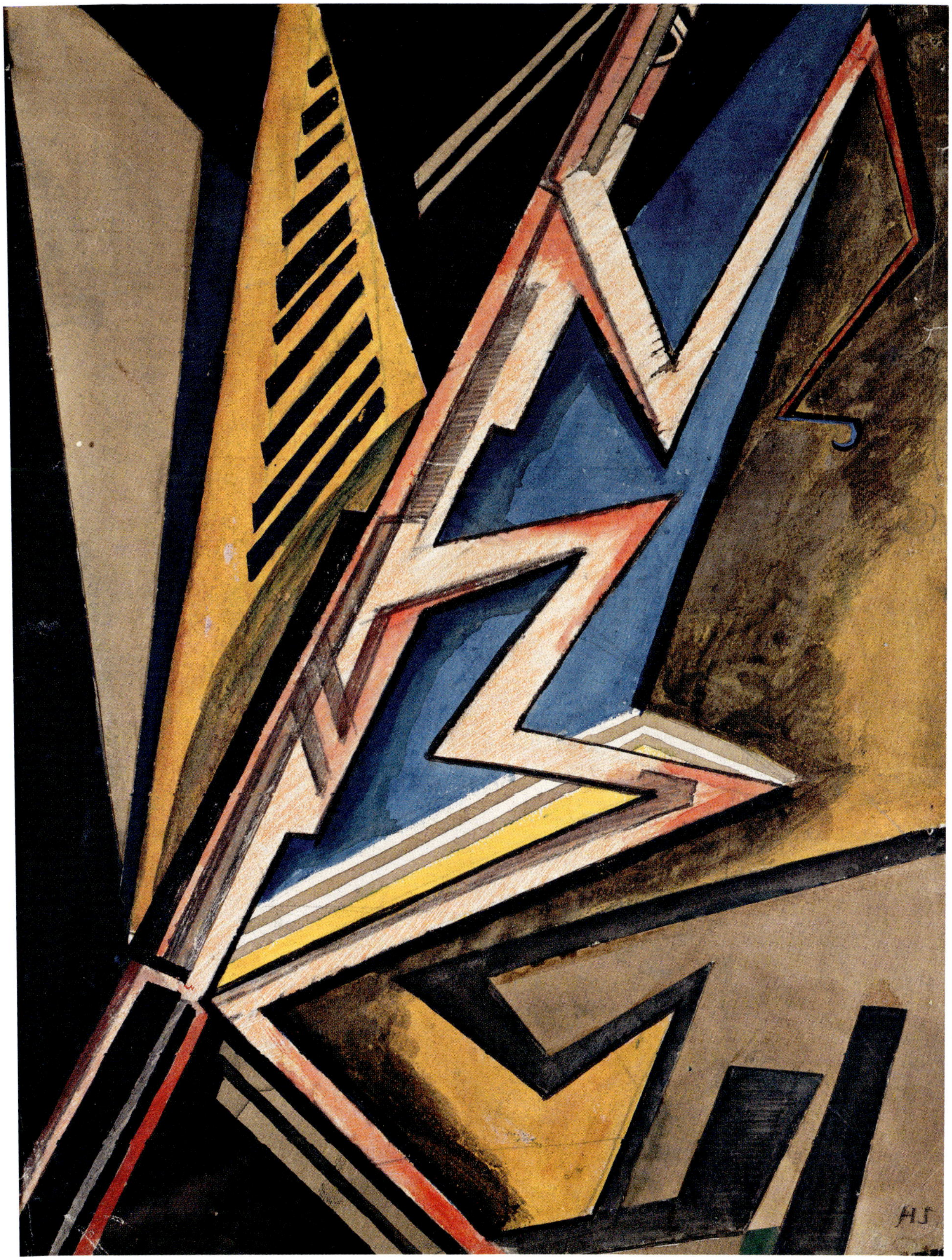
HS

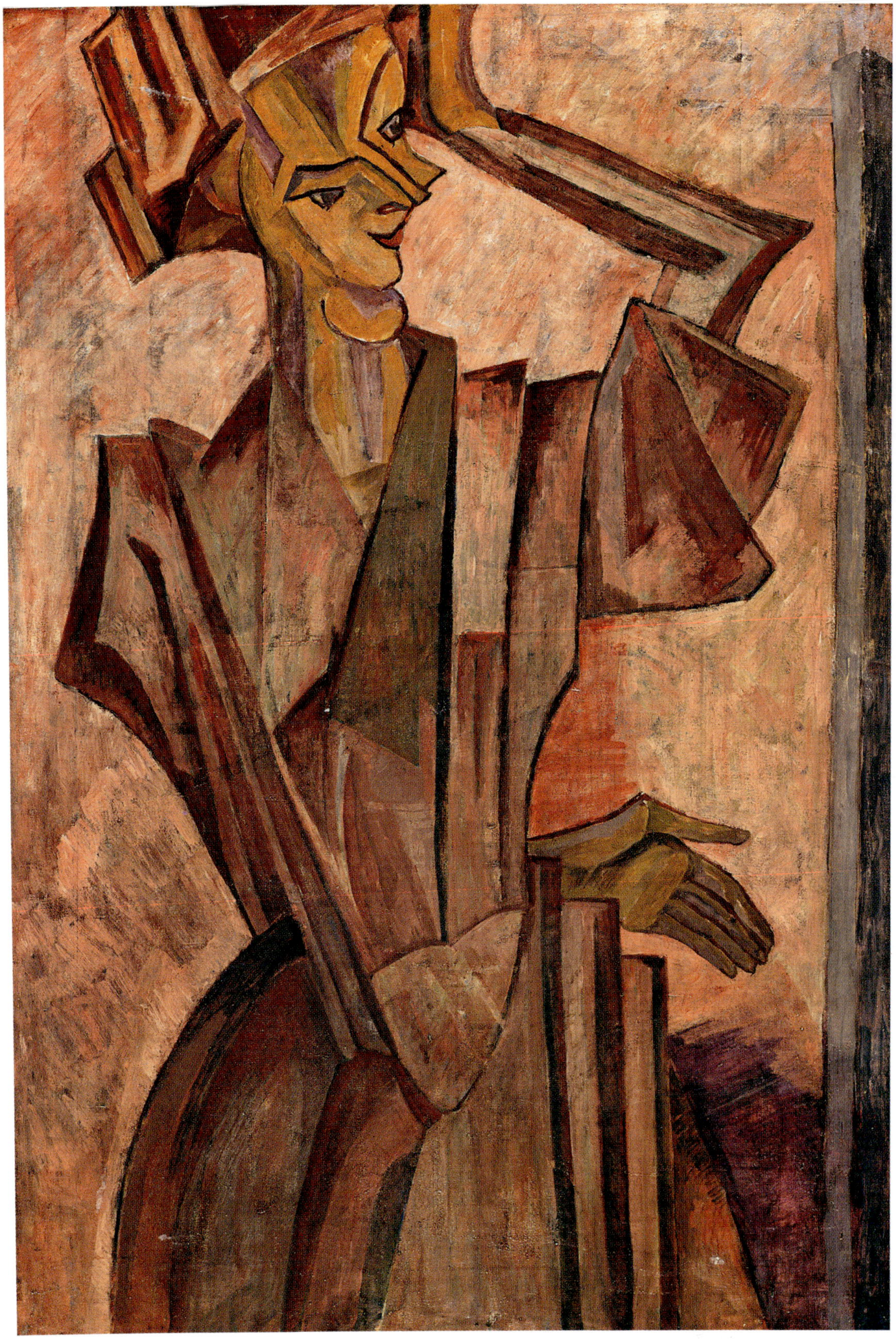

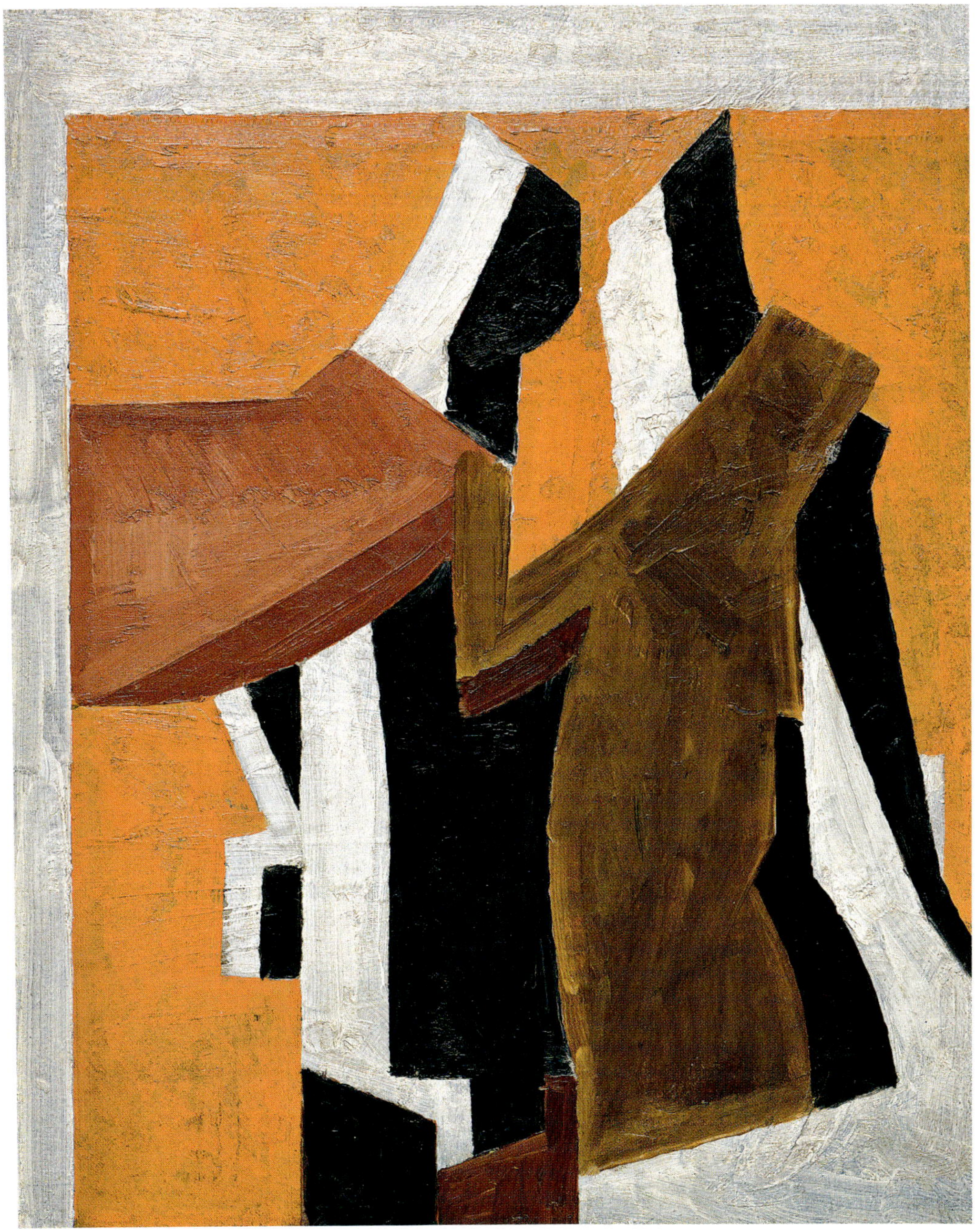

12
FREDERICK ETCHELLS
Woman at a Mirror
1913
oil on canvas
115.2 x 76.9 cm
Manchester City Galleries

13
DAVID BOMBERG
Composition with Figures
*c.*1912–13
oil on wood panel
41 × 32.8 cm
The Whitworth Art Gallery,
The University of Manchester

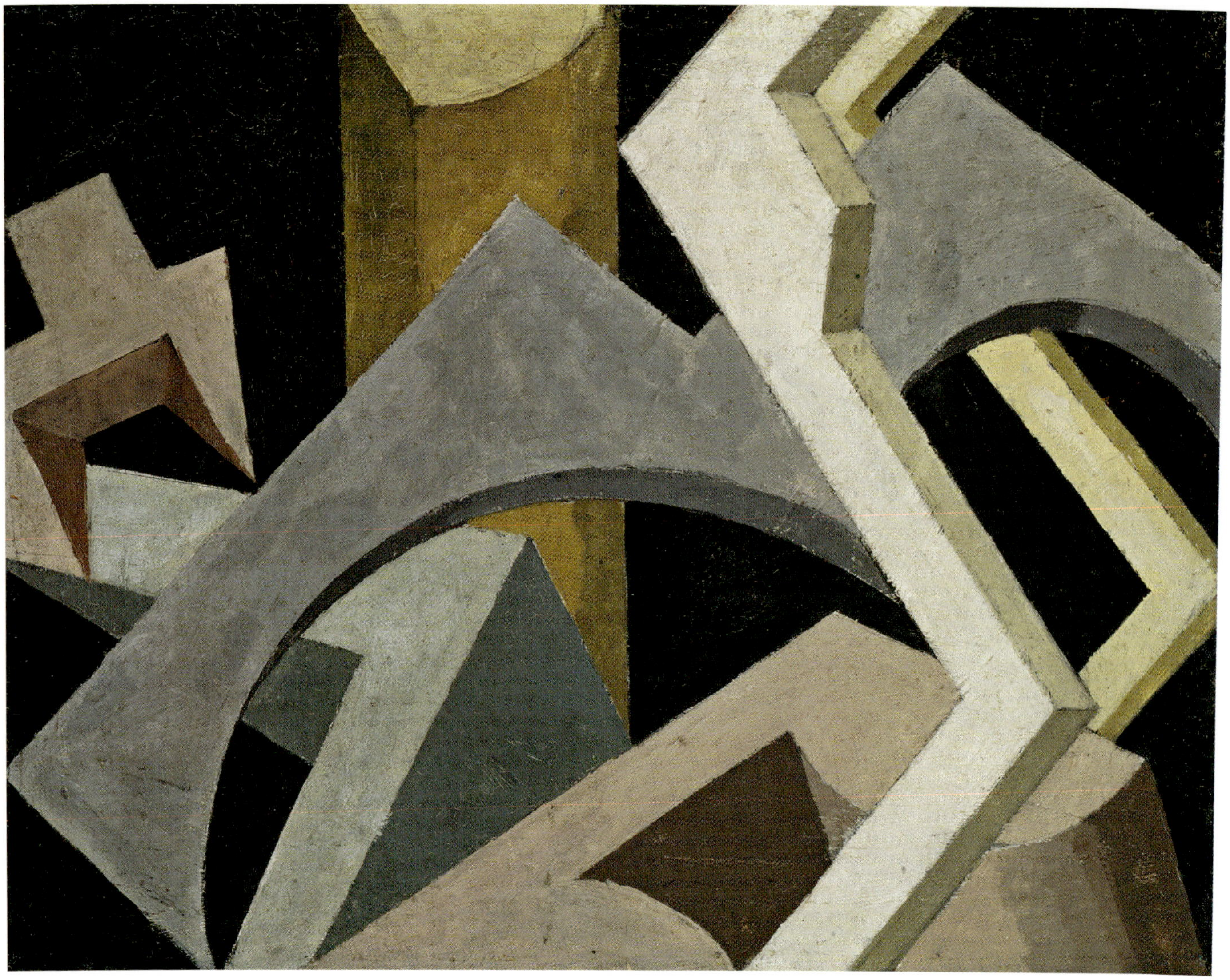

14
JESSICA DISMORR
Abstract Composition
*c.*1915
oil on wood
41.3 × 50.8 cm
Tate, London

15
LAWRENCE ATKINSON
Vorticist Composition
*c.*1914–15
oil on canvas
106.5 × 85 cm
Dr. and Mrs. Jeffrey Sherwin

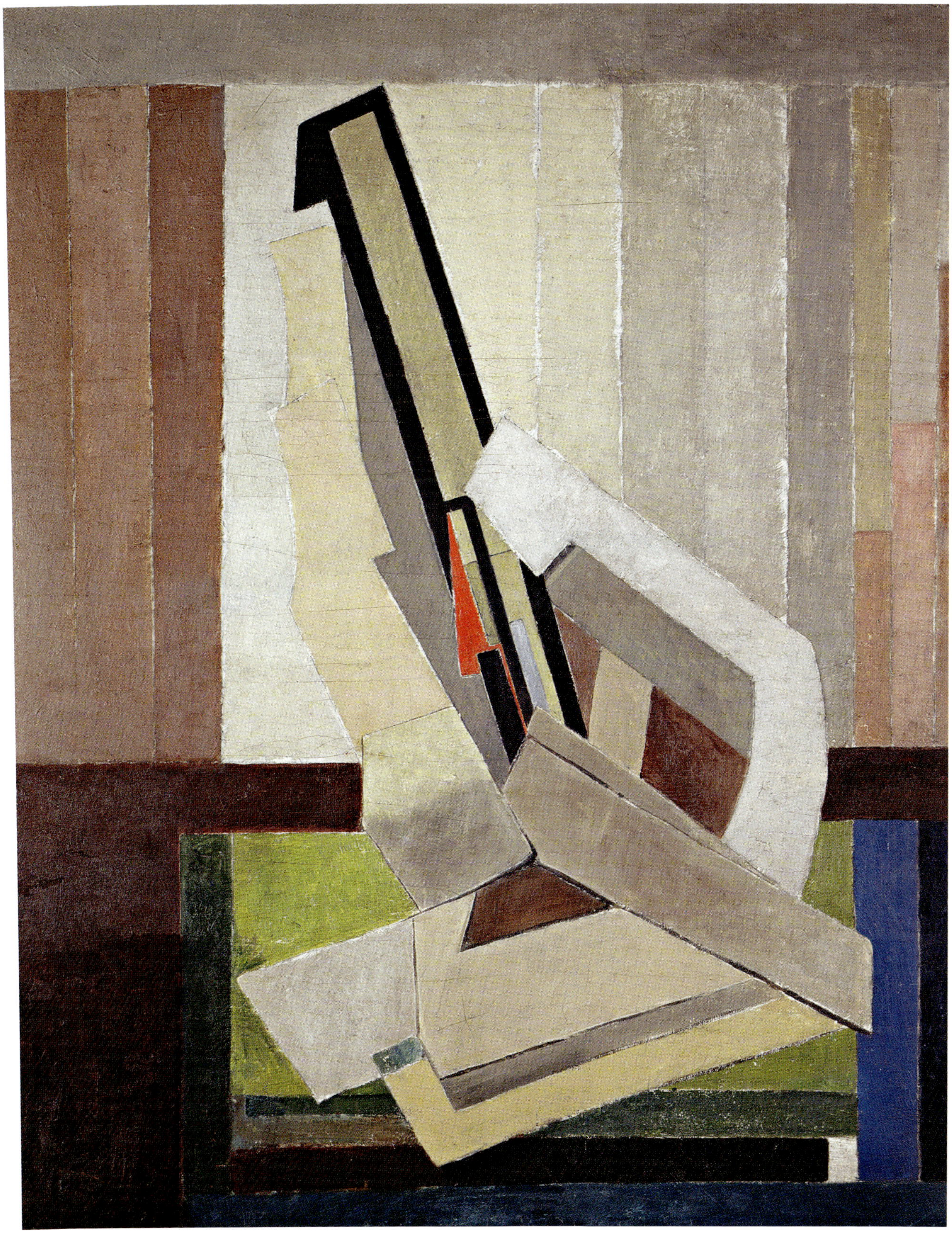

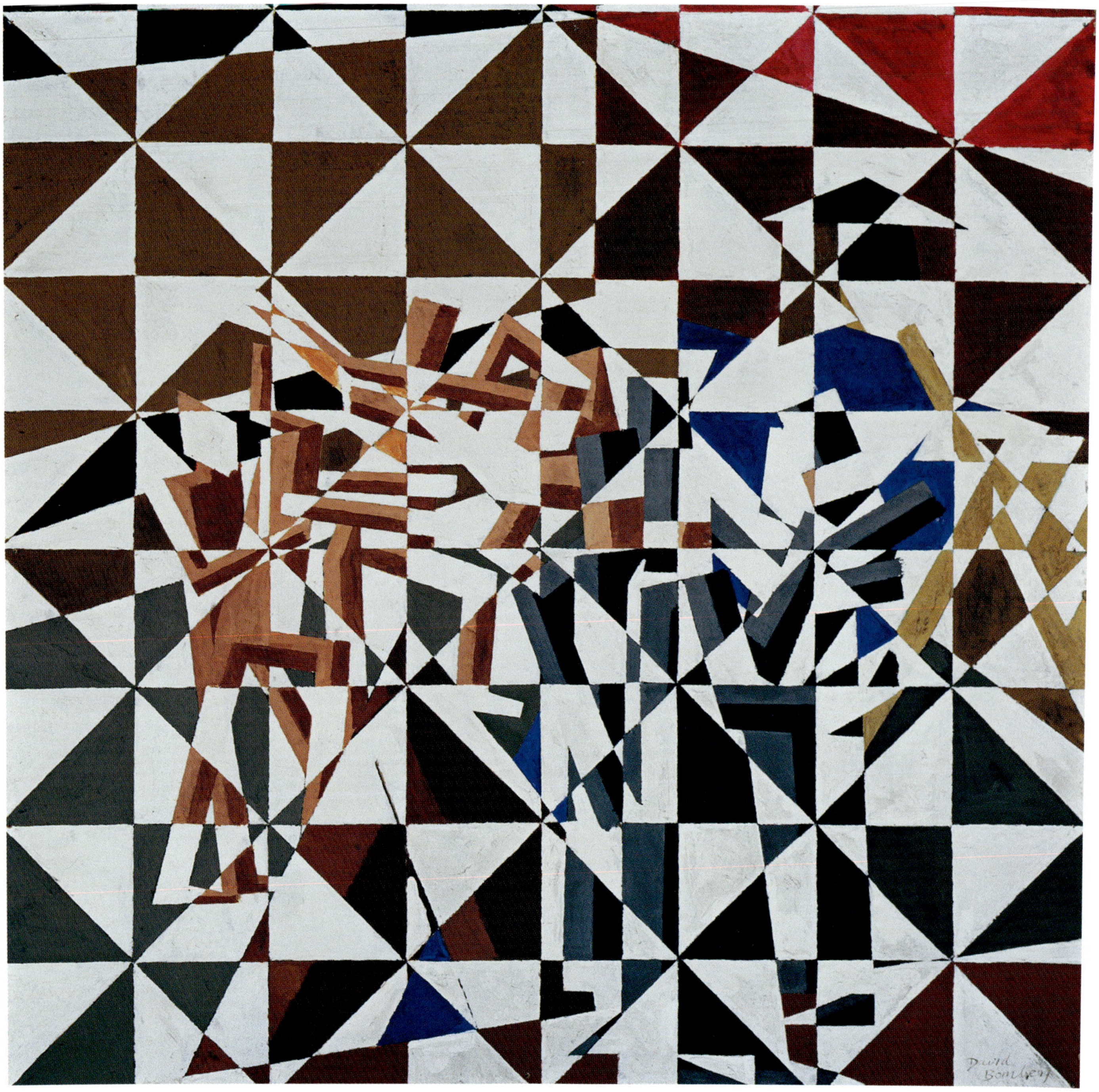

16
DAVID BOMBERG
Ju-Jitsu
*c.*1913
oil on board
61.9 × 61.9 cm
Tate, London

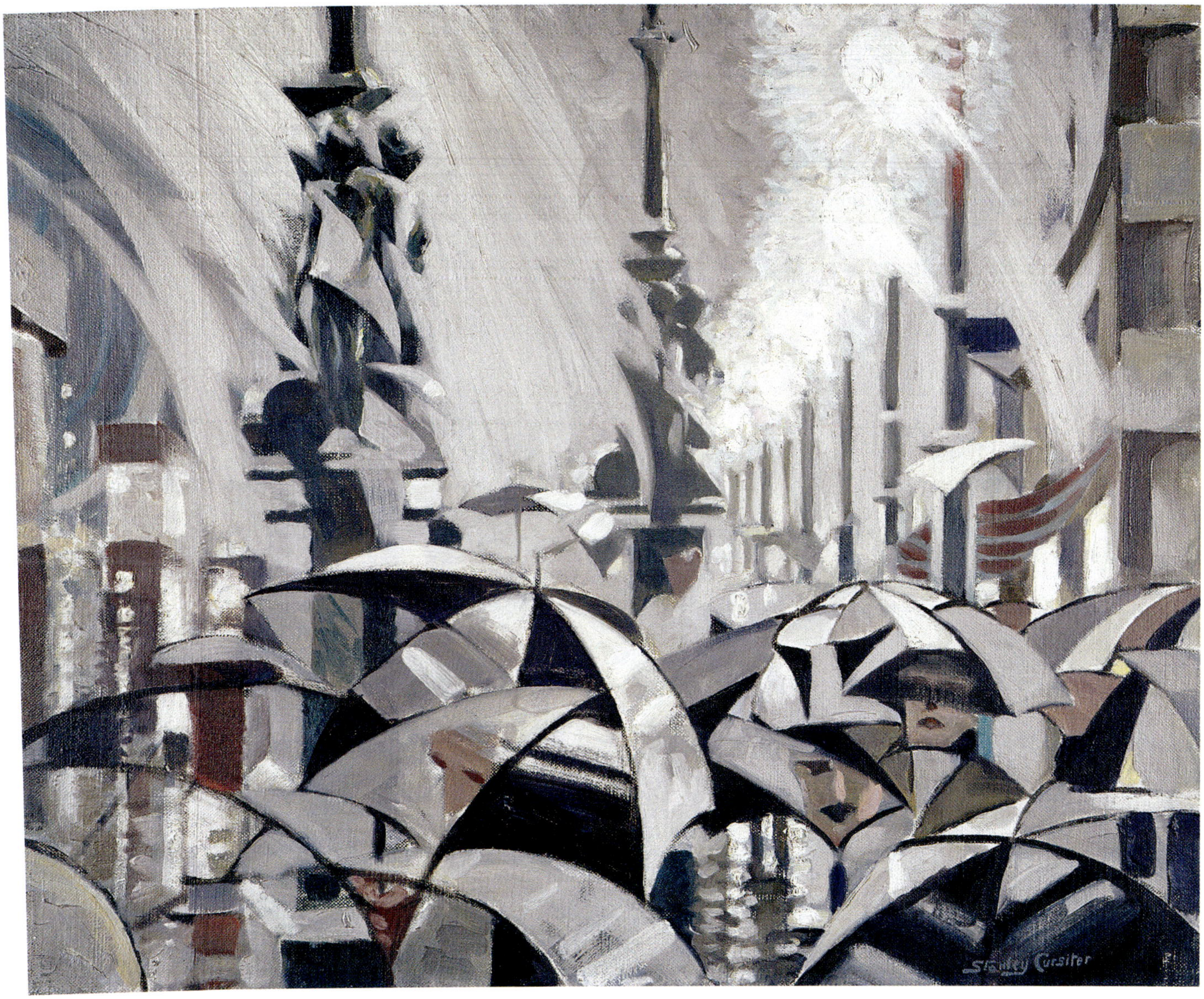

17
STANLEY CURSITER
Rain on Princes Street
1913
oil on canvas
51.4 × 61 cm
McManus Galleries, Dundee City
Council Leisure and Arts

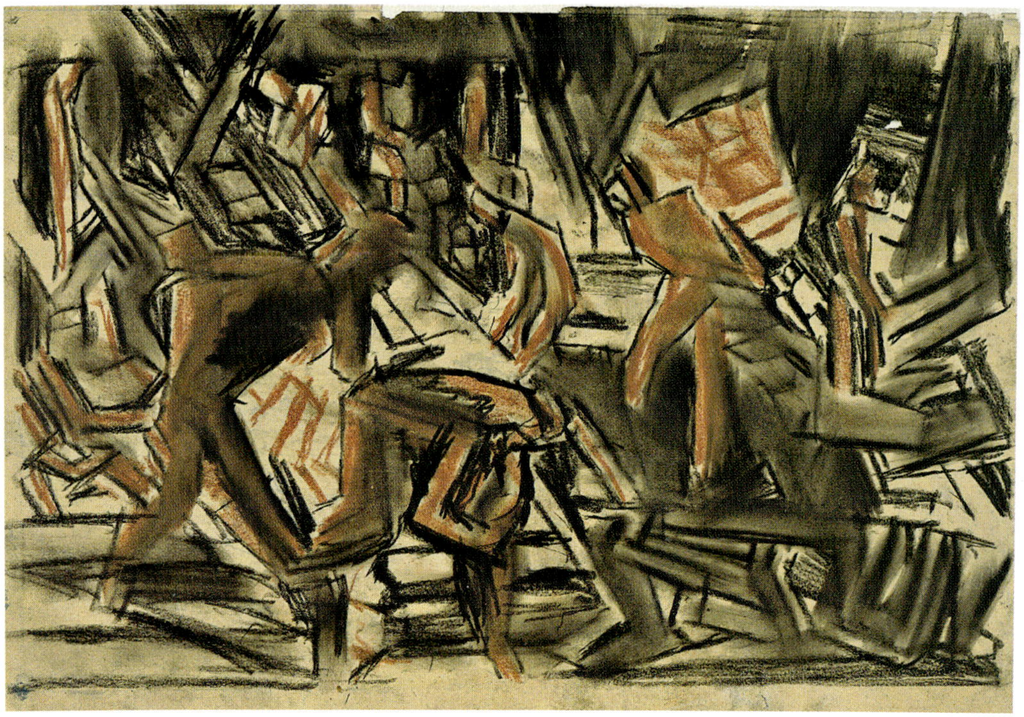

18
DAVID BOMBERG
Study for 'Sappers at Work, A Canadian Tunnelling Company'
1918
black and red chalk on paper
27.9 × 40.6 cm
The Whitworth Art Gallery,
The University of Manchester

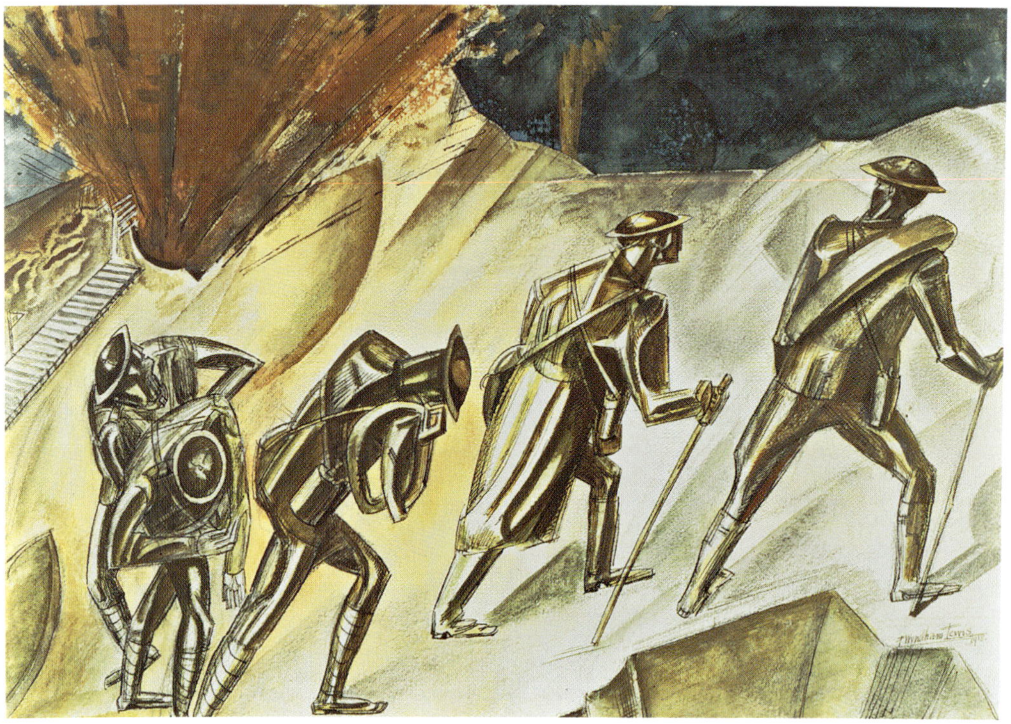

19
WYNDHAM LEWIS
Officers and Signallers
1918
ink, watercolour and gouache
on paper
25.4 × 35.6 cm
Imperial War Museum

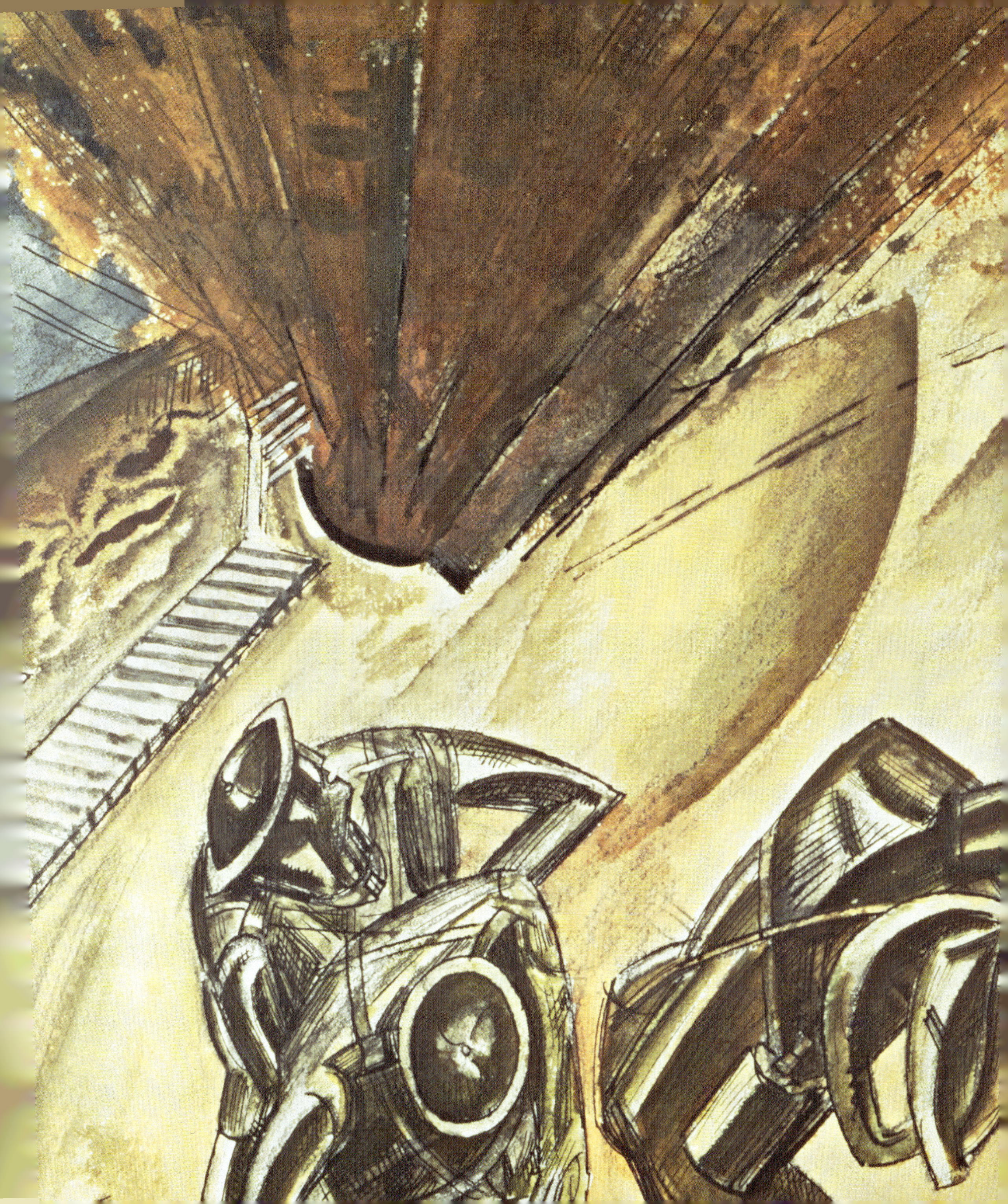

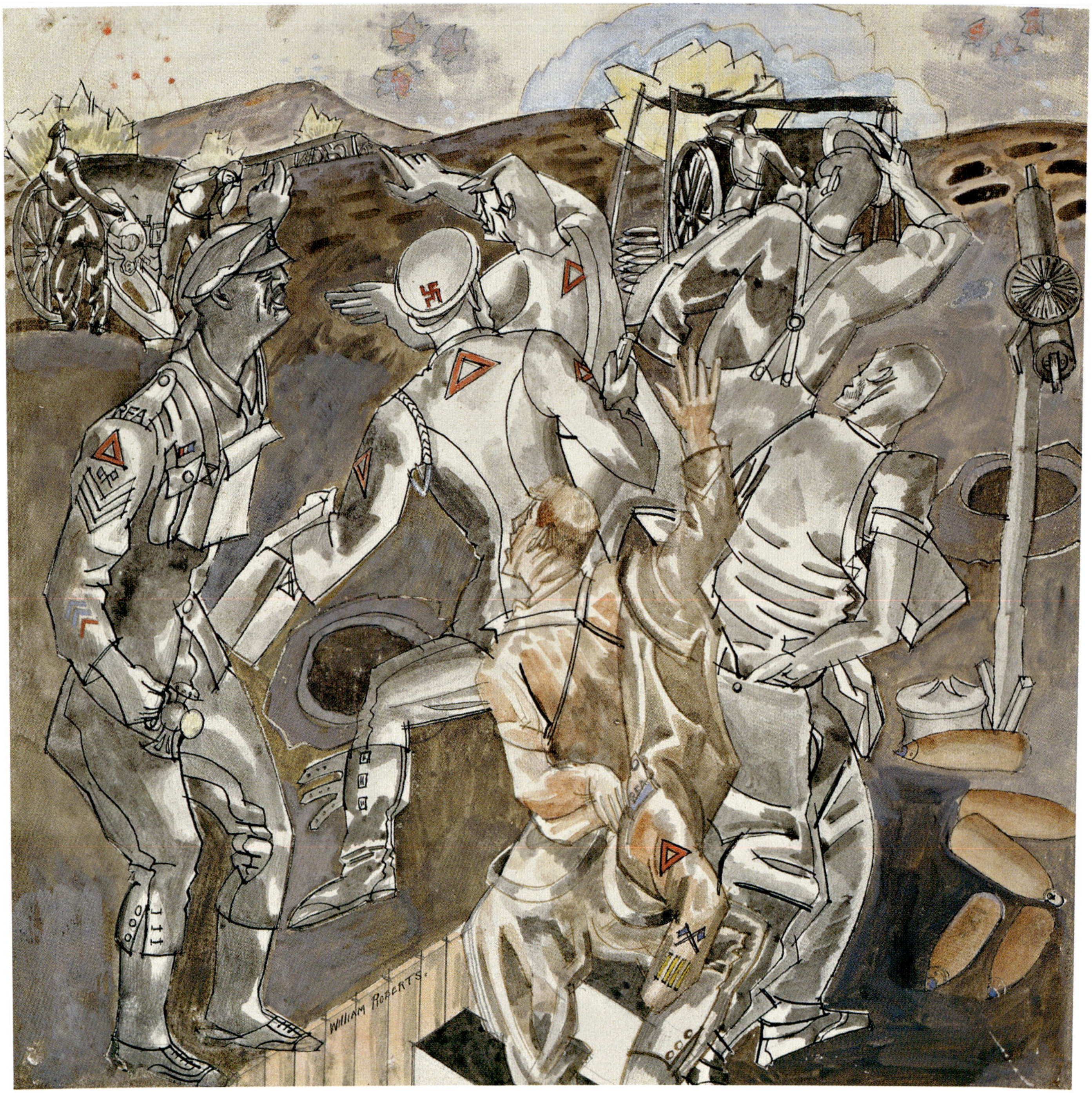

20
WILLIAM ROBERTS
Gunners Turning Out for an SOS: Battery Action at Night
1918
pencil and watercolour on paper
32.3 × 32.3 cm
Imperial War Museum

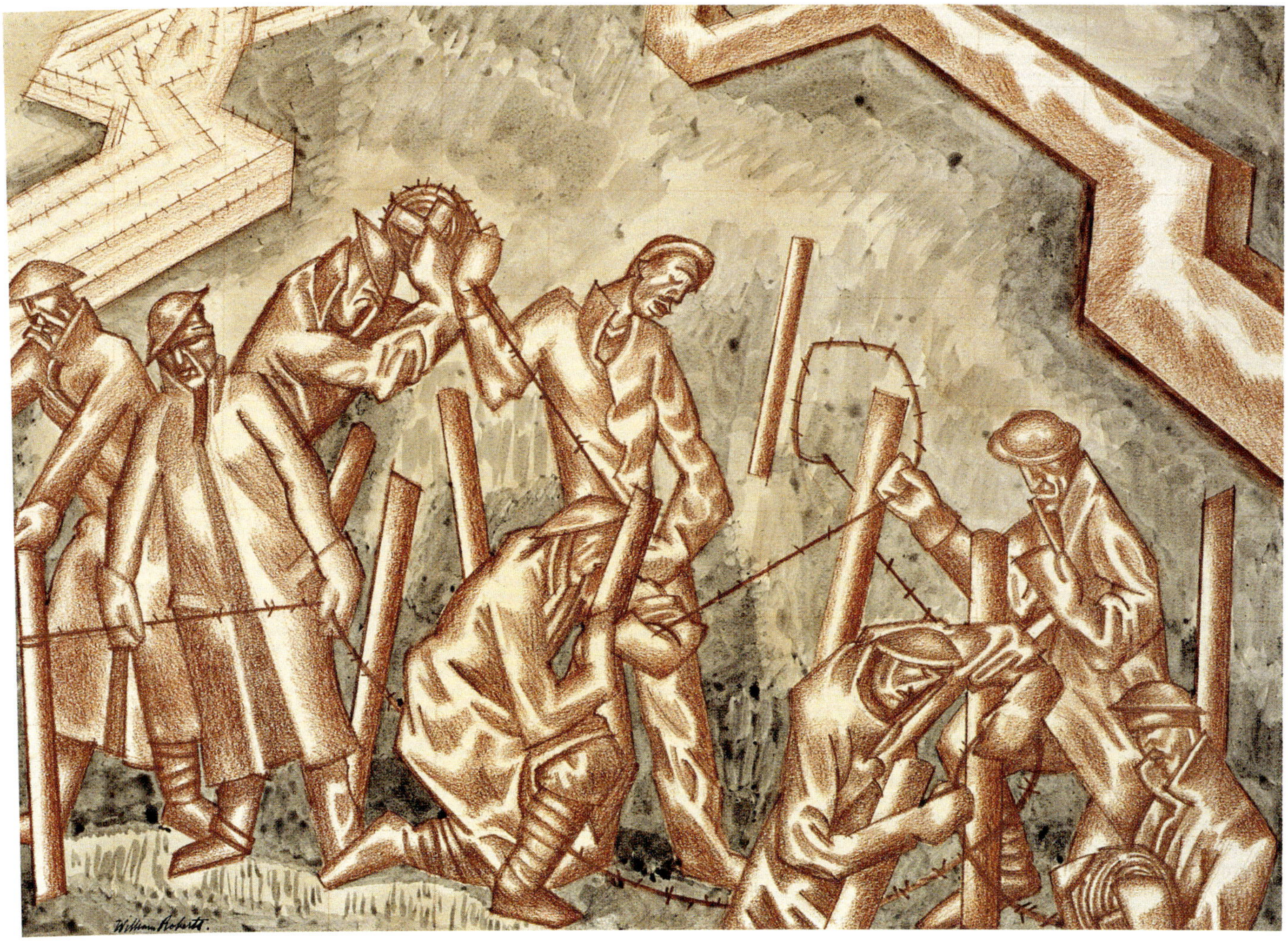

21
WILLIAM ROBERTS
The Wiring Party
1918
black ink wash and red pastel on paper
28 × 38 cm
Dr. and Mrs. Jeffrey Sherwin

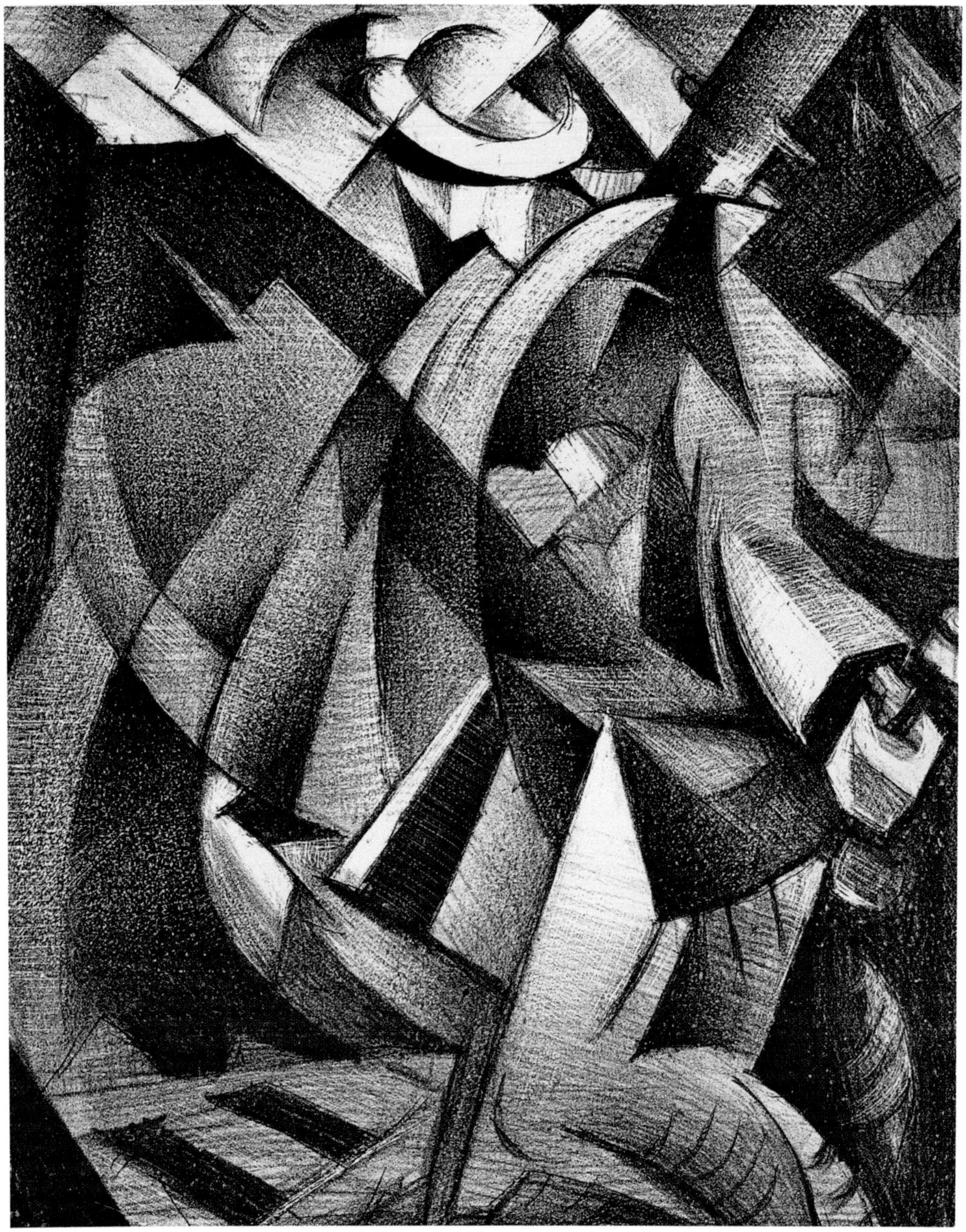

22
C. R. W. NEVINSON
The Bomber
1918
lithograph
28.6 × 22.3 cm
The British Museum

23
GINO SEVERINI
Dancer (Ballerina + Sea)
1913
oil, gouache, black wash and pastel on board
75.5 × 50.5 cm
Estorick Collection, London

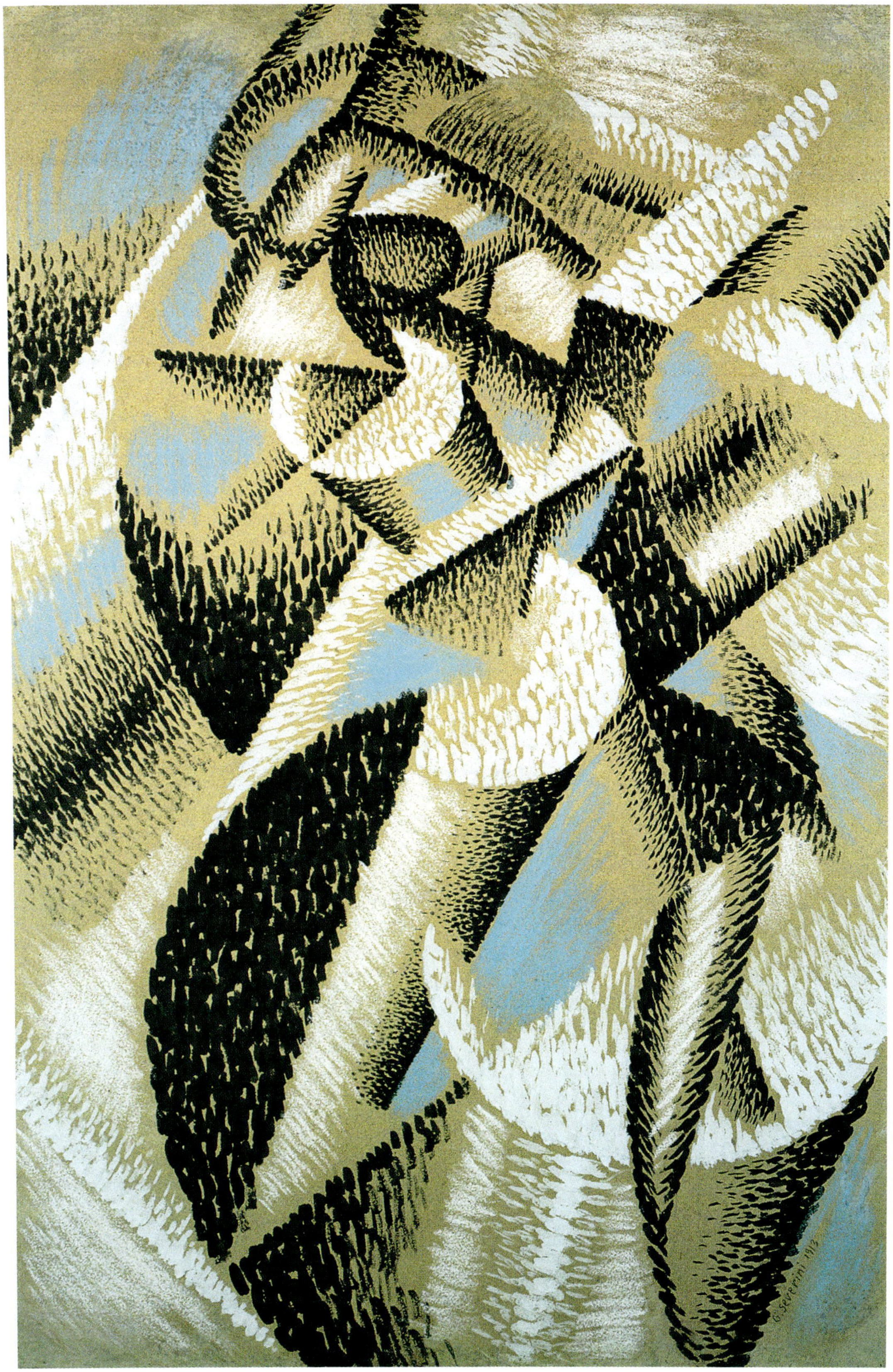

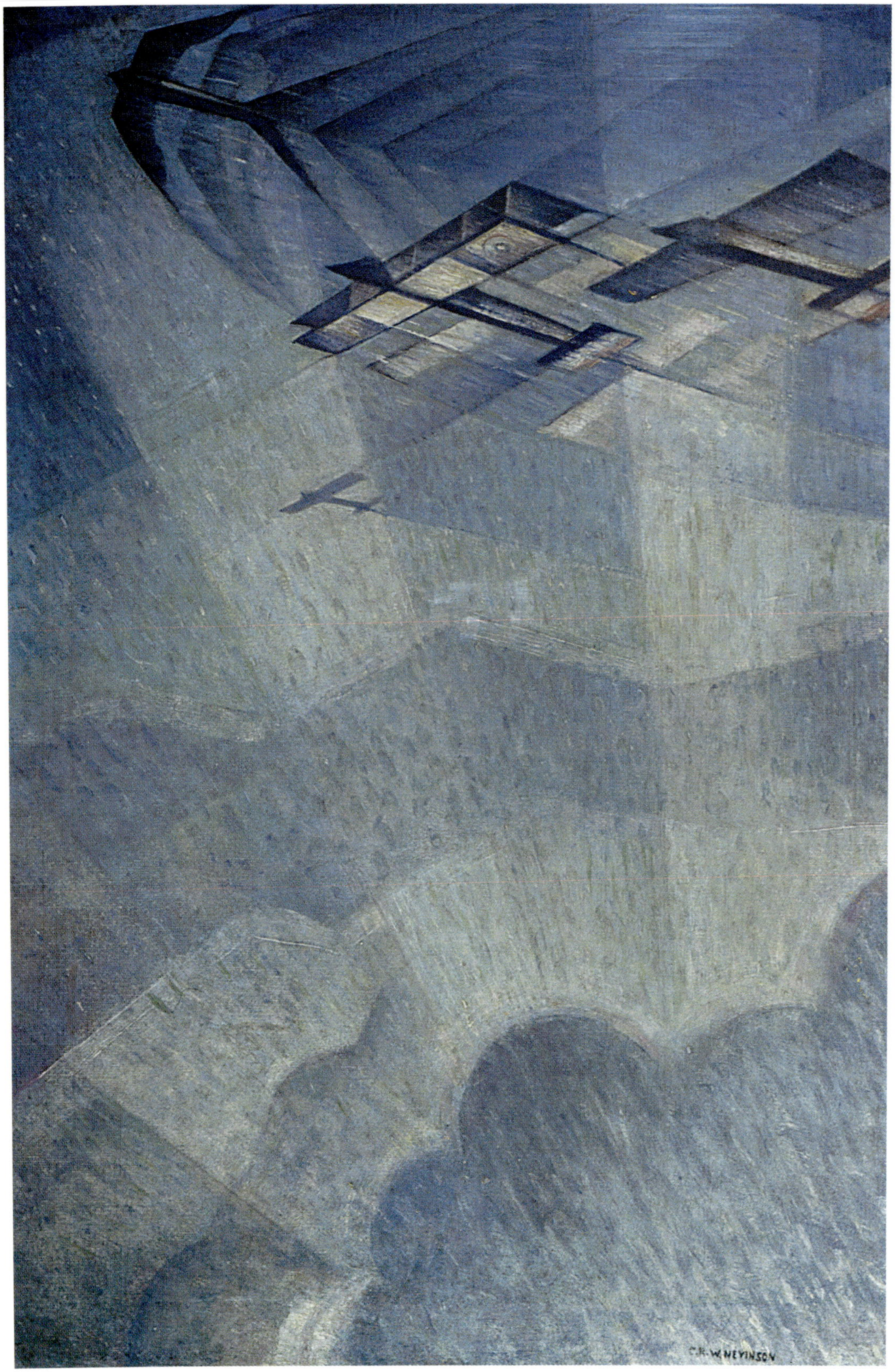
C.R.W. NEVINSON

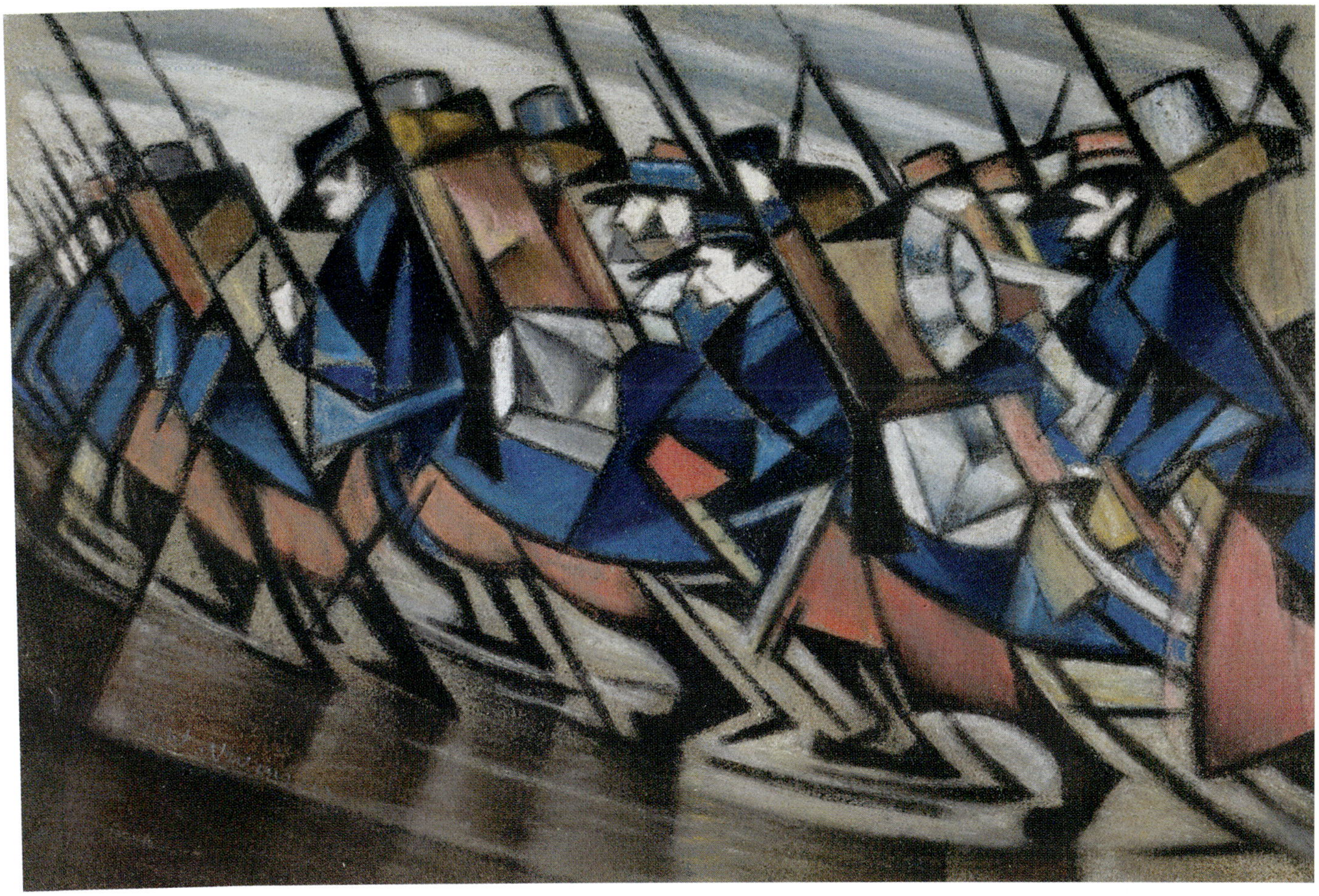

24
C. R. W. NEVINSON
Marching Men
1914–15
pastel on paper
13.9 × 20.3 cm
Imperial War Museum

25
C. R. W. NEVINSON
Taube Pursued by Commander Samson
1915
oil on canvas
85.7 × 49.5 cm
Courtesy of the Trustees of the
Royal Air Force Museums

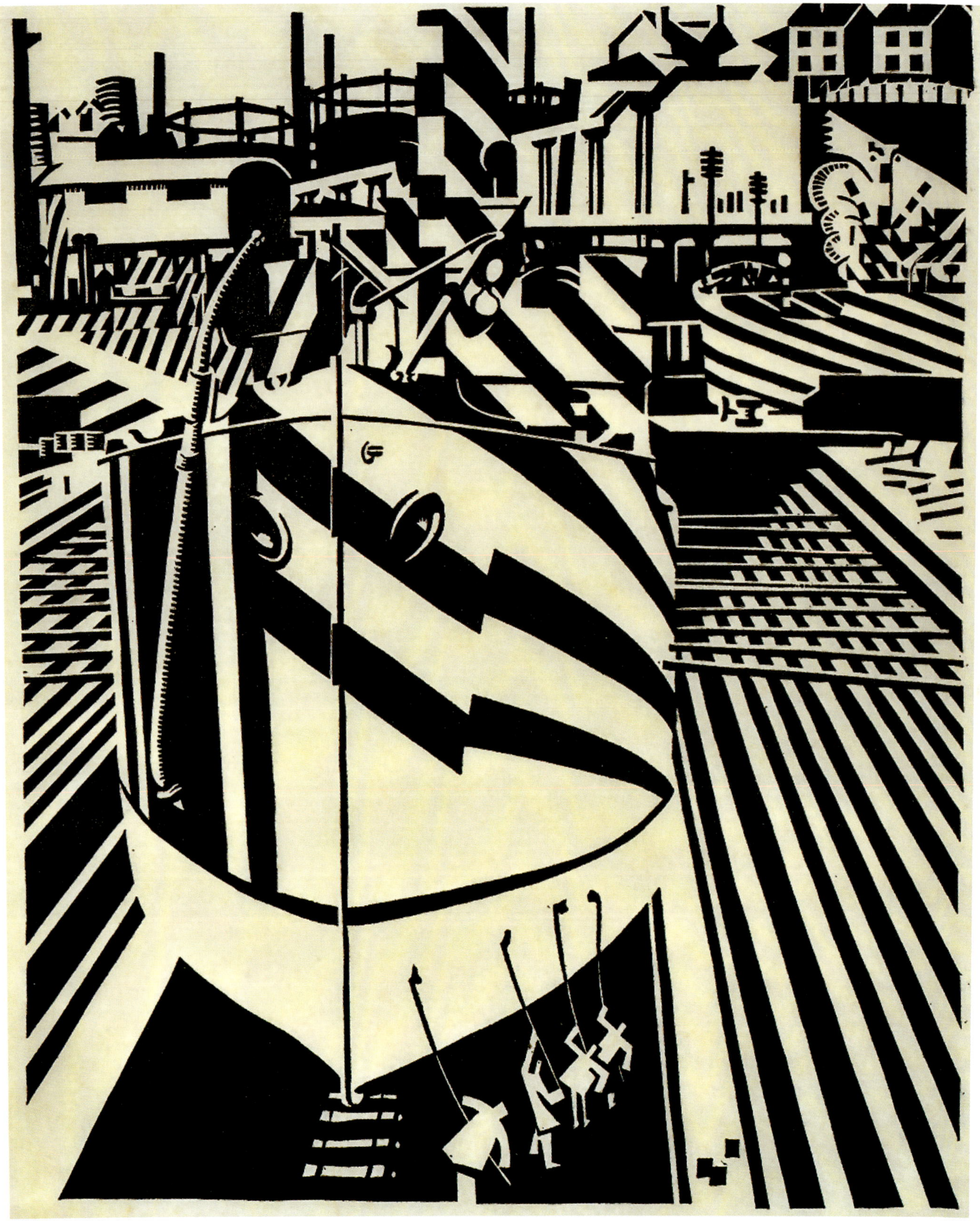

26
EDWARD WADSWORTH
Liverpool Shipping
1918
woodcut
25.9 × 20.1 cm
The British Museum

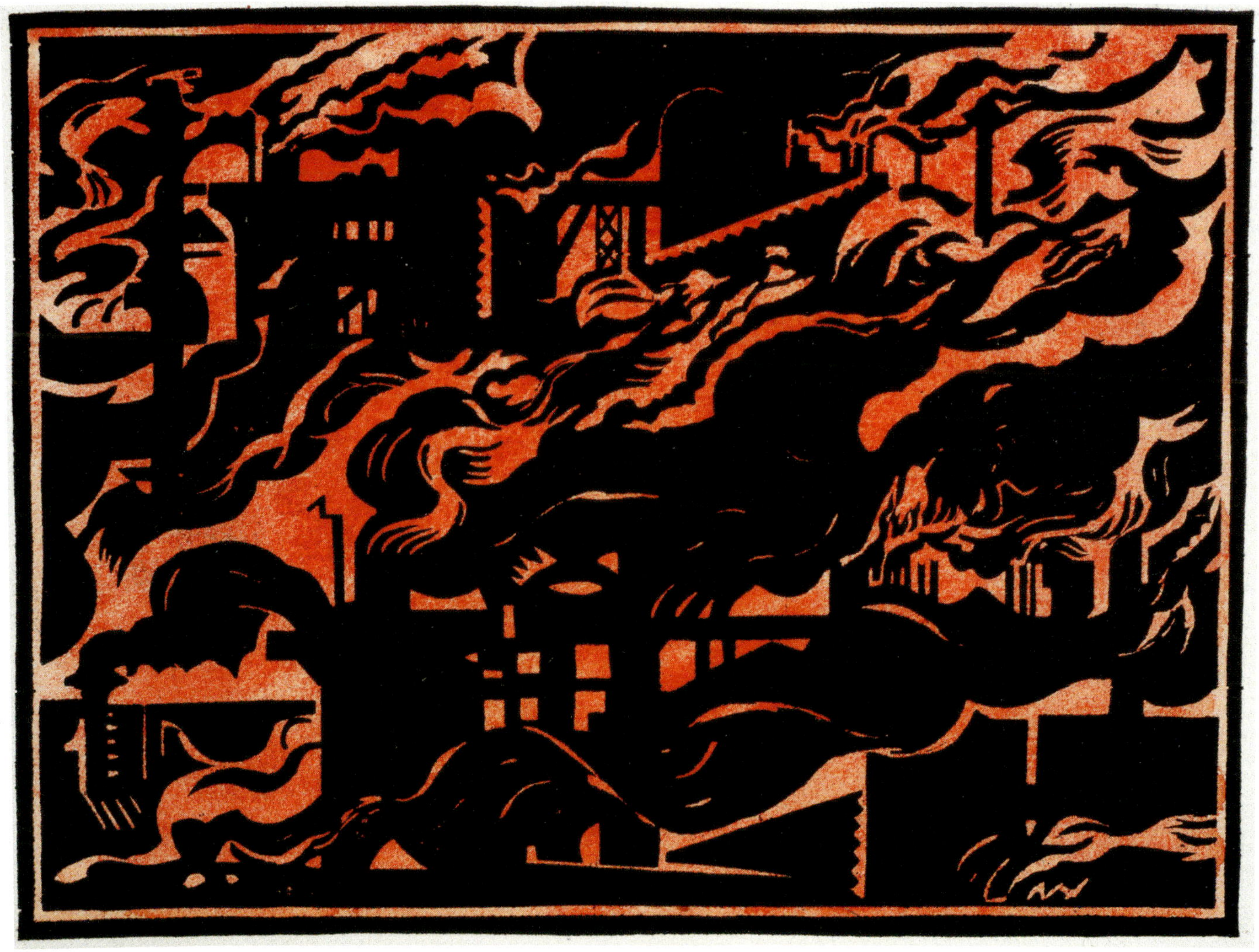

27
EDWARD WADSWORTH
Blast Furnaces 2
1919
woodcut
13.8 × 18.1 cm
The British Museum

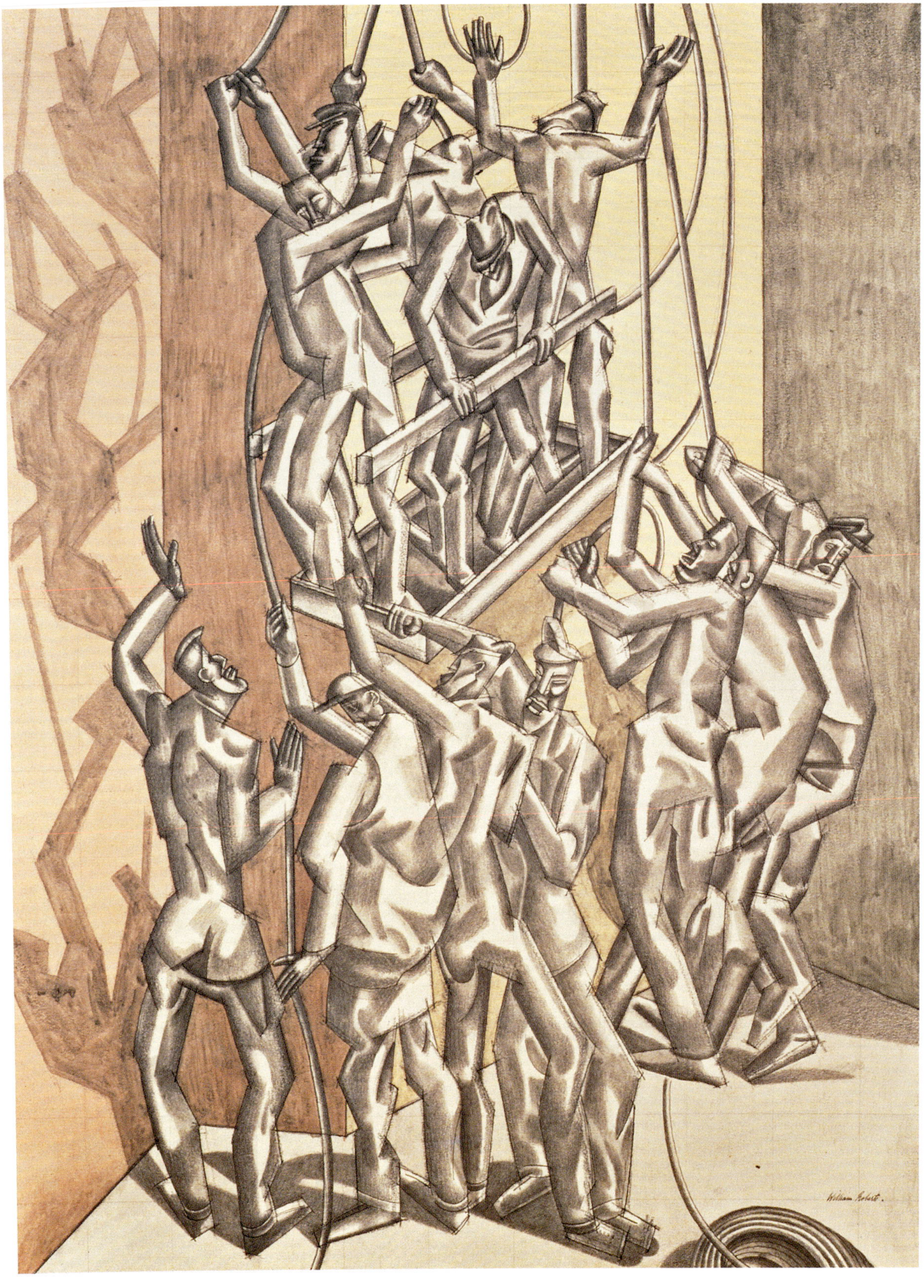

28
WILLIAM ROBERTS
The Travelling Cradle
1919
ink and watercolour on paper
58.8 × 43 cm
Southampton City Art Gallery

29
WILLIAM ROBERTS
Athletes Exercising in a Gymnasium
1920
pencil, watercolour and ink on paper
45.1 × 35.9 cm
Tate, London

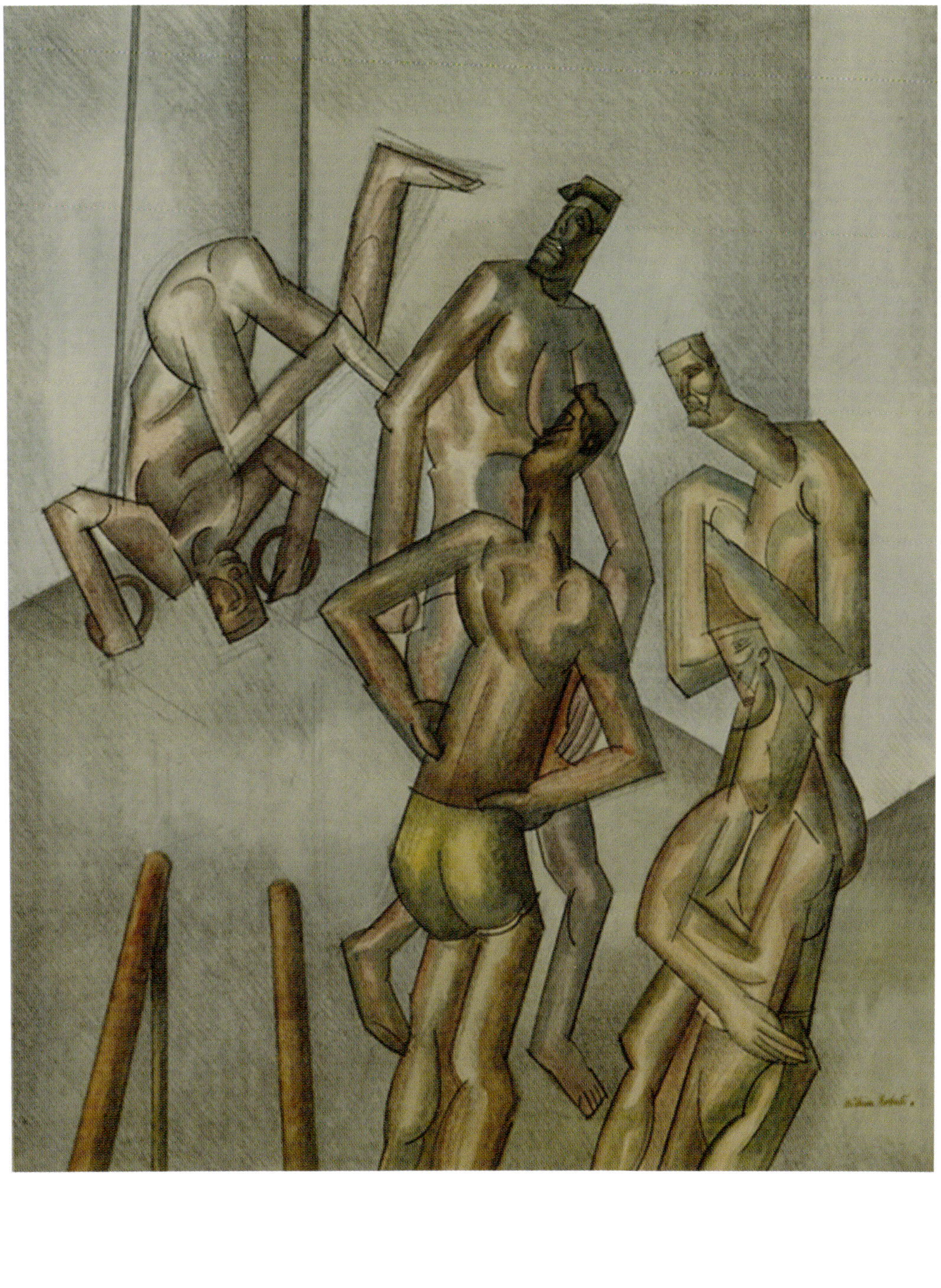

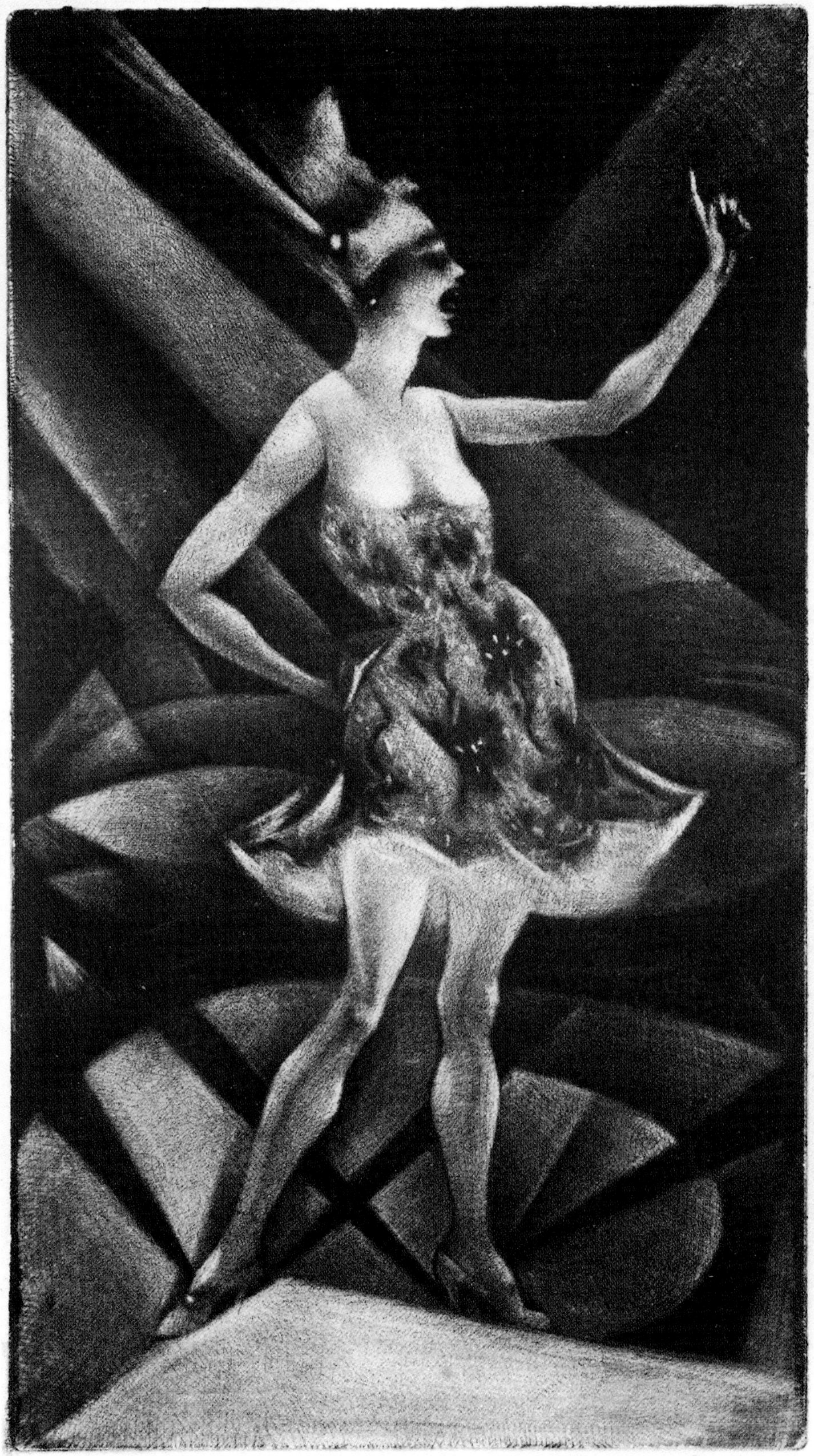

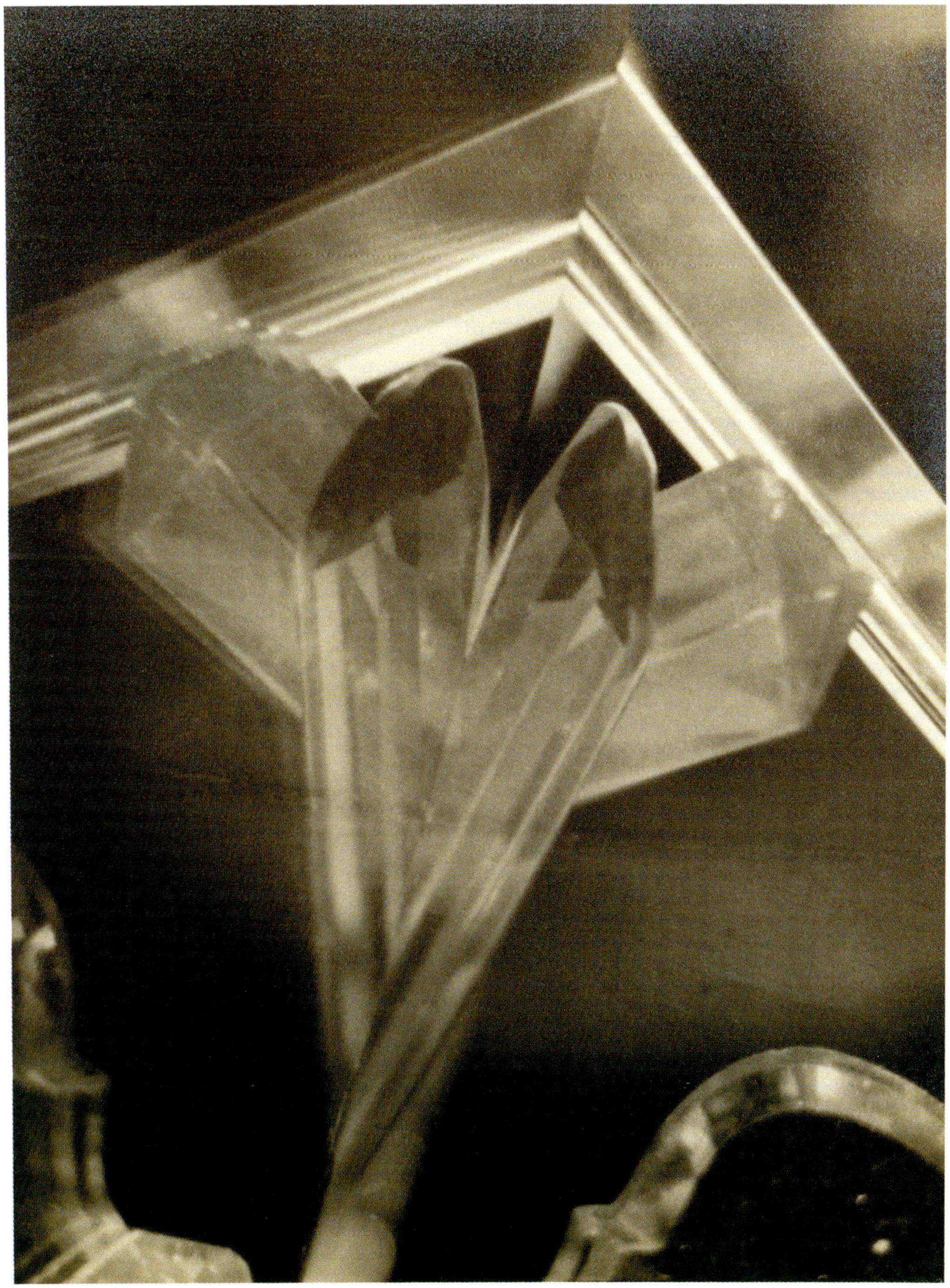

30
C. R. W. NEVINSON
The Roof Gardens
1919
mezzotint
21.1 × 11.6 cm
Private collection

31
ALVIN LANGDON COBURN
Vortograph
*c.*1916
photograph
30 × 21 cm
Courtesy of the Royal Photographic Society Collection at the National Museum of Photography, Film and Television

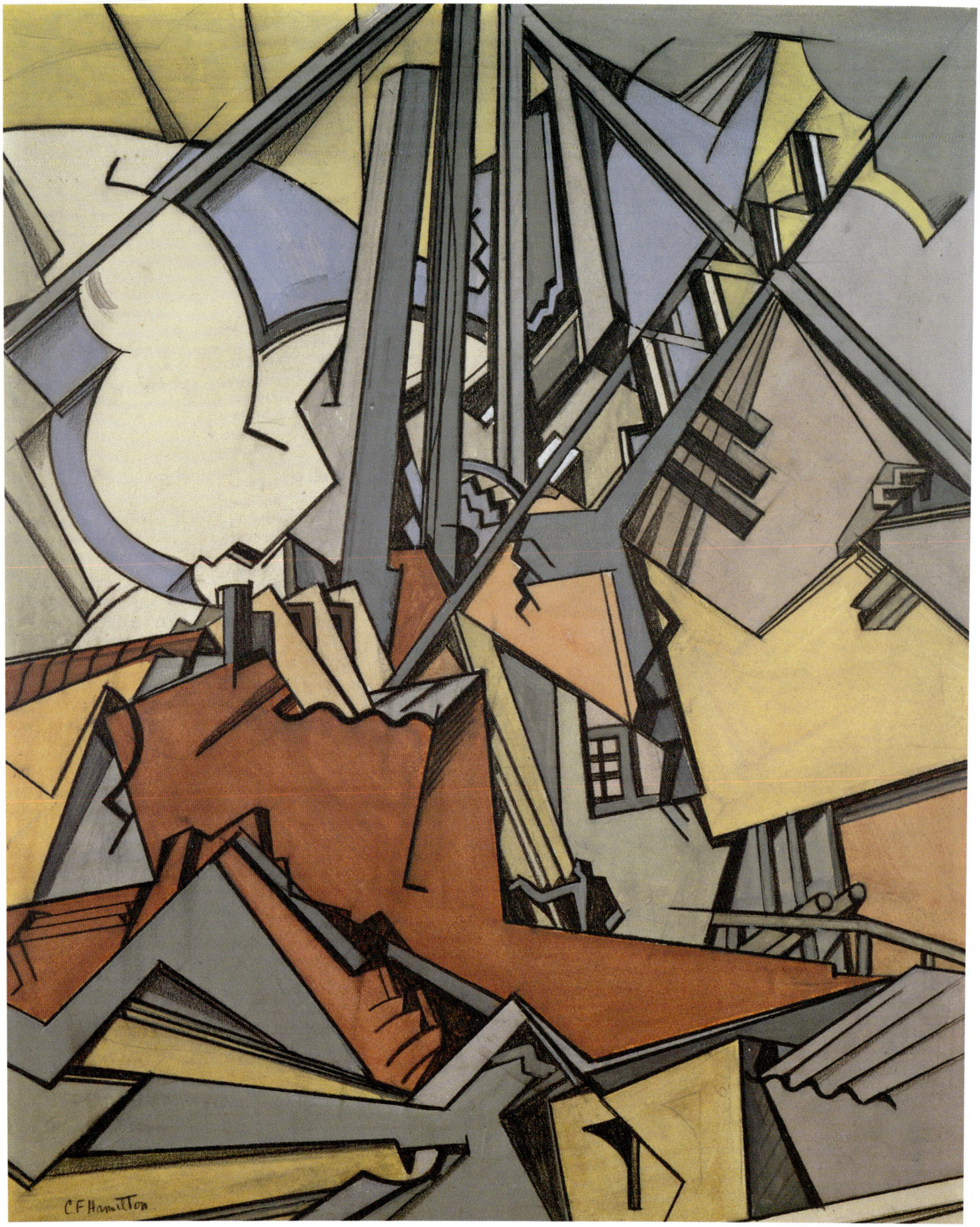
C F Hamilton

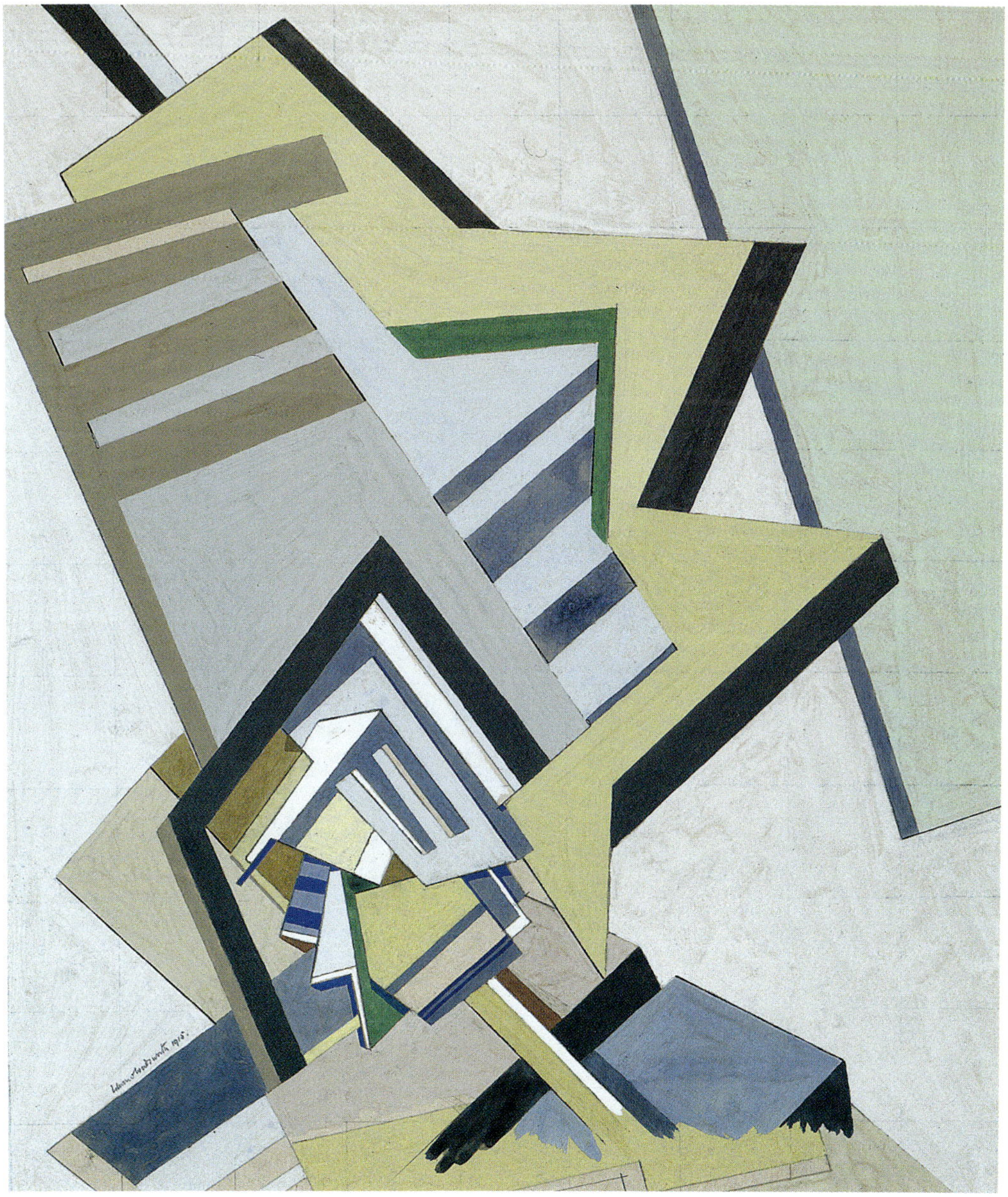

32
CUTHBERT HAMILTON
Reconstruction
1919–20
pencil, crayon and gouache
on paper
55.9 × 41.9 cm
Tate, London

33
EDWARD WADSWORTH
Abstract Composition
1915
gouache, ink and pencil on paper
41.9 × 34.3 cm
Tate, London

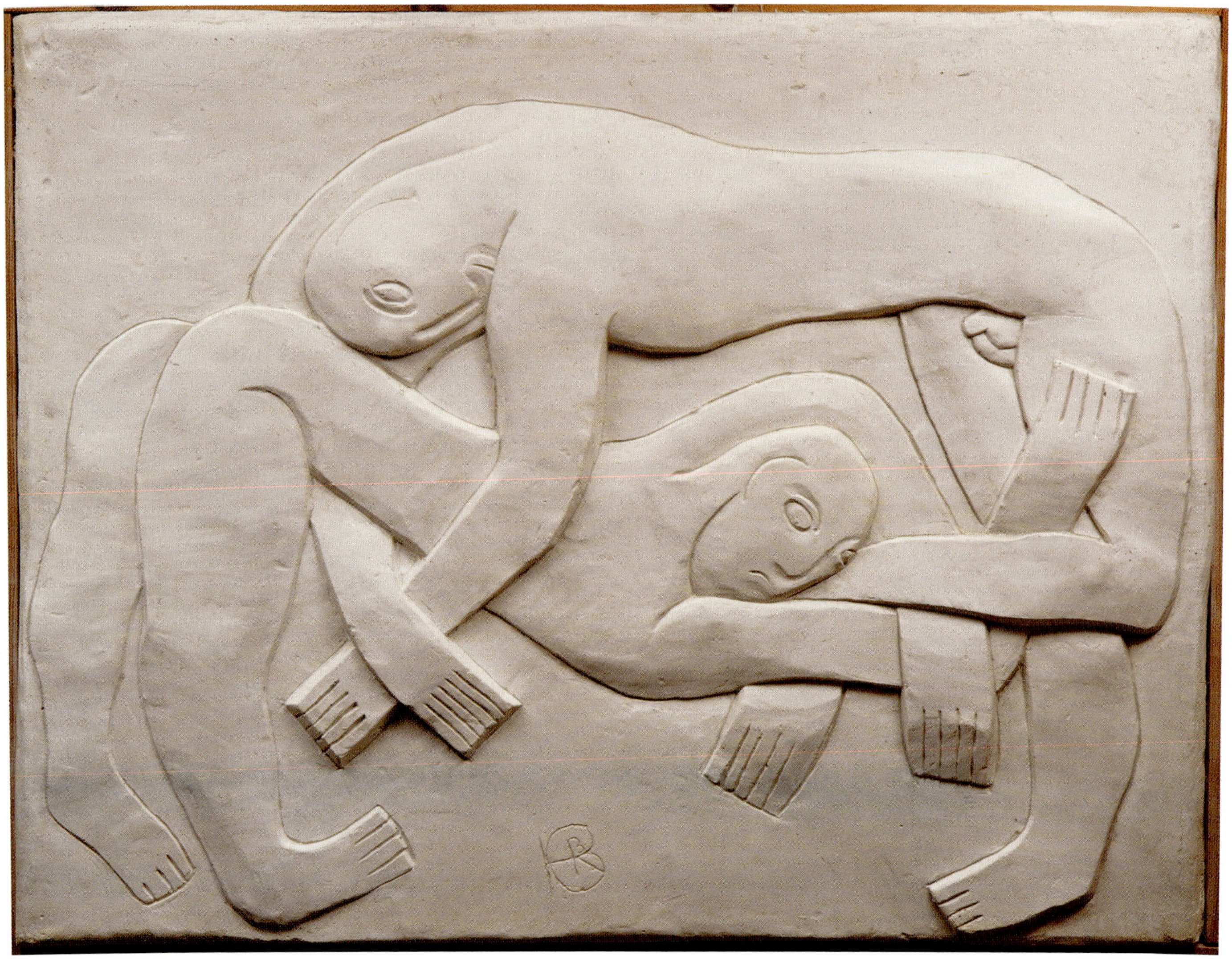

34
HENRI GAUDIER-BRZESKA
Wrestlers
plaster low-relief
1913
76 × 97 cm
Dr. and Mrs. Jeffrey Sherwin

35
FRANK DOBSON
Drawing for carving 'Toilet' (Front view)
1919
pencil, brown ink and red chalk
on paper
30.6 × 22.7 cm
Manchester City Galleries

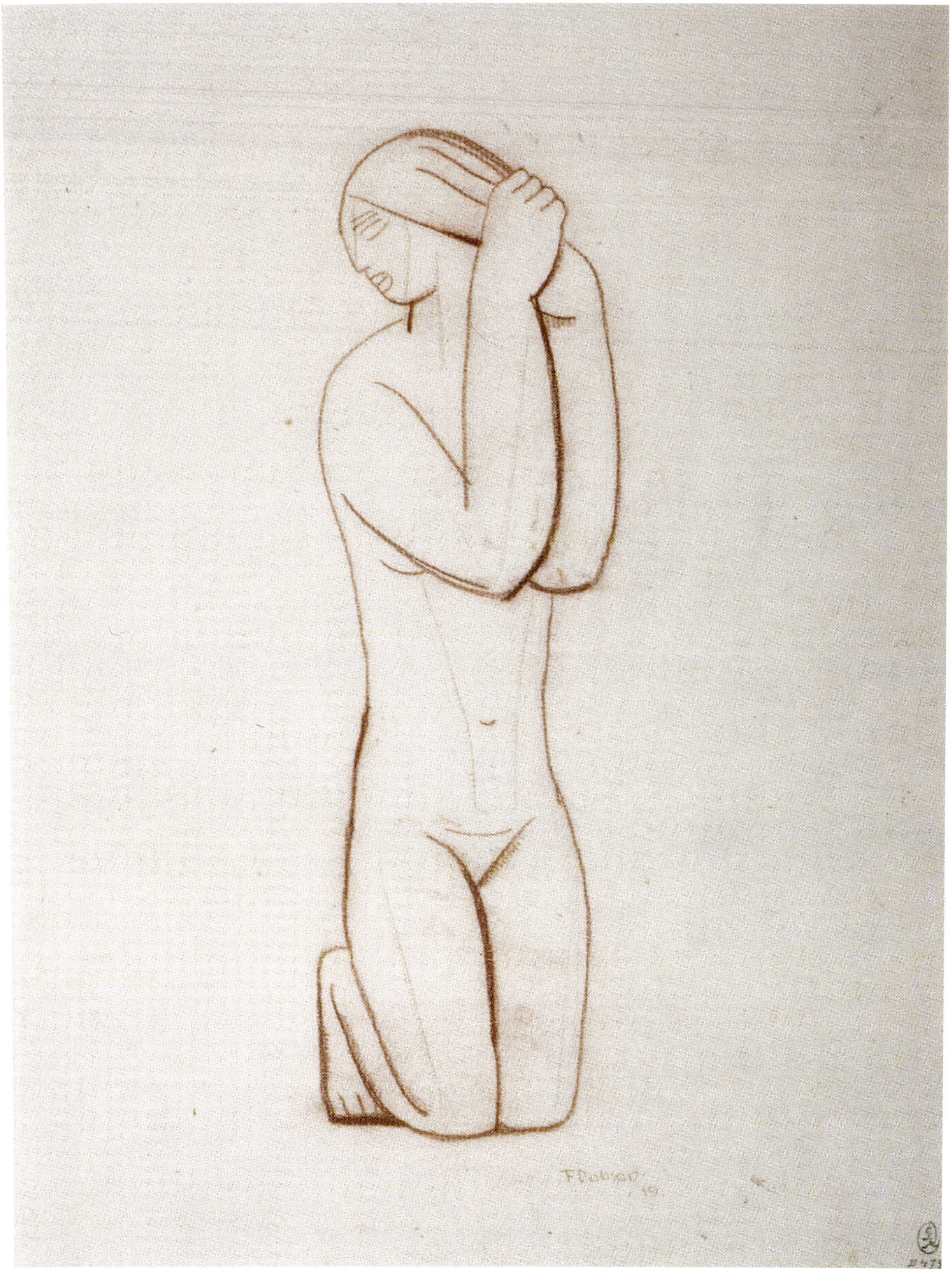
F Dobson
/19.

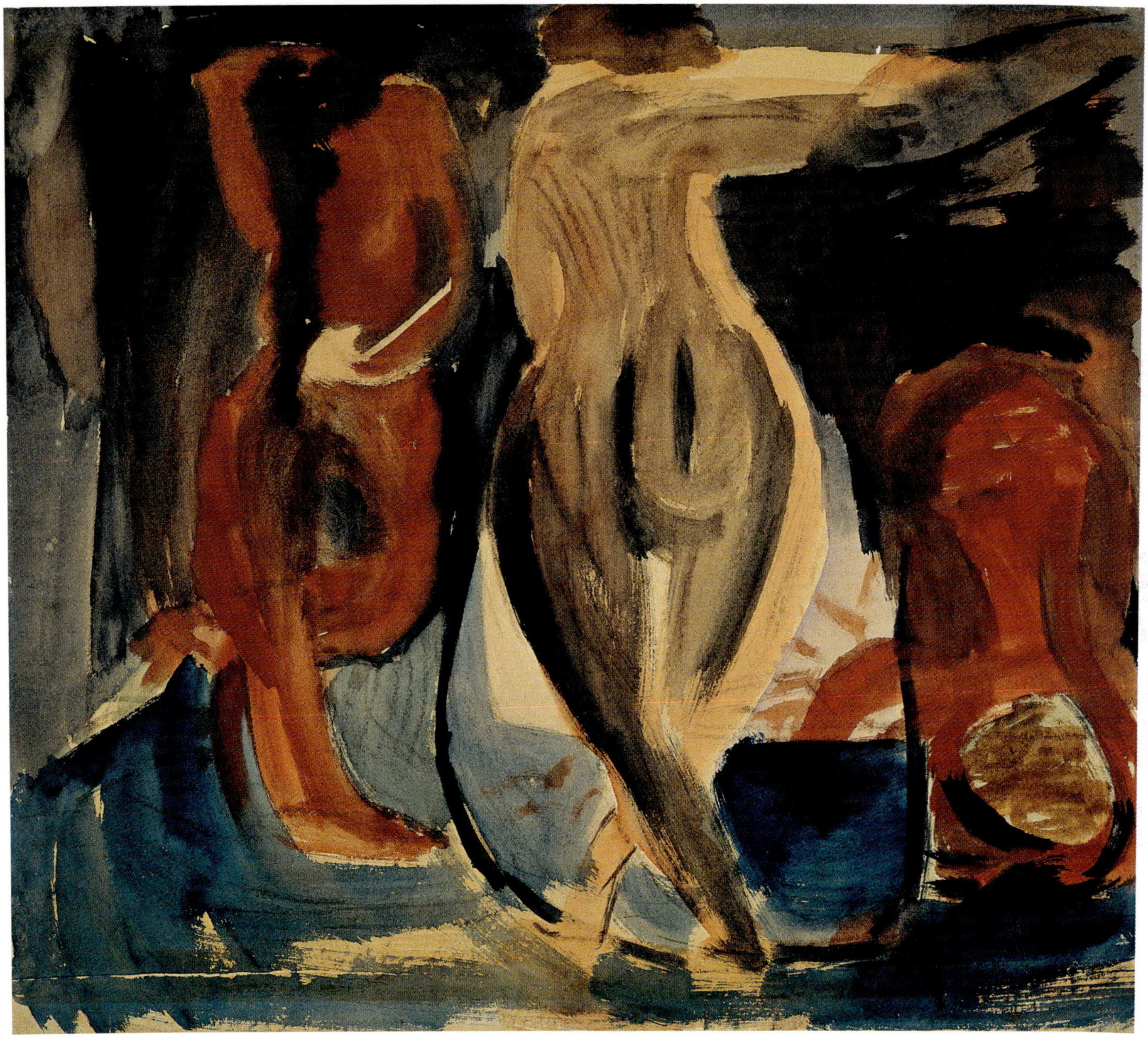

36
DAVID BOMBERG
Two Nude Figures Dancing
1920
watercolour and charcoal on paper
51.1 × 55.6 cm
The British Museum

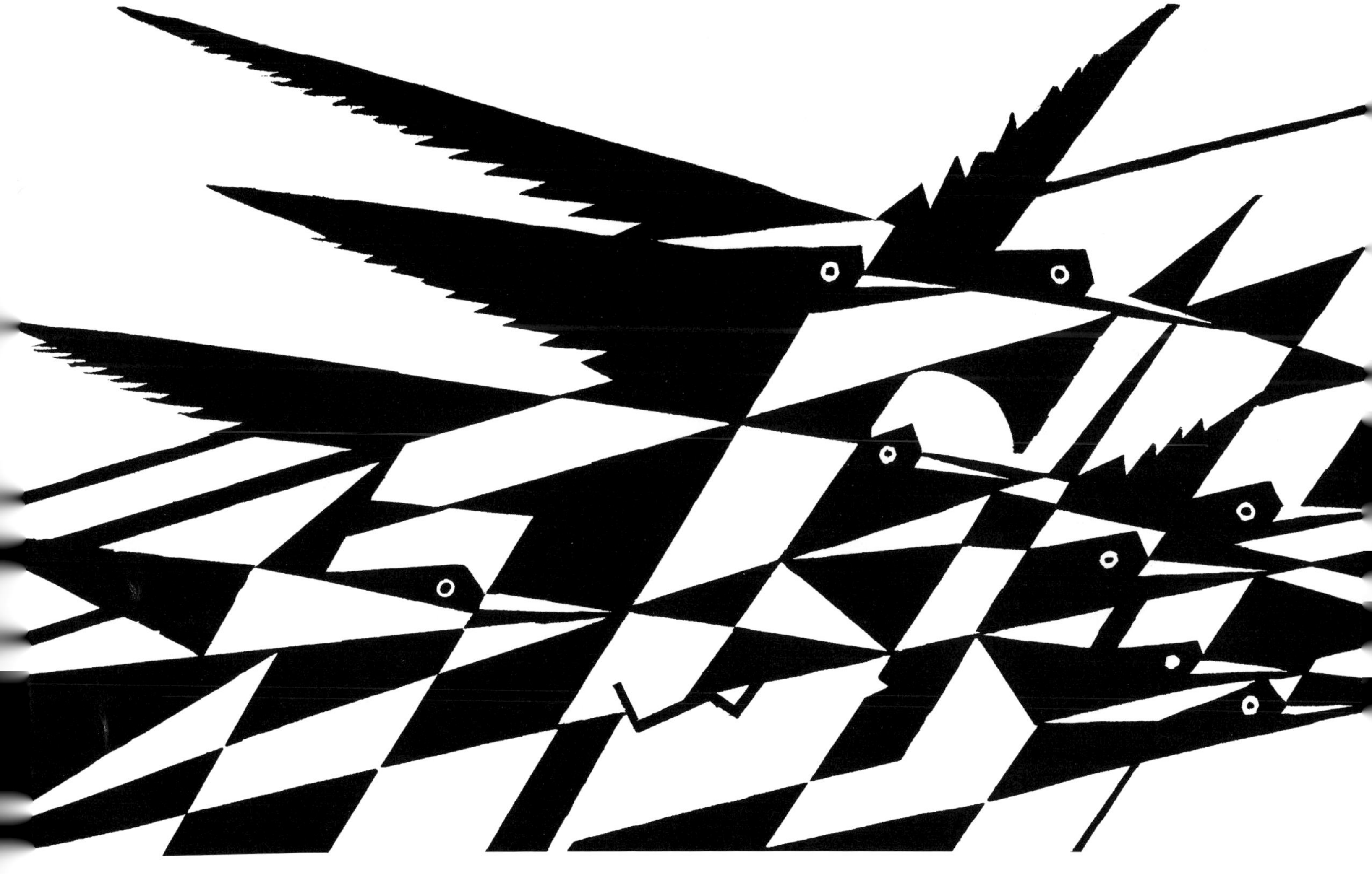

37
EDWARD McKNIGHT KAUFFER
Flight
1917
woodcut
14 × 23 cm
The British Museum

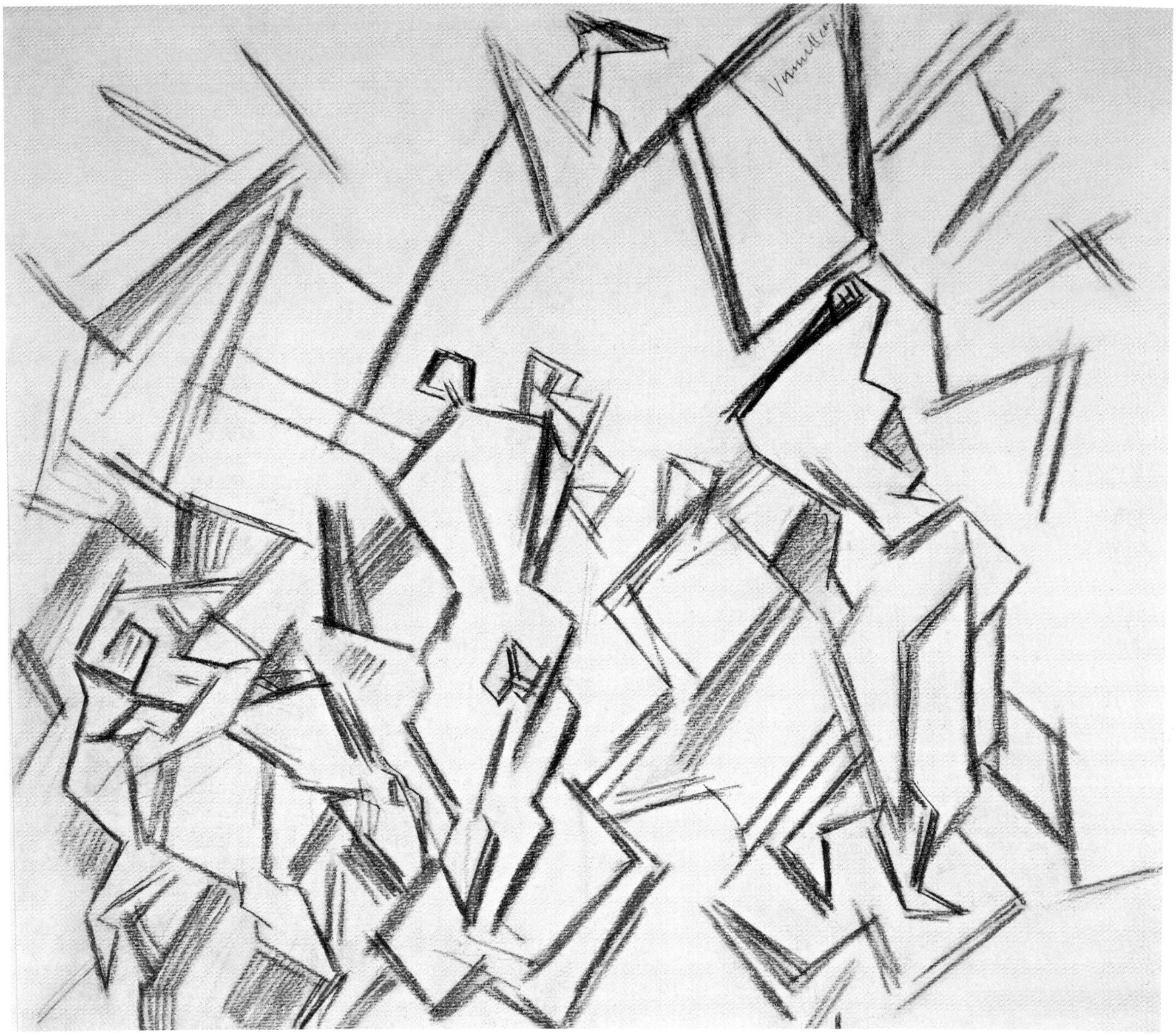

38
WYNDHAM LEWIS
Vorticist Figure Composition
*c.*1914
charcoal and ink on paper
38 × 68 cm
Private collection

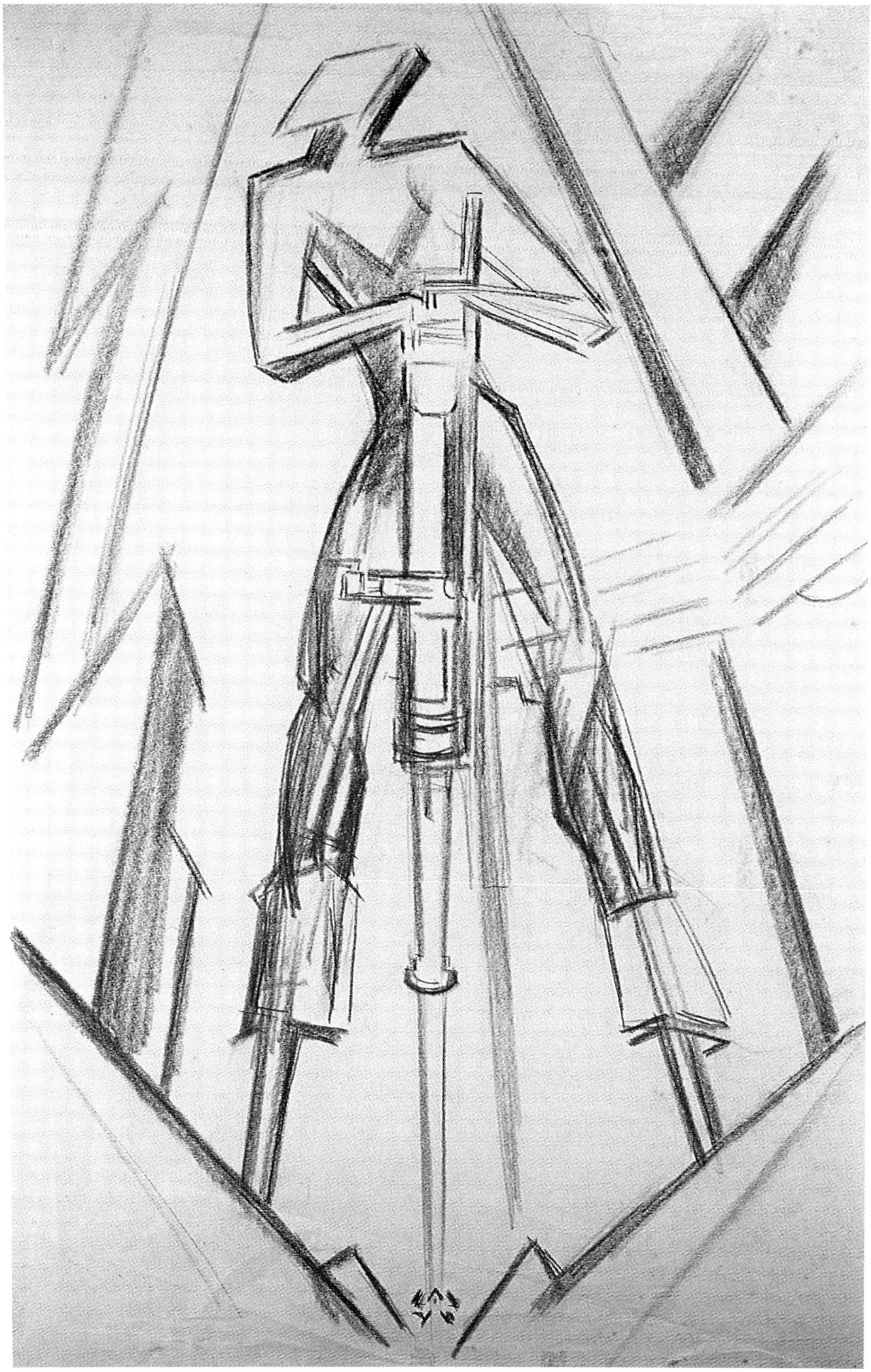

39
JACOB EPSTEIN
Study for 'The Rock Drill'
1913
charcoal on paper
67.5 × 42.5 cm
The Garman Ryan Collection,
The New Art Gallery, Walsall

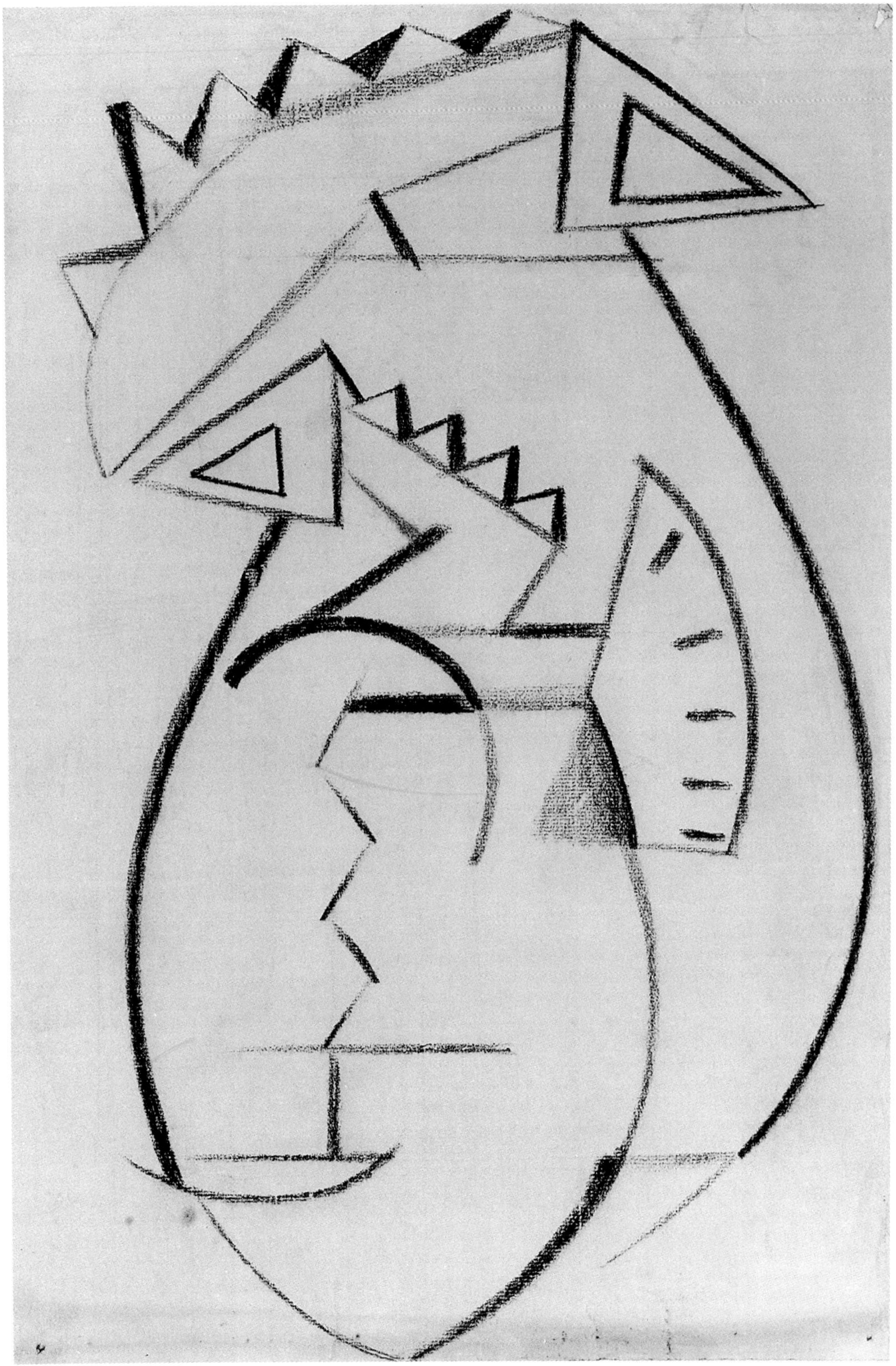

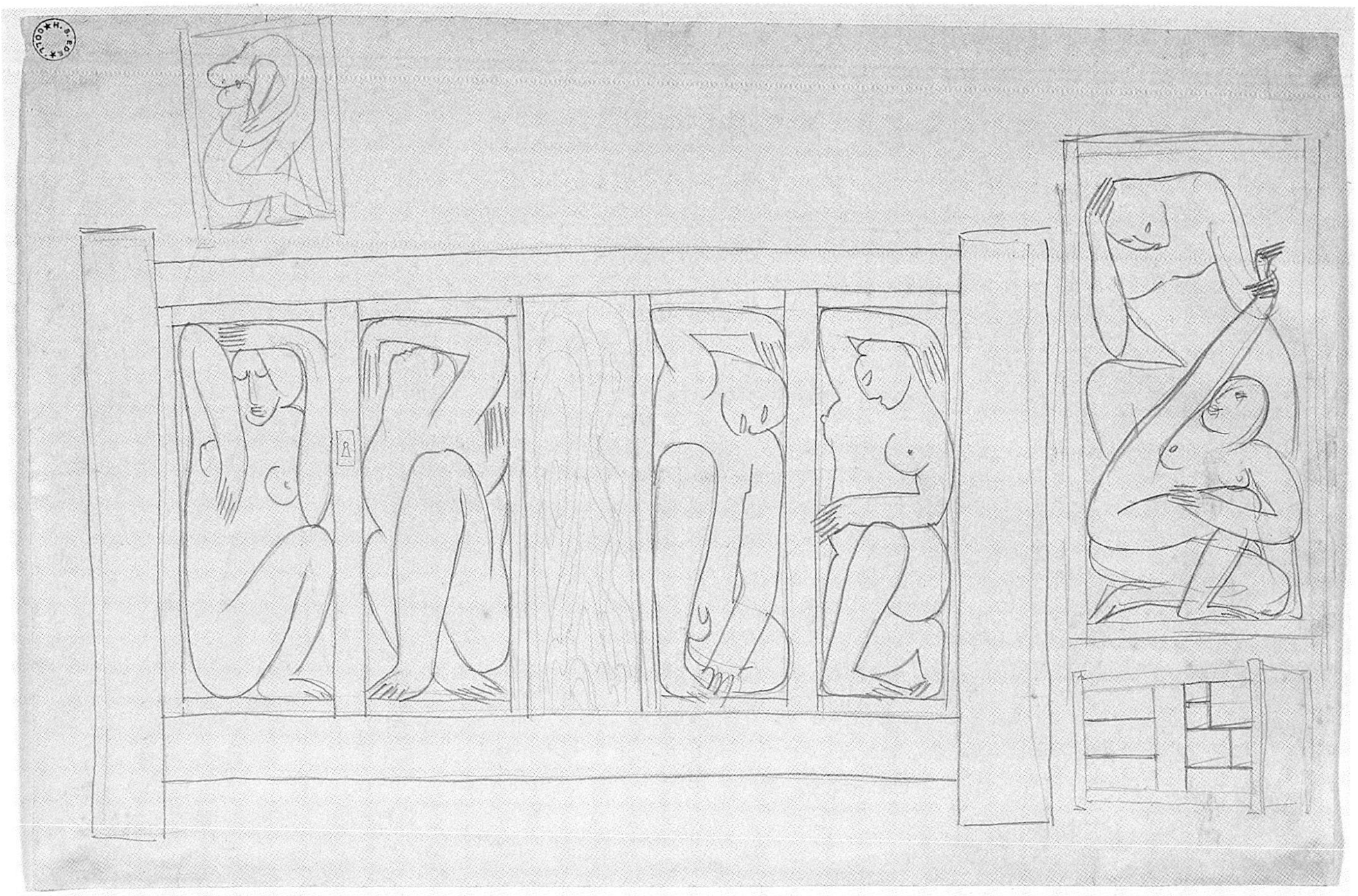

40
HENRI GAUDIER-BRZESKA
Sketch of a cabinet for the Omega Workshop
1913
pencil, ink and pastel on paper
25.7 × 38.1 cm
Dr. and Mrs. Jeffrey Sherwin

41
HENRI GAUDIER-BRZESKA
Design for a Vorticist Ornament
1914
black conté crayon on ingres paper
48.3 × 31.6 cm
National Museums & Galleries of Wales

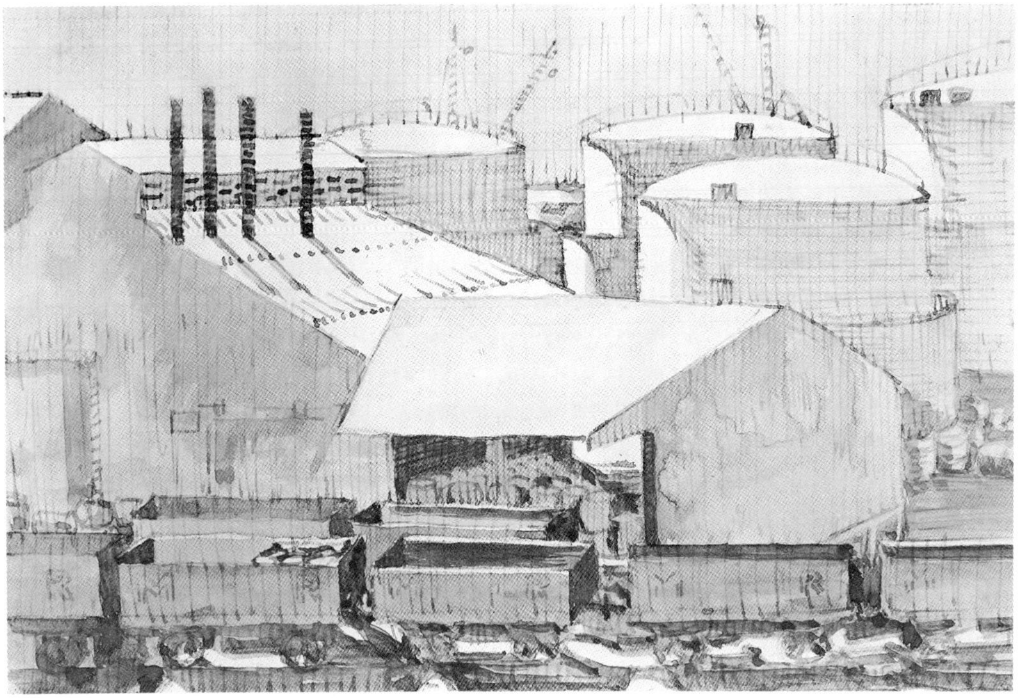

42
EDWARD WADSWORTH
The Gas Works
c.1910–11
ink and watercolour on paper
14.7 × 20.1 cm
The Whitworth Art Gallery,
The University of Manchester

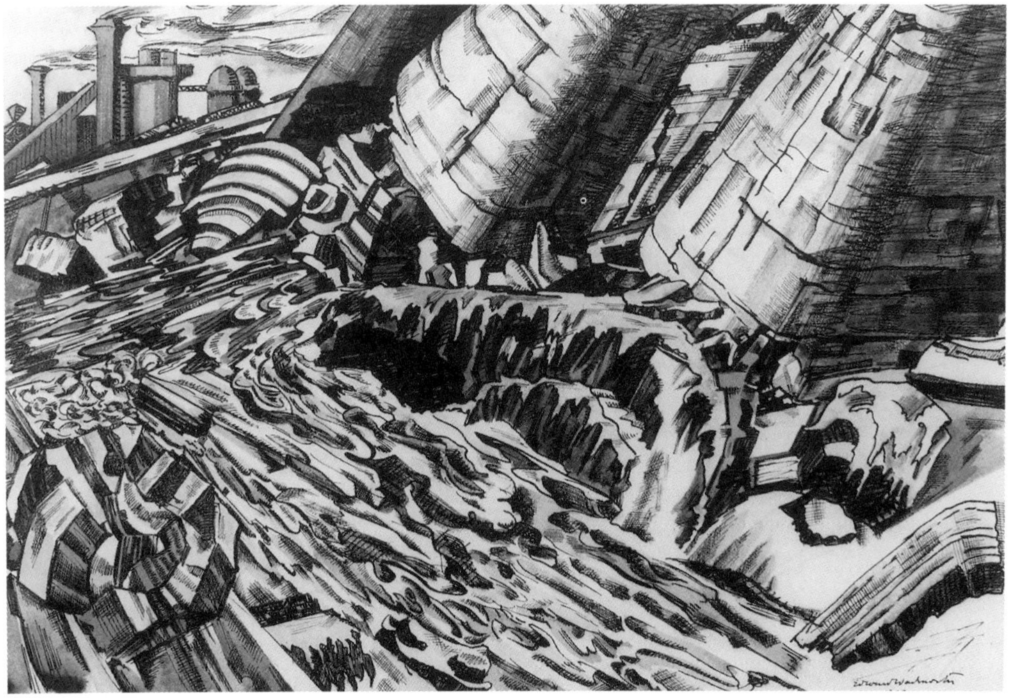

43
EDWARD WADSWORTH
Blast Furnaces
1919
black ink and watercolour on paper
28.3 × 41.1 cm
Manchester City Galleries

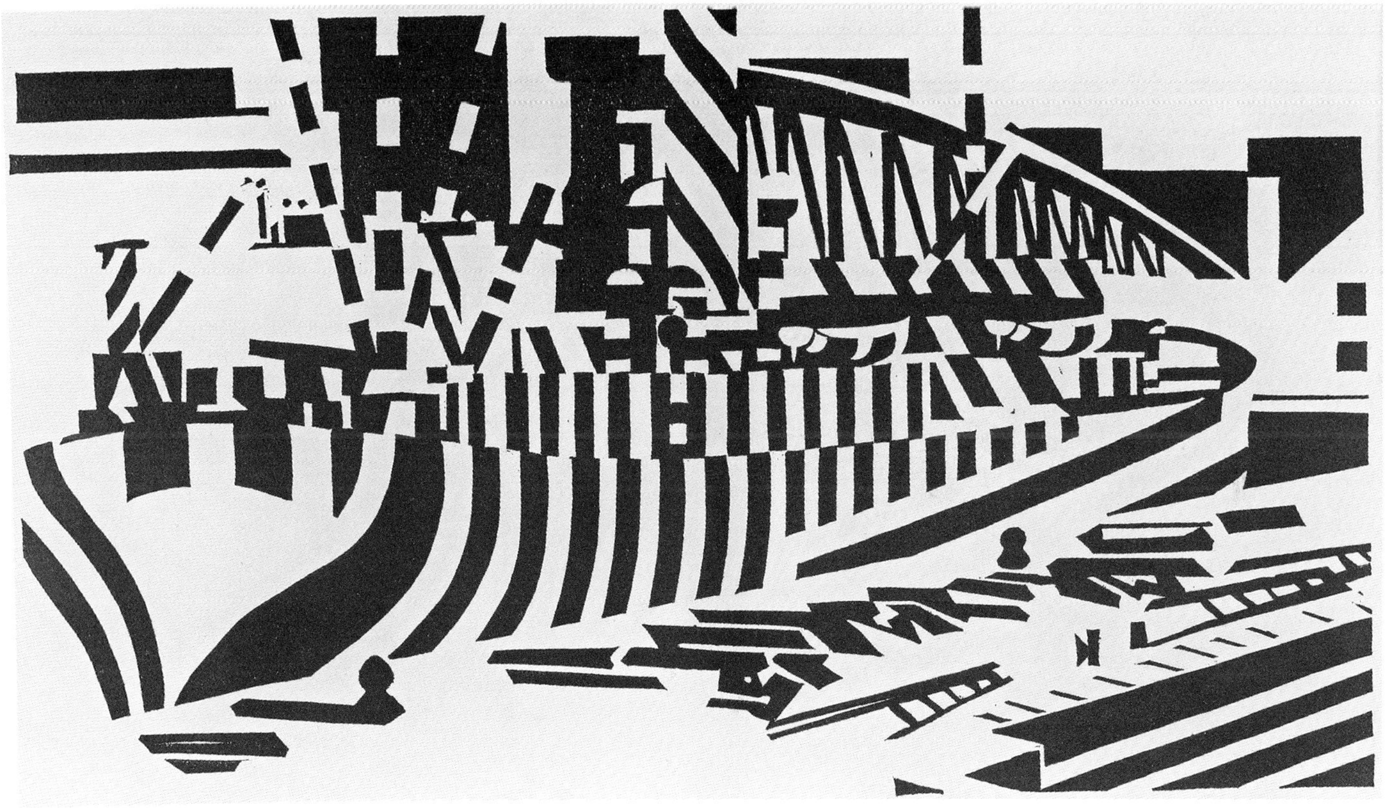

44
EDWARD WADSWORTH
Dazzled Ship in Dry Dock
1918
woodcut
12.7 × 21.6 cm
The Whitworth Art Gallery,
The University of Manchester

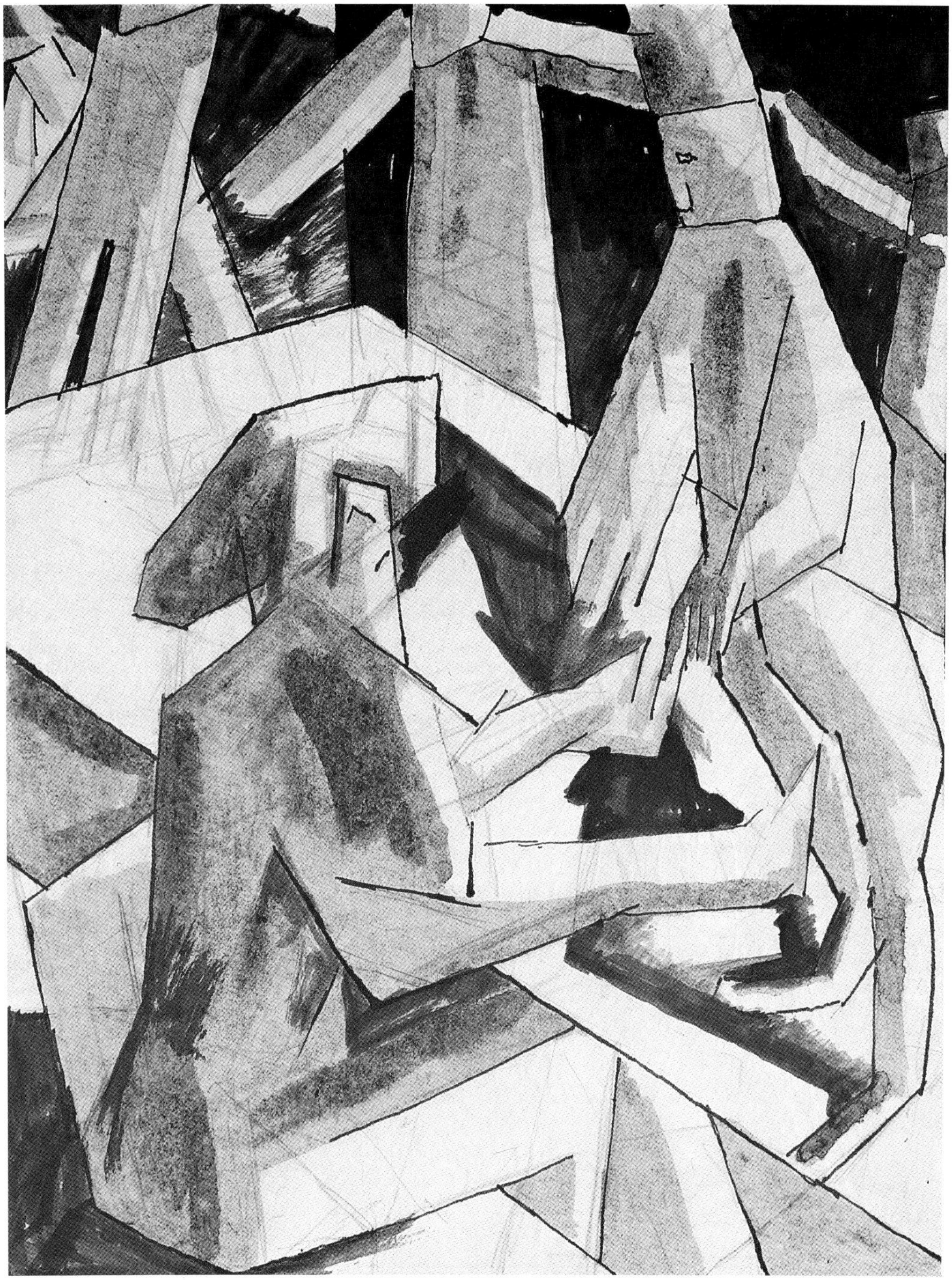

45
WILLIAM ROBERTS
The Boxing Match, Novices
1914
pencil, ink and watercolour on paper
50.9 × 35.6 cm
The Whitworth Art Gallery, The University of Manchester

46
DAVID BOMBERG
The Players
c.1914
pencil and ink wash on paper
26 × 20 cm
Dr. and Mrs. Jeffrey Sherwin

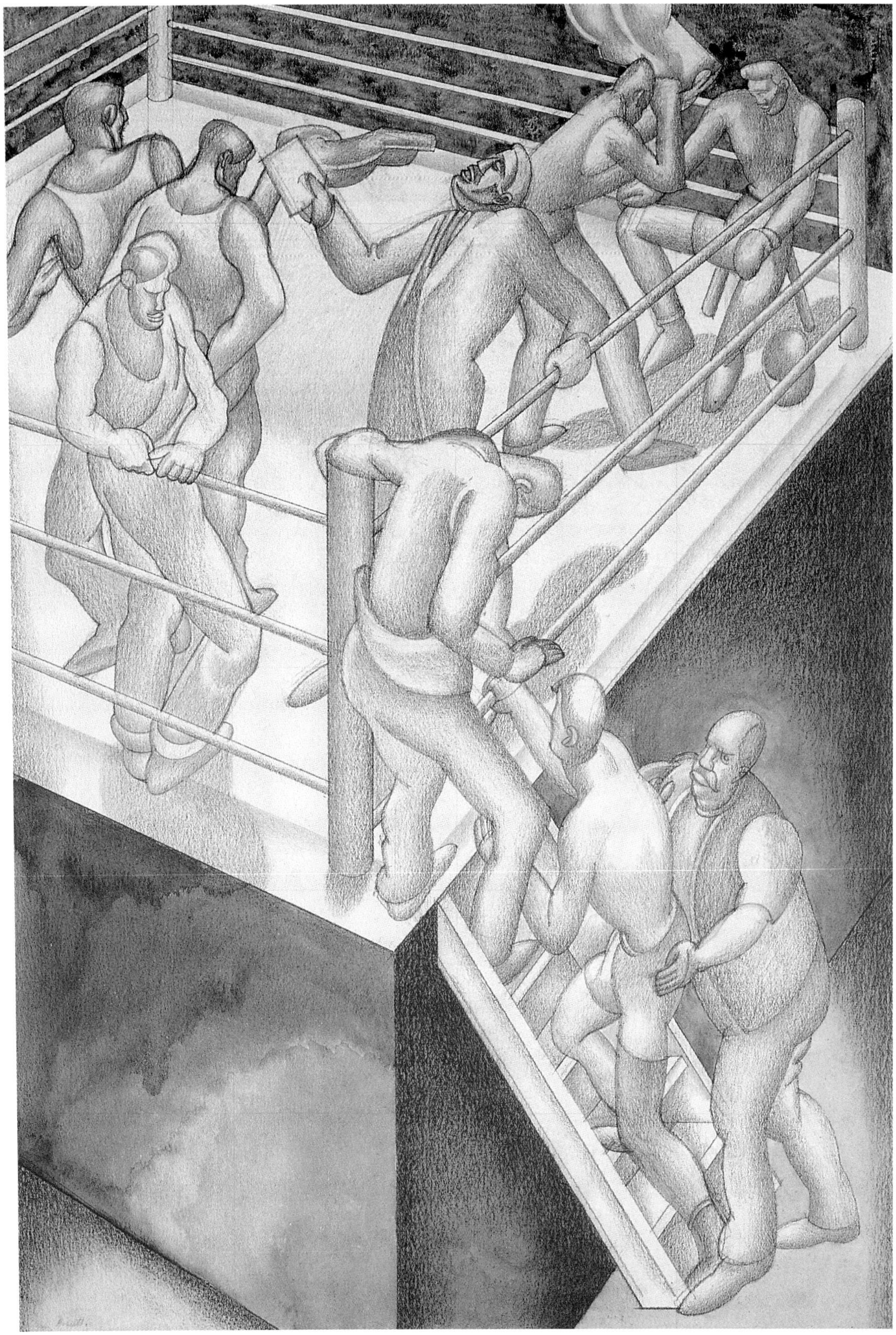

47
WYNDHAM LEWIS
Girl Reclining
*c.*1919
ink on paper
38.1 × 55.9 cm
Tate, London

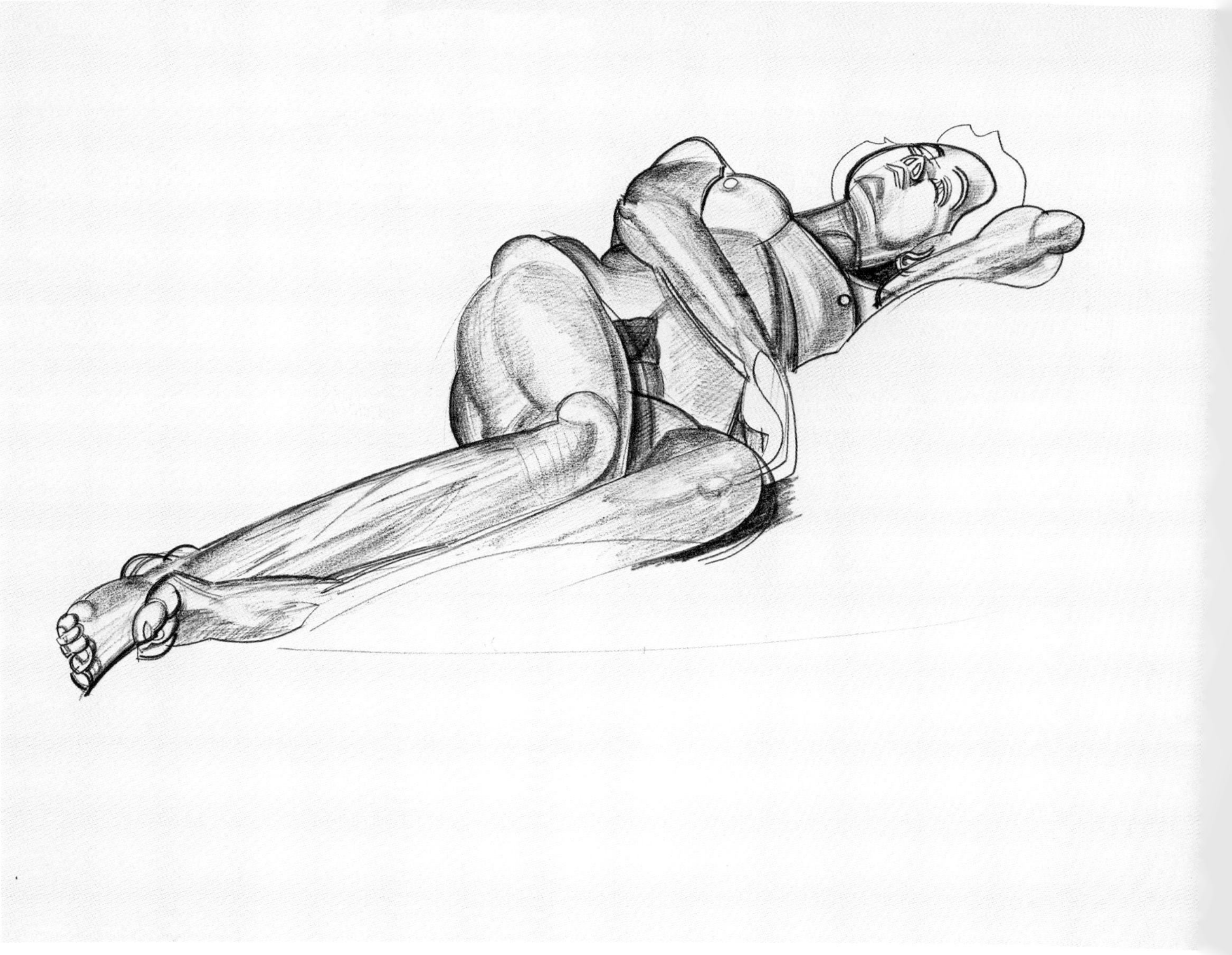

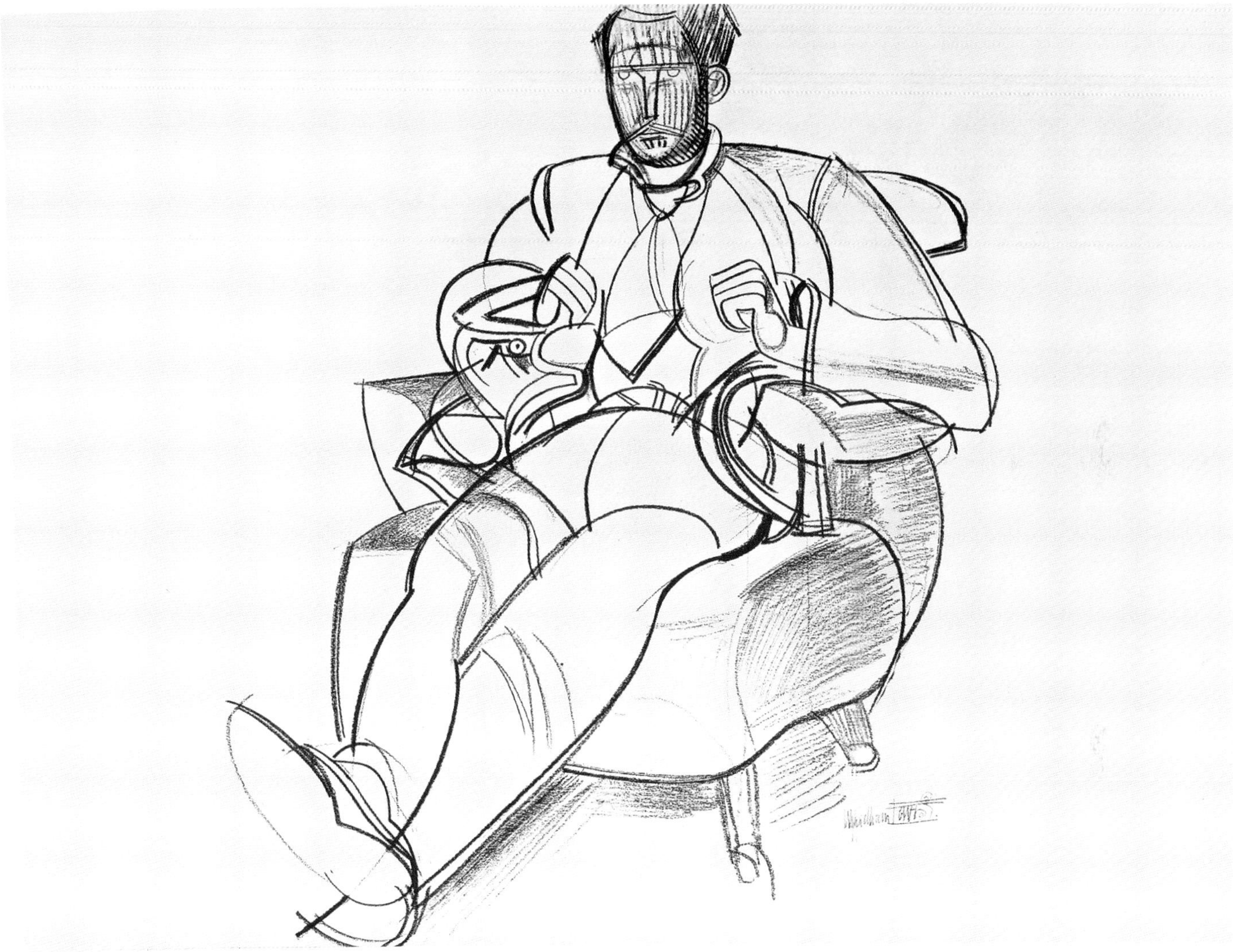

48
WYNDHAM LEWIS
Portrait of Ezra Pound, Seated
*c.*1920
black chalk on paper
38 × 50.6 cm
Manchester City Galleries

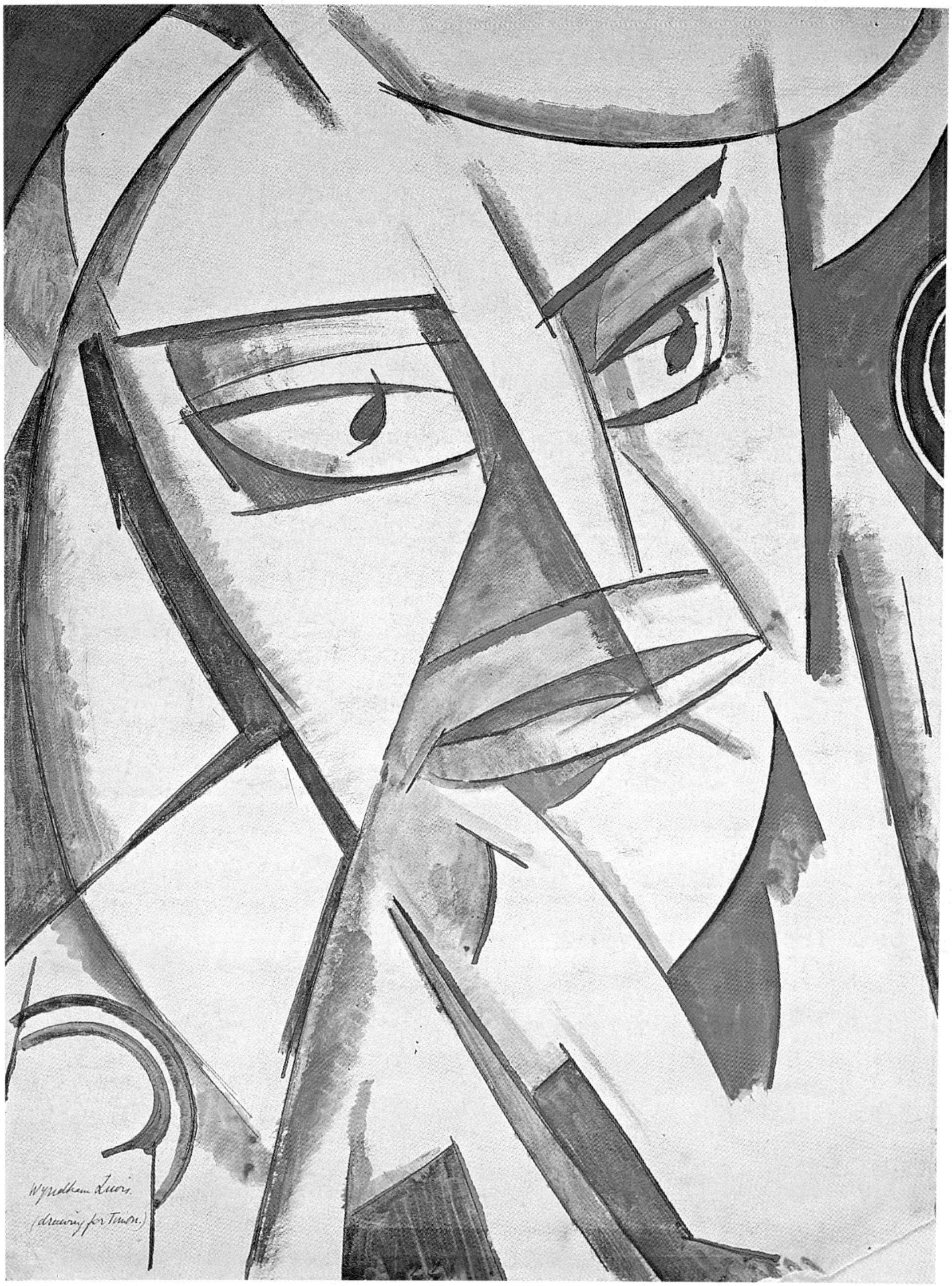

49
WYNDHAM LEWIS
Study of a head for 'Timon of Athens'
c.1912
ink and watercolour on paper
35 × 20 cm
Private collection

50
JACOB KRAMER
The Philosopher
1922
lithograph
47 × 31 cm
Dr. and Mrs. Jeffrey Sherwin

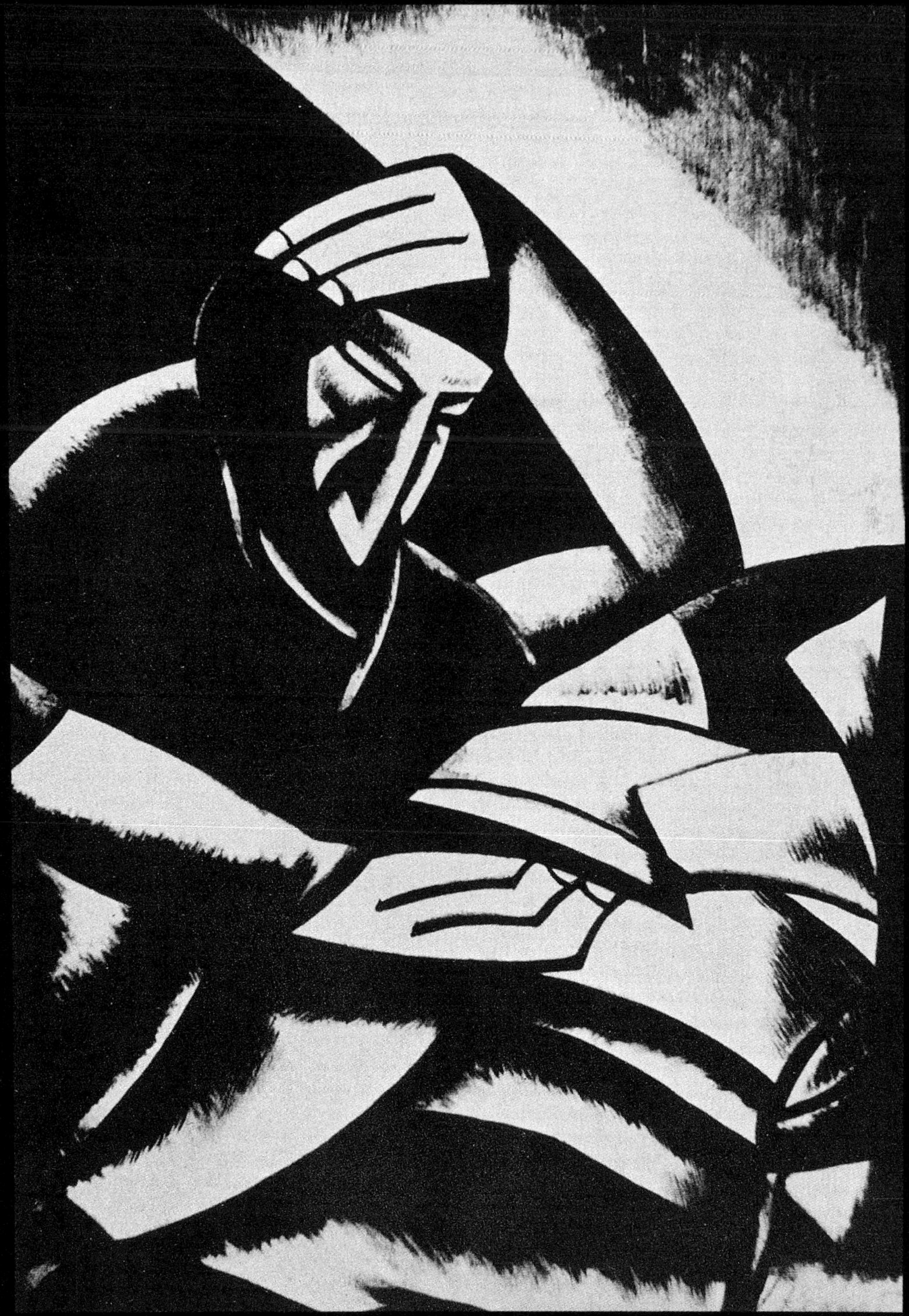

LIST OF WORKS

All measurements in centimetres, height before width

Umberto Boccioni (1882–1916)
Modern Idol
1911
oil on panel
60 × 58.4 cm
Estorick Collection, London
Exhibited: *The Italian Futurist Painters*, Sackville Gallery, London, March 1912
[*plate 7*]

Edward Wadsworth (1889–1949)
The Gas Works
c.1910–11
ink and watercolour on paper
14.7 × 20.1 cm
The Whitworth Art Gallery, The University of Manchester
[*plate 42*]

Wyndham Lewis (1882–1957)
Study of a Head for 'Timon of Athens'
c.1912
ink and watercolour on paper
35 × 20 cm
Private collection
[*plate 49*]

Gino Severini (1883–1966)
Dancer (Ballerina + Sea)
1913
oil, gouache, black wash and pastel on board
75.5 × 50.5 cm
Estorick Collection, London
Exhibited: *Futurist Paintings*, Marlborough Gallery, London, April–May 1913
[*plate 23*]

Wyndham Lewis (1882–1957)
The Vorticist
1912
watercolour, ink and chalk on paper
42.2 × 32.2 cm
Southampton City Art Gallery
[*plate 8*]

C. R. W. Nevinson (1889–1946)
Dance Hall Scene
c.1913–14
gouache and pencil on paper
22.2 × 19.7 cm
Tate, London
Exhibited: Allied Artists Association Salon, Holland Park, London, June 1914
[*plate 6*]

David Bomberg (1890–1957)
Composition with Figures
c.1912–13
oil on wood panel
41 × 32.8 cm
The Whitworth Art Gallery, The University of Manchester
[*plate 13*]

Frederick Etchells (1886–1973)
Woman at a Mirror
1913
oil on canvas
115.2 × 76.9 cm
Manchester City Galleries
[*plate 12*]

Henri Gaudier-Brzeska (1891–1915)
Sketch of a cabinet for the Omega Workshop
1913
pencil, ink and pastel on paper
25.7 × 38.1 cm
Dr. and Mrs. Jeffrey Sherwin
[*plate 40*]

Jacob Epstein (1880–1959)
Study for 'The Rock Drill'
1913
charcoal on paper
67.5 × 42.5 cm
The Garman Ryan Collection, The New Art Gallery, Walsall
[*plate 39*]

Henri Gaudier-Brzeska (1891–1915)
Wrestlers
plaster low-relief
1913
76 × 97 cm
Dr. and Mrs. Jeffrey Sherwin
[*plate 34*]

David Bomberg (1890–1957)
Ju-Jitsu
c.1913
oil on board
61.9 × 61.9 cm
Tate, London
Exhibited: Chenil Gallery, London, July 1914
[*plate 16*]

Giacomo Balla (1871–1958)
Speeding Automobile
1913
coloured crayons and pencil on paper
25 × 28.5 cm
Estorick Collection, London
Exhibited: *Futurist Pictures and Sculptures*, Doré Gallery, London, April–May 1914
[*plate 5*]

Stanley Cursiter (1887–1976)
Rain on Princes Street
1913
oil on canvas
51.4 × 61 cm
McManus Galleries, Dundee City Council Leisure and Arts
[*plate 17*]

Ardegno Soffici (1879–1964)
Landscape
c.1913–14
woodcut
26 × 18 cm
Estorick Collection, London
Exhibited: *Futurist Pictures and Sculptures*, Doré Gallery, London, April–May 1914
[*plate 3*]

Edward Wadsworth (1889–1949)
Mytholmroyd
c.1914
two-colour woodcut
38 × 30.4 cm
The Whitworth Art Gallery, The University of Manchester
Exhibited: Twenty-One Gallery, London, March 1914
[*plate 1*]

Henri Gaudier-Brzeska (1891–1915)
Design for a Vorticist Ornament
1914
black conté crayon on ingres paper
48.3 × 31.6 cm
National Museums & Galleries of Wales
[*plate 41*]

David Bomberg (1890–1957)
The Players
c.1914
pencil and ink wash on paper
26 × 20 cm
Dr. and Mrs. Jeffrey Sherwin
[*plate 46*]

Henri Gaudier-Brzeska (1891–1915)
Doorknocker
c.1914
brass
17.7 × 18.8 cm
Kettle's Yard, University of Cambridge
[*plate 4*]

William Roberts (1895–1980)
The Boxing Match, Novices
1914
pencil, ink and watercolour on paper
50.9 × 35.6 cm
The Whitworth Art Gallery, The University of Manchester
Exhibited: New English Art Club, London, May–June 1914
[*plate 45*]

Wyndham Lewis (1882–1957)
Two Vorticist Figures
c.1913–14
ink and watercolour on paper
24.7 × 31.9 cm
The British Museum
[*plate 9*]

Helen Saunders (1885–1963)
Vorticist Composition (Study for 'Cannon'?)
c.1915
ink and watercolour on paper
38 × 30 cm
Private collection
[*plate 11*]

Wyndham Lewis (1882–1957)
Vorticist Figure Composition
c.1914
charcoal and ink on paper
38 × 68 cm
Private collection
[*plate 38*]

Helen Saunders (1885–1963)
Vorticist Composition: Black and Khaki (?)
c.1915
ink and watercolour on paper
25.5 × 18 cm
Private collection
[*plate 10*]

C. R. W. Nevinson (1889–1946)
Marching Men
1914–15
pastel on paper
13.9 × 20.3 cm
Imperial War Museum
Exhibited: London Group, Goupil Gallery, London, March 1915
[*plate 24*]

Jessica Dismorr (1885–1939)
Abstract Composition
c.1915
oil on wood
41.3 × 50.8 cm
Tate, London
[*plate 14*]

C. R. W. Nevinson (1889–1946)
Taube Pursued by Commander Samson
1915
oil on canvas
85.7 × 49.5 cm
Courtesy of the Trustees of the Royal Air Force Museums
Exhibited: London Group, Goupil Gallery, London, March 1915
[*plate 25*]

Lawrence Atkinson (1873–1931)
Vorticist Composition
c.1914–15
oil on canvas
106.5 × 85 cm
Dr. and Mrs. Jeffrey Sherwin
Exhibited: *Abstract Sculpture and Painting*, Eldar Gallery, London, May 1921
[*plate 15*]

Edward Wadsworth (1889–1949)
Abstract Composition
1915
gouache, ink and pencil on paper
41.9 × 34.3 cm
Tate, London
[*plate 33*]

Alvin Langdon Coburn (1882–1966)
Vortograph
c.1916
photograph
30 × 21 cm
Courtesy of the Royal Photographic Society Collection at the National Museum of Photography, Film and Television
Exhibited: Camera Club, London, February 1917
[*plate 31*]

Edward McKnight Kauffer (1890–1954)
Flight
1917
woodcut
14 × 23 cm
The British Museum
[*plate 37*]

C. R. W. Nevinson (1889–1946)
The Bomber
1918
lithograph
28.6 × 22.3 cm
The British Museum
Exhibited: Leicester Galleries, London, March–April 1918
[*plate 22*]

Wyndham Lewis (1882–1957)
Officers and Signallers
1918
ink, watercolour and gouache on paper
25.4 × 35.6 cm
Imperial War Museum
Exhibited: *Guns*, Goupil Gallery, London, February 1919
[*plate 19*]

William Roberts (1895–1980)
Gunners Turning Out for an SOS: Battery Action at Night
1918
pencil and watercolour on paper
32.3 × 32.3 cm
Imperial War Museum
Exhibited: Burlington House, London, December 1919–February 1920
[*plate 20*]

David Bomberg (1890–1957)
Study for 'Sappers at Work, A Canadian Tunnelling Company'
1918
black and red chalk on paper
27.9 × 40.6 cm
The Whitworth Art Gallery, The University of Manchester
Exhibited: Burlington House, London, January 1919
[*plate 18*]

William Roberts (1895–1980)
The Wiring Party
1918
black ink wash and red pastel on paper
28 × 38 cm
Dr. and Mrs. Jeffrey Sherwin
Exhibited: New English Art Club, London, June 1919
[*plate 21*]

Edward Wadsworth (1889–1949)
Dazzled Ship in Dry Dock
1918
woodcut
12.7 × 21.6 cm
The Whitworth Art Gallery, The University of Manchester
Exhibited Adelphi Gallery, London, March 1919
[*plate 44*]

C. R. W. Nevinson (1889–1946)
Southwark
1918
mezzotint
22.5 × 15 cm
The British Museum
Exhibited: Keppel Gallery, New York, April–May 1919
[*plate 2*]

Edward Wadsworth (1889–1949)
Liverpool Shipping
1918
woodcut
25.9 × 20.1 cm
The British Museum
Exhibited: Adelphi Gallery, London, March 1919
[*plate 26*]

Wyndham Lewis (1882–1957)
Girl Reclining
*c.*1919
ink on paper
38.1 × 55.9 cm
Tate, London
[*plate 47*]

Frank Dobson (1886–1963)
Drawing for carving 'Toilet' (Front view)
1919
pencil, brown ink and red chalk on paper
30.6 × 22.7 cm
Manchester City Galleries
Exhibited: *Group X*, Heal's Mansard Gallery, London, March–April 1920
[*plate 35*]

C. R. W. Nevinson (1889–1946)
The Roof Gardens
1919
mezzotint
21.1 × 11.6 cm
Private collection
Exhibited: Leicester Galleries, London, October 1919
[*plate 30*]

William Roberts (1895–1980)
The Travelling Cradle
1919
ink and watercolour on paper
58.8 × 43 cm
Southampton City Art Gallery
[*plate 28*]

Edward Wadsworth (1889–1949)
Blast Furnaces
1919
black ink and watercolour on paper
28.3 × 41.1 cm
Manchester City Galleries
Exhibited: *The Black Country*, Leicester Galleries, London, January 1920
[*plate 43*]

Edward Wadsworth (1889–1949)
Blast Furnaces 2
1919
woodcut
13.8 × 18.1 cm
The British Museum
Exhibited: *The Black Country*, Leicester Galleries, London, January 1920
[*plate 27*]

Cuthbert Hamilton (1885–1959)
Reconstruction
1919–20
pencil, crayon and gouache on paper
55.9 × 41.9 cm
Tate, London
Exhibited: *Group X*, Heal's Mansard Gallery, London, March–April 1920
[*plate 32*]

William Roberts (1895–1980)
Athletes Exercising in a Gymnasium
1920
pencil, watercolour and ink on paper
45.1 × 35.9 cm
Tate, London
Exhibited: *Group X*, Heal's Mansard Gallery, London, March–April 1920
[*plate 29*]

David Bomberg (1890–1957)
Two Nude Figures Dancing
1920
watercolour and charcoal on paper
51.1 × 55.6 cm
The British Museum
[*plate 36*]

Wyndham Lewis (1882–1957)
Portrait of Ezra Pound, Seated
*c.*1920
black chalk on paper
38 × 50.6 cm
Manchester City Galleries
Exhibited: *Tyros and Portraits*, Leicester Galleries, London, April 1921
[*plate 48*]

Jacob Kramer (1892–1962)
The Philosopher
1922
lithograph
47 × 31 cm
Dr. and Mrs. Jeffrey Sherwin
[*plate 50*]

PRINTED MATERIAL

Blast (published July 1914)
Estorick Collection, London

Blast: War Number (published July 1915), cover by Wyndham Lewis
Estorick Collection, London

The Sky Pilot, cover by Lawrence Atkinson for *Wheels* magazine, 1918
Private collection

Russian Ballet, book of colour lithographs by David Bomberg, 1919
Private collection

Gun Drill, cover by William Roberts for *Wheels* magazine, 1919
Private collection

The Black Country, book illustrated by Edward Wadsworth, 1920
Private collection

Modern Woodcutters no.4, book illustrated by Edward Wadsworth, 1921
Private collection

Dazzle Painting: Kunst als Camouflage, Camouflage als Kunst, Albert Roskam (Rotterdam, 1987)
Lent by Alexander Hollweg

CHRONOLOGY

Compiled by Jonathan Black

20 February 1909: The 'Founding and Manifesto of Futurism', written by Filippo Tommaso Marinetti (1876–1944), was published in *Le Figaro*.

July 1909: Louis Blériot flew across the Channel, from France to England, in 37 minutes.

April 1910: Marinetti gave his first public lecture in England, to the all-female audience of the Lyceum Club at 138 Piccadilly. The Secretary of the Club was Margaret Wynne Nevinson.

August 1910: Excerpts from the February 1909 'Founding and Manifesto of Futurism' were reprinted in *Tramp* magazine, edited by Douglas Goldring.

8 November 1910: 'Manet and the Post-Impressionists' opened at 7 Grafton Street, London.

14 June 1911: First Camden Town Group exhibition opened in London. Exhibitors included Walter Richard Sickert (1860–1942), Charles Ginner (1878–1952) and Wyndham Lewis (1882–1957).

26 October 1911: The first bombing raid from the air was carried out by an Italian aircraft over the Libyan city of Tripoli.

October 1911: While students at the Slade School of Art, C. R. W. Nevinson (1889–1946) and Edward Wadsworth (1889–1949) formed a group calling itself the 'Neo-Primitives'. The group admired paintings by so-called Italian 'primitives' such as Paolo Uccello (1397–1475), Piero della Francesca (*c.*1415/20–92), Domenico Ghirlandaio (1449–94), Sandro Botticelli (1445–1510) and Luca Signorelli (*c.*1440/50–1523).

February 1912: First exhibition of Futurist Painting took place in Paris. Umberto Boccioni (1882–1916), Gino Severini (1883–1966), Luigi Russolo (1885–1947), Carlo Carrà (1881–1966) and Giacomo Balla (1871–1958) exhibited.

March 1912: First Futurist Exhibition in England held at the Sackville Gallery, 28 Sackville Street, London. Marinetti and Boccioni visit London. Boccioni, Severini, Russolo and Carrà exhibited.

June 1912: C. R. W. Nevinson and Edward Wadsworth finished their studies at the Slade School of Art.

26 June 1912: The Cave of the Golden Calf opened 9 Heddon Street, London. Owned by Frida Strindberg, the Cave was decorated by Percy Wyndham Lewis (1882–1957), Jacob Epstein (1880–1959), Charles Ginner, Spencer Gore (1878–1914), Eric Gill (1882–1940) and Cuthbert Hamilton (1884–1959). The Cave went bankrupt in February 1914.

July 1912: Lewis exhibited a huge canvas, influenced by Futurism, entitled *Kermesse* at the 5th Allied Artists Salon, Royal Albert Hall.

5 October 1912: The 'Second Post-Impressionist Exhibition' opened at the Grafton Galleries.

January 1913: American poet Ezra Pound described London as a 'vortex'. Nevinson introduced to Lewis by Wadsworth.

15 March 1913: *Lacerba* published Marinetti's 'The Battle of Adrianople: October 1912'.

7 April–7 May 1913: Severini held a solo exhibition at the Marlborough Gallery, 34 Duke Street, St. James's. While in London, Severini met Nevinson.

11 May 1913: Marinetti published his Manifesto 'Destruction of Syntax – Imagination without Strings – Words in Freedom' in Milan.

June 1913: William Roberts (1895–1980) left the Slade, after entering in 1911.

June–July 1913: Boccioni exhibited 11 'plastic ensembles' at the Galérie Boétie, Paris.

8 July 1913: Official opening of the Omega Workshops, founded by Roger Fry, at 33 Fitzroy Square, London. Members included Lewis, Wadsworth, Frederick Etchells (1886–1973), Cuthbert Hamilton, John (or Jock) Turnbull, Duncan Grant, Vanessa Bell, Henri Gaudier-Brzeska (1891–1915) and Nina Hamnett. The Workshops closed in June 1919.

October 1913: 'Post-Impressionists and Futurists' exhibition held at the Doré Gallery, 35 New Bond Street. Exhibitors include Lewis, Nevinson, Wadsworth, Hamilton, Etchells and Jacob Epstein.

5 October 1913: Lewis, Wadsworth, Etchells and Hamilton left the Omega Workshops after a violent dispute with Roger Fry.

November 1913: London Group created.

16–20 November 1913: Marinetti gave poetry recitals at the Cave of the Golden Calf, the Poetry Bookshop, Clifford Inn Hall and at the Doré Gallery.

17 November 1913: Wadsworth wrote to Lewis that Nevinson has suggested the name *Blast* as the title for the new avant-garde arts magazine Lewis wishes to publish the following year.

18 November 1913: A dinner held in honour of Marinetti at the Florence Restaurant, Rupert Street, London. Lewis, Nevinson, Wadsworth, Hamilton and Etchells were present.

December 1913: William Roberts exhibited his first 'Cubist' oil, *The Return of Ulysses*, at the New English Art Club.

16 December 1913–14 January 1914: Exhibition 'English Post Impressionists, Cubists and Others' held at Brighton Art Gallery. Lewis, Nevinson, Wadsworth, Hamilton, Etchells, Roberts, David Bomberg (1890–1957) and Epstein exhibited together in the same room.

26 February 1914: Private view of murals and decorations painted by Lewis for the dining room of Lady Drogheda, 40 Wilton Crescent, London.

6 March 1914: Private view of the First London Group exhibition held at the Goupil Gallery. Among the exhibitors were Bernard Adeney (1878–1966), Bomberg (1890–1957), Epstein, Etchells, Hamilton, Lewis, Nevinson and Wadsworth.

30 March 1914: The Rebel Art Centre opened at 38 Great Ormond Street. The Centre was funded by Kate Lechmere and members included Etchells, Hamilton, Lewis, Nevinson and Wadsworth.

1 April 1914: First advertisement for *Blast* appeared in the British press, in the magazine *The Egoist*. *Blast* claimed it would champion: 'Cubism, Futurism, Imagisme and all Vital Forms of Modern Art'.

Late April–May 1914: Second Futurist group exhibition held in London, at the Doré Gallery. Ardegno Soffici (1879–1964) and Balla exhibited for the first time in London. Other exhibitors included Boccioni, Carrà, Marinetti, Russolo and Severini.

30 April 1914: At 8.45 pm Marinetti performed 'The Siege of Adrianople: October 1912' at the Doré Gallery with assistance from Nevinson.

8 May–20 June 1914: 20th Century Art exhibition opened at the Whitechapel Art Gallery, London. Exhibitors included Bomberg, Etchells, Gaudier-Brzeska, Lewis, Nevinson, Roberts and Wadsworth.

7 June 1914: Marinetti's and Nevinson's 'Vital English Art' manifesto was published in the *Observer*. The manifesto identified the following as 'pioneers' of 'vital English Art': Lawrence Atkinson (1873–1931), David Bomberg, Jacob Epstein, Frederick Etchells, Cuthbert Hamilton, Nevinson, Roberts, Wadsworth and Wyndham Lewis. Marinetti gave his address as: 'Italian Futurist Movement (Milan)' and Nevinson as: 'Art Rebel Centre (London)'.

12 June 1914: Marinetti's and Nevinson's lectures on Futurism, at the Doré Gallery, New Bond Street, were interrupted by Lewis, Wadsworth, Epstein, Hulme, Gaudier-Brzeska and 5 other Rebel Art Centre members.

13 June 1914: *Blast* advertised, in the *Spectator*, as 'The Manifesto of the Vorticists – The English Parallel Movement to Cubism and Expressionism' [and] Death Blow to Impressionism and Futurism.'

14 June 1914: 'Vital English Art' roundly condemned in a letter to the *Observer* written by Lewis and signed by him and Wadsworth, Roberts, Bomberg, Etchells, Atkinson, Hamilton, Gaudier-Brzeska, Richard Aldington and Ezra Pound.

15–20 June 1914: *Intonarumori* concerts were held at the London Coliseum with music by Russolo, Ugo Piatti and Paolo Buzzi (1874–1956) and recitals by Marinetti.

28 June 1914: Archduke Franz Ferdinand, heir to the Austro-Hungarian Empire, and his wife were assassinated in Sarajevo by a Serbian terrorist Gavrilo Princip.

2 July 1914: publication of *Blast* (dated 20 June 1914). The magazine, advertised as a quarterly, was priced at 2/6 a copy with 160 pages. The main 'Manifesto' was signed, in the following order, by Richard Aldington, Malcolm Arbuthnot, Lawrence Atkinson, Henri Gaudier-Brzeska, Jessica Dismorr (1885–1939), Cuthbert Hamilton, Ezra Pound, William Roberts, Helen Saunders (1885–1963), Edward Wadsworth and Wyndham Lewis.

28 July 1914: Austria-Hungary declared war on Serbia. The following morning, Austrian gunboats on the Danube began to shell Belgrade.

30 July 1914: An Exhibition of Futurist, Cubist and Post-Impressionist Paintings opened at the Scarborough School of Art, Vernon Place.

4 August 1914 (Midnight): Britain declared war on Imperial Germany.

17 August 1914: *Lacerba* and Marinetti began a campaign for Italy to enter the war on the side of the Entente Powers (Britain and France). Italy was still, technically, a member of the Triple Alliance (with Germany and Austria-Hungary).

20 September 1914: Carrà's 'Futurist Synthesis of War' was

published. It was signed by: Carrà, Marinetti, Boccioni, Russolo and Piatti.

13 November 1914–30 January 1915: Nevinson served with the Friends' Ambulance Unit in northern France and in Flanders.

December 1914: Roberts, Bomberg and Epstein met regularly at 8 Ormonde Terrace, Primrose Hill, at the home of lawyer and hunger marcher Stuart Gray. The three planned to exhibit together.

5 March 1915: Private view of a London Group exhibition at the Goupil Gallery. Exhibitors included Epstein (with *The Rock Drill*), Lewis, Nevinson (with *Returning to the Trenches* and *Ypres after the Second Bombardment*) and Wadsworth.

April 1915: During the Second Battle of Ypres, the Germans deployed poisoned gas for the first time in the history of warfare.

24 May 1915: Italy joined the Allied Powers and declared war on Austria-Hungary. In July 1915 Marinetti, Russolo, Boccioni, Sant'Elia, Piatti and Sironi volunteered to serve with the Lombard Volunteer Cyclists Battalion. This was converted into an Alpini battalion that saw action at the Battle of Monte Altissimo in October 1915. The battalion was disbanded in December 1915.

31 May 1915: First major Zeppelin raid on London took place.

1 June 1915–January 1916: Nevinson served as a Private in the Royal Army Medical Corps at the Third London General Hospital, Wandsworth.

5 June 1915: Henri Gaudier-Brzeska was killed in action, fighting with the French Army, at Neuville St. Vaast.

10 June 1915: Vorticism Exhibition opened at the Doré Gallery. The catalogue was written and signed by Wyndham Lewis. 'Vorticist Group' members were listed as Jessica Dismorr, Frederick Etchells, Henri Gaudier-Brzeska, William Roberts, Helen Saunders (as 'Sanders'), Edward Wadsworth and Percy Wyndham Lewis. 'Invitees' were Bernard Adeney, Lawrence Atkinson, Bomberg, Duncan Grant, Jacob Kramer (1892–1962) and Nevinson.

20 July 1915: *Blast: War Number (Review of the Great English Vortex)* was published. The magazine reproduced works by Etchells, Nevinson and Roberts.

11 January–1 February 1916: An exhibition of 'Paintings and Ornament by Wyndham Lewis (Vorticist)' was held at the Restaurant La Tour Eiffel, 1 Percy Street, London.

15 January–1 February 1916: Severini's 'First Futurist Exhibition of the Plastic Art of War' was held at the Galerie Boutet de Monvel, Paris.

February 1916: Lewis and Roberts volunteered for the Royal Artillery. Lewis eventually became an officer in the Royal Garrison Artillery and Roberts a Private in the Royal Field Artillery. Lewis served in France, May–November 1917 and Roberts, August 1916–April 1918.

1 July–22 November 1916: Battle of the Somme.

August 1916: Boccioni killed in a riding accident.

August 1916–August 1917: Wadsworth served with Naval Intelligence in the Royal Naval Volunteer Reserve on the eastern Aegean island of Lemnos.

26 September–4 November 1916: Nevinson held his first solo exhibition, at the Leicester Galleries, Leicester Square, London.

October 1916: Alvin Langdon Coburn (1882–1966) and Ezra Pound devised the 'Vortograph'.

10 January 1917: The one and only Vorticist show in USA opened at the Penguin Club, 8 East 15th Street New York. 75 works by Lewis, Wadsworth, Roberts, Etchells, Dismorr and Saunders.

February 1917: Coburn exhibited his 'Vortographs' at the Camera Club, London.

June 1917: Marinetti was wounded in the leg, fighting on the Isonzo.

31 July–10 November 1917: Battle of Passchendæle.

September 1917–May 1918: 1,428 people were killed or wounded during German bombing raids on London.

October 1917: Bolshevik coup in Russia. The Royal Navy employed Wadsworth as part of its 'Dazzle' camouflage programme.

December 1917: Russolo was seriously wounded during fighting at Monté Grappa on the Asiago Front. Lewis was appointed an official war artist by the Canadian War Records Scheme.

2 March–5 April 1918: Nevinson held second solo exhibition, devoted to his official war art, at the Leicester Galleries.

8–10 August 1918: British and Dominion Forces defeat Germans at the Battle of Amiens.

11 November 1918: Defeat of Imperial Germany.

January 1919: Nevinson declared he was no longer a 'Futurist'.

4 January 1919: Canadian War Memorials Scheme exhibition opened at Burlington House. Among the exhibitors were Lewis, Wadsworth, Roberts, Hamilton, Etchells Nevinson, Bomberg and Turnbull.

February 1919: Lewis held his first solo exhibition, 'Guns', at the Goupil Gallery, London.

March 1919: Wadsworth exhibited 31 woodcuts and 4 drawings at the Adelphi Gallery, 9 Duke Street, near the Embankment, London.

23 March 1919: Marinetti was present at the meeting in Milan that led to the creation of the Italian Fascist movement.

29 April–17 May 1919: Nevinson held an exhibition of his prints at the Keppel Gallery, 4 East 39th Street, New York.

July 1919: Versailles Peace Treaty signed.

3 September 1919: Lewis wrote to John Quinn that he had recently formed a group of ten painters who were going to exhibit together. He also hoped to publish a third issue of *Blast* in November.

25 October 1919: Nevinson's third solo exhibition opened at the Leicester Galleries, London.

December 1919–February 1920: 'Nation's War Paintings And Other Records' opened at Burlington House. Among the exhibitors were Nevinson, Lewis, Wadsworth, Roberts, Frank Dobson (1886–1963) and Stanley Spencer.

January 1920: Wadsworth held an exhibition of 39 'Black Country' drawings at the Leicester Galleries. Many of the drawings were reproduced in a book, *The Black Country*, with a foreword by Arnold Bennett, published in September 1920.

26 March–24 April 1920: 'Group X' exhibition held at Heal's Mansard Gallery, Tottenham Court Road. Exhibitors were Dismorr, Dobson, Etchells, Charles Ginner, Hamilton, Wyndham Lewis, Roberts, E. McKnight Kauffer, John Turnbull and Wadsworth.

10 November–4 December 1920: Nevinson held an exhibition of his New York images at the Bourgeois Galleries, 668 Fifth Avenue at 53rd Street, New York.

April 1921: Lewis's exhibition 'Tyros and Portraits' held at the Leicester Galleries.

May 1921: Lawrence Atkinson held an exhibition entitled 'Abstract Sculpture and Painting' at the Eldar Gallery, 40 Great Marlborough Street, London.

November 1923: Roberts held his first solo exhibition at the Chenil Galleries, London.

1924: Noel Coward's *The Vortex* was performed in London and proved to be a scandalous success.

EXCERPTS FROM KEY TEXTS

Selected by Jonathan Black

1. We intend to sing the love of danger, the habit of energy and fearlessness.

3. Up to now, literature has exalted a pensive immobility, ecstasy and sleep. We intend to exalt aggressive action, a feverish insomnia, the racers stride, the mortal leap, the punch and the slap.

4. We affirm that the world's magnificence has been enriched by a new beauty: the beauty of speed. A racing car whose hood is adorned with great pipes, like serpents of explosive breath – a roaring car that seems to ride on grapeshot is more beautiful than the *Victory of Samothrace*.

7. Except in struggle, there is no more beauty. No work without an aggressive character can be a masterpiece.

9. We will glorify war – the world's only hygiene – militarism, patriotism, the destructive gesture of freedom-bringers, beautiful ideas worth dying for and scorn for women.

11. We will sing of great crowds, excited by work, by pleasure, and by riot; we will sing of the multi-coloured, polyphonic, tides of revolution in the modern capitals; we will sing of the vibrant nightly fervour of arsenals and shipyards blazing with violent electric moons; greedy railway stations that devour smoke-plumed serpents; factories hung on clouds by the crooked lines of their smoke; bridges that stride the rivers like giant gymnasts, flashing in the sun with a glitter of knives; adventurous steamers that sniff the horizons; deep-chested locomotives whose wheels paw the tracks like the hooves of enormous, steel horses bridled by tubing; and the sleek flight of planes whose propellers chatter in the wind like banners and seem to cheer like an enthusiastic crowd.

It is from Italy that we launch through the world this violently unsettling, incendiary manifesto of ours. With it, today, we establish Futurism, because we want to free this land from its smelly gangrene of professors, archaeologists, ciceroni and antiquarians ... The oldest of us is thirty: so we have at least a decade for finishing our work. When we are forty, other, younger and stronger men will probably throw us in the wastebasket, like useless manuscripts – we want it to happen! ... Art, in fact, can be nothing but violence, cruelty and injustice.

Taken from *The Founding and Manifesto of Futurism* by F. T. Marinetti. Published in *Le Figaro*, 20 February 1909.

We must breathe in the tangible miracles of contemporary life – the iron network of speedy communications which envelops the earth, the transatlantic liners, the dreadnoughts, those marvellous flights which furrow our skies, the profound courage of our submarine navigators and the spasmodic struggle to conquer the unknown. How can we remain insensible to the frenetic life of our great cities and to the exciting new psychology of night-life; the feverish figures of the bon viveur, the cocotte, the apache and the absinthe-drinker? ... We declare war on all artists and all institutions which insist on hiding behind a façade of false modernity ... We condemn as insulting to youth ... The neurasthenic cultivation of hermaphroditic archaism which they rave about in Florence ...

Taken from *The Manifesto of the Futurist Painters*, dated 11 February 1910 and signed by Boccioni, Carrà, Russolo, Balla and Severini.

We are young and our art is violently revolutionary ... It is only possible to react against Impressionism by surpassing it ... The simultaneousness of states of mind in the work of art: that is the intoxicating aim of our art ... the simultaneousness of the ambient ... the dislocation and dismemberment of objects, the scattering and fusion of details, freed from accepted logic, and independent from one another. In order to make the spectator live in the centre of the picture ... the picture must be the synthesis of *what one remembers* and of *what one sees* ... what must be rendered is the *dynamic sensation* ... the particular rhythm of each object, its inclination, its movement or ... its interior force.

Taken from *The Exhibitors to the Public*, dated 5 February 1912 and signed by Boccioni, Carrà, Russolo, Balla and Severini.

Following the laws of a new concept of harmony they [objects] will be encapsulated inside the muscular lines of a body. In this way, the cogs of a machine might easily appear out of the armpits of a mechanic, or the lines of a table could cut a reader's head in two, or a book with its fanned out pages could intersect the reader's stomach. LET'S SPLIT OPEN OUR FIGURES AND PLACE THE ENVIRONMENT INSIDE THEM ... [We] destroy the literary and traditional 'dignity' of marble and bronze statues ... Insist that even twenty types of materials can be used in a single work of art in order to achieve plastic movement ... glass, wood, cardboard, iron, cement, hair, leather, cloth, mirrors, electric lights, etc.

Taken from *The Technical Manifesto of Futurist Sculpture* by Umberto Boccioni. Published in *Poesia*, 11 April 1912.

Important modifiers of our sensibility: 1. Acceleration of life to today's swift pace ... 3. Dread of quiet living, love of danger, and an attitude of daily heroism ... 10. A modification in the idea of war, which has become the necessary and bloody test of a people's force ... 12. Man multiplied by the Machine. New mechanical sense, a fusion of instinct with the efficiency of motors and conquered forces. 13. ... idealism of Sport. Idea and love of the 'record'. 14. New tourist sensibility bred by ocean liners and great hotels, Passion for the city ... Ridicule of the 'holy green silence' and the ineffable landscape ... 16. A loathing of curved lines ... Love for the straight line and the tunnel. The habit of visual foreshortening and visual synthesis caused by the speed of trains and cars that look down on cities and countrysides ... Love of speed, abbreviation, and the summary.

Taken from *Destruction of Syntax – Imagination Without Strings – Words-in-Freedom* by F. T. Marinetti. Published in *Lacerba*, 15 June 1913.

AGAINST 1. The worship of tradition and the conservatism of the Academies, the commercial acquiescence of English artists, the effeminacy of their art and their complete absorption towards a purely decorative sense. 2. The pessimistic, sceptical and narrow views of the English public, who stupidly adore the pretty-pretty, the commonplace, the soft, sweet and mediocre, the sickly revivals of Medievalism, the Garden Cities, with their curfews and artificial battlements, the Maypole Morris dances, Aestheticism, Oscar Wilde, the Pre-Raphaelites, Neo-Primitives and Paris. 3. The proverbial snob who ignores, or despises, all English daring, originality and invention, but welcomes eagerly all foreign originality and daring ... 5. The indifference of the King, the State and the politicians towards all arts. 6. The English notion that Art is a useless pastime, only fit for women and schoolgirls, that artists are poor deluded fools to be pitied and protected and Art a ridiculous complaint, a mere topic for table-talk ... 8. The old grotesque idea of genius – drunken, filthy, ragged, outcast ... the synonym of Art, Chelsea, the Montmartre of London: the Post-Rossettis with long hair under their sombreros and other passéist filth ... 11. ... Take care children. Mind the Motors. Don't go too quick. Wrap yourselves up well. Mind the draughts. Be careful of the lightning. Forward! HURRAH for motors! HURRAH for speed! HURRAH for draughts! HURRAH for lightning!

WE WANT 1. To have an English Art that is strong, virile and anti-sentimental. 2. That English artists strengthen their Art by a recuperative optimism, a fearless desire for adventure, a heroic instinct of discovery, a worship of strength and a physical and moral courage, all sturdy virtues of the English race ... 4. To create a powerful advance guard, which alone can save English Art, now threatened by the traditional conservatism of Academies and the habitual indifference of the public. This will be an exciting stimulant, a violent incentive for creative genius, a constant inducement to keep alive the fires of invention, and of Art ... 5. A rich and powerful country, like England, ought, without question, to support, defend and glorify its advance guard of artists, no matter how advanced or how extreme, if it intends to deliver its Art from inevitable death.

Taken from *A Futurist Manifesto. Vital English Art* by F. T. Marinetti and C. R. W. Nevinson. Published in the *Observer*, 7 June 1914.

LONG LIVE THE VORTEX!: To make the rich of the community shed their education skin, to destroy politeness, standardisation and academic, that is civilised, vision, is the task we have set ourselves ... It is not necessary to be an outcast Bohemian, to be unkempt or poor, any more than it is necessary to be rich or handsome, to be an artist ... AUTOMOBILISM (Marinetteism) bores us ... Wilde gushed twenty years ago about the beauty of machinery ... The 'poor' are detestable animals! They are only picturesque ... for the sentimentalist or the romantic!

Manifesto – I: BLAST first (from politeness) ENGLAND ... DISMAL SYMBOL, set round our bodies, of effeminate lout within. VICTORIAN VAMPIRE, the LONDON cloud sucks the Town's heart ... SO MUCH VAST MACHINERY TO PRODUCE ... 5. BLAST SPORT ... 6. BLAST years 1837 to 1900 ... BLAST Frank Brangwyn ... Galsworthy ... Dean Inge ... Croce ... C. B. Fry ...

Bergson ... Edward Elgar ... Weiniger [sic] ... Beecham (Pills, Opera, Thomas) ... Sydney Webb ... British Academy ... Annie Besant ... Joseph Holbrooke ... Clan Strachey ... 2. BLESS the HAIRDRESSER ... 3. BLESS ENGLISH HUMOUR ... 4. BLESS FRANCE, Female Qualities, Females ... BLESS Carson ... Cromwell ... Frank Rutter ... James Joyce ... Henry Newbolt ... Frank Harris ... W. L. George ... George Robey ... Bandsman Rice ... Petty Officer Curran ... Konody ... Lewis Hind

Manifesto – II: We are Primitive Mercenaries in the Modern World ... The artist of the modern movement is a savage (in no sense an 'advanced', perfected, democratic, Futurist individual of Mr. Marinetti's limited imagination) ... *Manifesto V:* No great ENGLISH Art need be ashamed to share some glory with France, to-morrow it may be with Germany, where the Elizabethans did before it ... *Manifesto VI:* The Modern World is due almost entirely to Anglo-Saxon genius, – its appearance and its spirit. Machinery, trains, steam-ships, all that distinguishes externally our time, came far more from here than anywhere else ... *Manifesto VII:* Once this consciousness towards the new possibilities of expression in present life has come, however, it will be more the legitimate property of Englishmen than of any other people in Europe ... They are the inventors of this bareness and hardness, and should be the great enemies of Romance ... The Latins are at present, for instance, in their 'discovery' of sport, their Futuristic gush over machines, aeroplanes, etc., the most romantic and sentimental 'moderns' to be found. It is only the second-rate people in France or Italy who are thorough revolutionaries. In England, on the other hand, there is no vulgarity in revolt.

[*signed*] R. Aldington, Arbuthnot, L. Atkinson, Gaudier-Brzeska, J. Dismorr, C. Hamilton, E. Pound, W. Roberts, H. Sanders [sic], E. Wadsworth, Wyndham Lewis

Futurism, Magic and Life: Killing somebody must be the greatest pleasure in existence ... Some people enjoy best by proxy, some by masturbation; others prefer to do things themselves ...

The New Egos: We all to-day (possibly with a coldness reminiscent of the insect-world) are in each other's vitals – overlap, intersect, and are Siamese to any extent. THE ACTUAL HUMAN BODY BECOMES OF LESS IMPORTANCE EVERY DAY ... Dehumanization is the chief diagnostic of the Modern World.

Our Vortex II: The Vorticist is at his maximum point of energy when stillest. The Vorticist is not the Slave of Commotion, but its Master. *III:* In a Vorticist Universe we don't get excited at what we have invented. *IV:* Our Vortex is proud of its polished sides. Our Vortex desires the immobile rythm [sic] of its swiftness.

Vortex Pound: The Turbine: All experience rushes into this vortex. All the energized past, all the past that is living and worthy to live. All MOMENTUM, which is the past bearing upon us, RACE, RACE-MEMORY, instinct charging the PLACID, NON-ENERGIZED FUTURE. Futurism is the disgorging spray of a vortex with no drive behind it, DISPERSAL. VORTICISM is art before it has spread itself into a state of flacidity [sic], of elaboration, of secondary applications.

Taken from *Blast*, dated 20 June 1914 and published by John Lane, 2 July 1914.

By Vorticism we mean (a) ACTIVITY as opposed to the tasteful PASSIVITY of Picasso; (b) SIGNIFICANCE as opposed to the dull or anecdotal character to which the Naturalist is condemned; (c) ESSENTIAL MOVEMENT AND ACTIVITY (such as the energy of the mind) as opposed to the imitative cinematography, the fuss and hysterics of the Futurists ... Artists today have an immense commercialised mass of painting and every form of art to satisfy and destroy. There has never been such a load of sugary, cheap, anecdotal and, in every way, pitiable muck poured out by the ton ... Were the walls of London carpeted with abstractions, rather than the present mass of work that falls between two stools, the design usually weakened to explain some point, the effect architecturally would be much better and the Public taste could thus be educated in a popular way to appreciate the essentials of design better than picture galleries have ever done. As to popular acceptance of such abstract works as are found here [in the Vorticist exhibition], definite POPULAR acceptance should never be aimed at ...

Taken from *Note* by Wyndham Lewis in the catalogue of the Vorticist exhibition at the Doré Gallery, June 1915

Constantinople Our Star: The English sense of humour is a perpetual, soft, self-indulgent, (often maudlin) hysteria, that has weakened the brain of Britain more than any drug could ... If English women could only have their teeth drawn out, which protrude so much like a death's head ...

The European War and Great Communities: This blood-letting in mass, all at once, is so impressive and appalling. A steady dribble of blood, year by year, first in one corner and then in another, would not be noticed to the same extent ... Women's function, the manufacturing of children ... It takes the deft women we employ anything from twelve to sixteen years to fill and polish these little human cartridges and they of course get fond of them in the process ... The scale does not, by any means, flatter the individual. The sensation of immensity of horror and waste [at the Front] is too difficult to forget ... it is impossible for any individual regiment, or individual soldier, to get the necessary isolation and quality of uniqueness for their deed of gallantry.

Vortex Gaudier-Brzeska: This paltry mechanism, which serves as a purge to over-numerous humanity. This war is a great remedy. In the individual it kills arrogance, self-esteem, pride. It takes away from the masses numbers upon numbers of unimportant units ... I shall derive my emotions solely from the arrangement of surfaces. I shall present my emotions by the arrangement of my surfaces, the planes and lines by which they are defined.

C.31: When you watch an electric crane, swinging up with extraordinary grace and ease a huge weight, your instinct to admire this power is, subconsciously, a selfish one. It is a pity that there are not men so strong that they can lift a house up, and fling it across a river. *C.32:* In any heroic, that is, energetic representations of men to-day, this reflection of the immense power of machines will be reflected.

BLAST Brangwyn ... Orpen ... Mestrovic ... W. L. George ... Bevan and his dry rot ... BLESS Koyetzu, Rotatzu, Korin ... Bombardier Wells ...

Taken from *Blast: War Number, Review of the Great English Vortex.* Published by John Lane, 20 July 1915.

In the years before the war the accusation of decadence was frequently brought against the young men and the artists of the day. No charge has proved more false. Already, before the war, young artists in the Latin Countries and in England were seeking a wider inspiration than in the sickly worship of the nude and in the over-sensual broodings of the our elders which showed themselves in the literature and the art of the Yellow Book, in 'advanced' dramas and in some of the Pre-Raphaelites, a tendency largely due to trivial lives possessing no other conception of adventure, or emotion, than sex. The intensity of the present time is producing a vital art in England. In theatres and picture shop windows, it is true, an insipid and sentimental reaction against surrounding horrors is obvious, but a vital art may be trusted to overcome it. For the pressure of necessity is already compelling us to take up our natural position as pioneers in literature, art, science and industry – a position of initiative which over-prosperity, self-content and insularity had tempted us comfortably to forego.

Taken from *Note by the Artist* by C. R. W. Nevinson, in the exhibition catalogue *Pictures and Drawings of War by C. R. W. Nevinson (late Private RAMC),* Leicester Galleries, London, September 1916.

The public, surprised at finding eyes and noses in this exhibition, will begin by the reflection that the artist has conceded Nature, and abandoned those vexing diagrams by which he puzzled and annoyed. The case is really not quite like that. All that has happened is that in these things the artist has set himself a different task ... I never associated myself to the jejune folly that would tell you one week that a Polynesian totem was the only formula by which the mind of Man – the Modern Man ... might be expressed ... 'Abstract Art', expressionism, cubism, or what not, is a fanatic ... but perfectly sincere insistence on the fundamentals of design or colour ... I have attempted here only one thing: that is in a direct, ready formula to give an interpretation of what I took part in in France. I set out to do a series dealing with the Gunner's life from his arrival in the Depot to his life in the lines ... it is certain that the philosophy of the War, all the serious interpretation of it, has yet to be done ... all the War journalism, in painting and writing, will cease with the punctuality and *netteté* of a pistol shot when the war curtain goes down. It will then be the turn of those with experience of the subject, the inclination, the mood, to make the true record. Truth has no place in action. This show, then, pretends nothing, in extent: I make only the claim for it in kind that it attempts to give a personal and immediate expression of a tragic event. Experimentation is waived: I have tried to do with pencil and brush what story-tellers like Chekov and Stendhal did in their books.

Taken from *Foreword* by Wyndham Lewis, in the exhibition catalogue *Guns*, Goupil Gallery, London, February 1919.

In the matter of the graphic presentation of industrialism, Mr. Wadsworth does not confront an entirely uneducated public. Industrialism in its fiercer moods has been handled by artists before. It has been sentimentalised, with afflicting consequences. It has been transmogrified by stunt artists whose intention was to whack the public on the head ... I am not going to compare Mr. Wadsworth with other serious artists of industrialism ... Certainly, I am not going to state that Mr. Wadsworth is 'advanced'' for I have never yet seen anything more 'advanced' than, say, the Elgin marbles ... Mr. Wadsworth is very austere, and that, in particular, he has no use for that facile picturesqueness which any slick performer can paste over furnaces and slag heaps and grime ... He depends on his central vitalising emotion, and he allows no extrinsic facts ... to interfere with the expression of that emotion. His courage in this respect may disconcert the timid. And a good thing too!

Taken from *Note* by Arnold Bennett, in the exhibition catalogue *The Black Country, Drawings by Edward Wadsworth*, Leicester Galleries, London, January 1920.

The members of this group have agreed to exhibit together twice annually, firstly for motives of convenience, and with no theory or dogma that would be liable to limit the development of any member. Each member sails his own boat, and may lift his sails to any wind that may seem to him to promise a prosperous cruise ... Group X, on the other hand, is not in the nature of a piratic community. They are a band of peaceful traders – naturally armed to the teeth and bristling with every device to defend the legitimate and honourable trafficking that is the result of their enterprising toil ... it is probable that the merchandise marked X will be known for a certain quality rather than another. X will not, and is not meant to, signify *anything* that can be made ... there are many people to-day who talk glibly of the 'victory' of the Cubist, Vorticist or Expressionist movements and, in the next breath, of now putting the armour off and becoming anything that pays best, repairing wherever, after the stress of a few years, the softest time is to be secured ... If you should wish to relate the artists of Group X to something English, Rowlandson would be the figure they would indicate rather than [Ford] Madox Brown, as a model Islander. Also they would refer you to a time in English history when England formed part of Europe, participating intellectually in the life of France, Spain and Italy, rather than to the time when England took on a clammy cloak pf provincial narrowness, as occurred in the Victorian period.

Taken from *Foreword Group X* by Wyndham Lewis, in the exhibition catalogue *Group X*, Mansard Gallery, London, March–April 1920.

I have narrowed this exhibition to two phases of work. One is of work done directly in contact with nature, or with full information of the natural accidental form. The other phase is one which I have just entered, that of a series of pictures coming under the head of satire; grotesque scenes of a selected family or race of beings ... Most of the drawings are drawings from nature. It is important for an experimental artist and for experimental artists generally, to demonstrate that these activities are not the consequence of incompetence, as the enemies of these experiments so frequently assure the public ... My standpoint is that it is only a graceful dilettantism that desires to convert painting into a parlour game, a very intellectual dressmaker's hobby, or a wayward and slightly hysterical chess ... abstraction, or plastic music, is justified and at its best when its divorce from natural form or environment is complete, as in Kandinsky's expressionism, or in the experiments of the 1914 Vorticists ... Twenty years ago, 'art for art's sake' was the slogan ... Our present great general movement must be an emancipation towards complete human expression: but it is always liable in England to degenerate into a cultivated and snobbish game. My Tyros may help to frighten away this local bogy.

Taken from *Foreword* by Wyndham Lewis, in the exhibition catalogue *Tyros and Portraits*, Leicester Galleries, London, April 1921.

PLATE CREDITS

3, 5, 7, 23 Estorick Collection, London
1, 13, 18, 42, 44, 45 The Whitworth Art Gallery, The University of Manchester
12, 35, 43, 48 Manchester City Galleries
8, 28 Southampton City Art Gallery/Bridgeman Art Library
6, 14, 16, 29, 32, 33, 47 Tate, London 2004
15, 21, 34, 40, 46, 50 Dr. and Mrs. Jeffrey Sherwin
39 The Garman Ryan Collection, The New Art Gallery, Walsall
17 McManus Galleries, Dundee City Council Leisure and Arts
41 National Museums & Galleries of Wales
4 Kettle's Yard, University of Cambridge
2, 9, 22, 26, 27, 36, 37 The British Museum
10, 11, 38, 49 Private collection
19, 20, 24 Imperial War Museum
25 Royal Air Force Museum, Hendon
31 National Museum of Photography, Film and Television/Science and Society Picture Library
30 Fine Art Society plc, London

Copyright acknowledgements

1, 26, 27, 33, 42, 43, 44 Estate of Edward Wadsworth. All Rights Reserved, DACS 2004
8, 9, 38, 47, 48, 49 By Kind Permission of the Wyndham Lewis Memorial Trust
2, 22, 24, 25, 30 Courtesy of the Artist's Estate/Bridgeman Art Library
12, 31, Estate of the Artist
6, 13, 16, 18, 36, 46 Tate, London 2004
5, 17, 23 DACS 2004
10, 11 Brigid Peppin
19, 20 Crown Copyright/Imperial War Museum, London
35 Anne Garvey
39 Estate of Jacob Epstein
21, 28, 29, 45 The Estate of John David Roberts. By permission of the William Roberts Society

FIGURE ILLUSTRATION CREDITS

1, 14 David Thomson
2, 3 Estorick Collection, London
4 Manchester City Galleries
5, 13 Alex Hollweg
6, 7, 8, 9 Tate, London 2004
10 Leeds Museums and Galleries (City Art Gallery)
11, 12, 15 The Whitworth Art Gallery, The University of Manchester
16, 17 Private collection
18 Fine Art Society plc
19 Musée des Beaux Arts, Orléans
20 Hirschhorn Museum of Art, Washington DC
21, 22 Kettle's Yard, University of Cambridge
23 Private collection

Copyright acknowledgements

1, 5, 13, 14, 15 Estate of Edward Wadsworth. All Rights Reserved, DACS 2004
2, 3, 20 DACS 2004
4 By Kind Permission of the Wyndham Lewis Memorial Trust
6, 7, 8, 9 Tate, London 2004
10, 11 Courtesy of the Artist's Estate/Bridgeman Art Library
12, 18 Anne Garvey
16, 17 Brigid Peppin

Every effort has been made to trace the copyright holders of the material in this catalogue. The Estorick Collection apologises if any material has been reproduced without permission.